STUDIES IN WESTERN ART

LATIN AMERICAN ART,

and the Baroque Period in Europe

STUDIES IN WESTERN ART

ACTS OF THE TWENTIETH INTERNATIONAL
CONGRESS OF THE HISTORY OF ART

VOLUME III

PRINCETON, NEW JERSEY
PRINCETON UNIVERSITY PRESS
1963

FOREWORD

THIS volume, like its three companions, contains papers presented at the Twentieth International Congress of the History of Art, held in New York City September 7-12, 1961. The papers have been given their present form not simply as records of the proceedings of the Congress but as important contributions to the history of art. We have endeavored, therefore, to make them available to a wide audience. We have published them in full, with adequate illustration, and we have divided them into four volumes.* We hope that in this form they will find many more readers than if they appeared in the traditional single volume, which in this instance would have reached elephantine size and a proportionate price.

Inasmuch as the books will fall into the hands of historians and others who were not present at the Congress a word should be said about the contributors, and that entails a word about the organization of the Congress. The initial decisions were made by a Program Committee consisting of three European scholars, José Gudiol, Hans Hahnloser, and Jan van Gelder, and five Americans, who have continued to serve as the Editorial Associates of the present publication. This committee selected the topics of the twelve sessions and they invited scholars to act as chairmen of them. Each chairman then chose the speakers for his session, and also a group of historians—not more than twenty-five—to discuss the content of the papers in a meeting scheduled to follow the lectures. The lectures were open to all the 1200 *congressistes*; the discussion groups were limited to the speakers and the disputants.

These procedures were followed in all sessions, but within this framework the chairmen were free to shape their meetings as they saw fit. There were thus more lectures in some sessions than in others, and several chairmen asked scholars to speak briefly in the discussion meetings. On recommendation of the chairmen, a number of these briefer contributions are included in this publication. With the exception of two papers that were withheld

* The Table of Contents for each of the other volumes is listed in the Appendix to this volume.

v

by agreement with the authors, all of the papers read at the Congress appear in these volumes.

The publication of the Congress papers in this exceptionally complete form would not have been possible without grants in aid from the Arthur Houghton Foundation and the Clark Foundation. We are most grateful to both of them. We feel deeply indebted to our publisher, the Princeton University Press, and especially to its director, Mr. Herbert Bailey, Jr., and Miss Harriet Anderson, both of whom have taken an active part in the publication.

Mrs. Ida Rubin, Executive Secretary of the Congress, has served as Executive Editor, and undertook the large task of assembling the papers and preparing them for the press. She and her collaborator, Miss Irene Gordon, have our warmest thanks. In its last stages the publication has had the advantage also of the rare experience of a colleague who prefers to remain anonymous.

This foreword gives me a final opportunity to express again my appreciation of the work of the many friends and colleagues who collaborated in the preparation of the Congress. None gave so much time and effort, both before and after it, and none made such basic contributions, as my fellow members of the editorial board of this publication.

MILLARD MEISS
*President, International Committee
of the History of Art*

ACKNOWLEDGMENTS

For works of art owned by collections or museums, it is to be understood that the proprietor supplied the photograph unless another source is acknowledged. In other cases, acknowledgment is made to the following:

ACL: Held, Fig. 8
Aerofotos de México: Baird, Fig. 5
Alinari-Anderson: Wittkower, Figs. 19, 22
Bildarchiv d. Ost. Nationalbibliothek: Knap, Figs. 2, 6, 9, 12
Boonstra, Piet: Stechow, Fig. 4
Columbia University: Wittkower, Figs. 2, 3, 8, 10, 11,
    15-17, 20, 23
Justino Fernández and the Instituto Nacional de Antropoligía e
    Historia, Robertson, Fig. 6
Frequin, A.: Knab, Fig. 14
Gautherot, M.: Smith, Fig. 15
Inah, Mexico: Collier, Fig. 13
Kunstverlag Wolfrum, Vienna: Stechow, Fig. 6
Monumentos Coloniales, México: Baird, Figs. 1-4, 6, 7
Morgan Library: Stechow, Fig. 3
Novaes, M.: Smith, Figs. 1, 2, 5, 10, 14
Phaidon Press: Wittkower, Fig. 14
Smith, R. C.: Smith, 3, 4, 6-9, 11-13

CONTRIBUTORS

J. Q. VAN REGTEREN ALTENA, Kunsthistorisch Instituut der Universiteit van Amsterdam

DIEGO ANGULO IÑGUEZ, Instituto Diego Velazquez, Madrid

JOSEPH ARMSTRONG BAIRD, JR., University of California, Davis

ANTHONY BLUNT, The Courtauld Institute of Art, University of London

ALFREDO BOULTON, Caracas

MARIO T. BUSCHIAZZO, Universidad de Buenos Aires

MARGARET COLLIER, Yale University, New Haven

J. G. VAN GELDER, Kunsthistorisch Institut der Rijksuniversiteit te Utrecht

JULIUS S. HELD, Barnard College, Columbia University, New York City

E. HAVERKAMP-BEGEMANN, Yale University, New Haven

MICHAEL KITSON, The Courtauld Institute of Art, University of London

ECKHART KNAB, Gemäldegalerie der Akademie der bildenden Künste, Vienna

GEORGE KUBLER, Yale University, New Haven

RENSSELAER W. LEE, Princeton University

FRANÇOIS-GEORGES PARISET, University of Bordeaux

DONALD ROBERTSON, Tulane University, New Orleans

ROBERT C. SMITH, University of Pennsylvania, Philadelphia

WOLFGANG STECHOW, Oberlin College

RUDOLF WITTKOWER, Columbia University, New York City

CONTENTS

VOLUME III

CONTENTS

BAROQUE AND ANTIQUITY

INTRODUCTION

ANTHONY BLUNT

THE term "Baroque" has been used in many different senses during the last hundred years, and has been applied not only to the visual arts, but to literature and music. There has, in fact, been much confusion in the use of the word, partly because in these fields it has often been applied to styles that do not correspond to what is meant by Baroque in the visual arts. In literature, for instance, many works are called Baroque which the art historian might prefer to call Mannerist, and in music Bach is usually named as the typical Baroque composer, though it is hard to see a very close parallel between the Forty-Eight and the work of Rubens or Borromini.

Fortunately, we are not concerned here with the literary or musical aspects of the problem; and we are relieved of another burden in that we need not argue about the exact meaning of the word Baroque or the precise period to which we shall apply it. We need not spend time on deciding whether Maderno is proto-Baroque or Early Baroque, nor on defining the awkward frontier between Baroque and Rococo. It will be enough for us to agree on our use of terms, and I hope I shall not meet with strong opposition if I suggest that the word Baroque tends nowadays to be used in art history in two main senses, different but not really confusing: first, as a wide term covering the whole art of the seventeenth century and part of the eighteenth, and secondly, as a more precise term defining what may be considered the most characteristic of the styles which occurred in that period, that is to say, the art that arose in Italy about 1620, dominated Italian art until the advent of the classical revival in the mid-eighteenth century, and produced echoes of varying intensities in all other European countries—the art of Bernini, Borromini, and Pietro da Cortona. By extension, it is often and legitimately applied to works of other periods that share the characteristics of the art of Rome in the seventeenth century.

Certain participants in this session will be dealing with subjects that can be called Baroque in the wider sense, and will be considering, for instance, the attitude of Dutch and Flemish seventeenth-century artists toward ancient art or Velázquez' treatment of mythological themes.

The central core of our subject, however, is the attitude toward antiquity of those artists who can be called Baroque in the narrower sense, and this can, I believe, be most clearly seen by a comparison of their views with those of their rivals who claimed the title of Classical—a rivalry that came to a head in the famous quarrel between Pietro da Cortona and Sacchi in the Academy of St. Luke in the 1630's. It is this problem that I want to discuss in this introductory paper.

A child's approach to the problem of defining this difference would be to guess that the so-called classical artists made a greater use of antiquity than their Baroque rivals. This is, of course, manifestly untrue, and all artists in Italy in the seventeenth century, whatever their aesthetic creed, had an equal veneration for antiquity, both in regard to iconography and to formal qualities. The problem is to distinguish the uses they made of it.

In the matter of iconography it appears to me almost impossible to make any absolute distinction. If one limits the generalization to Italy, it would probably be true to say that classical artists were more learned in their allusions to ancient history and mythology than those who represented the Baroque party; that is to say, Poussin, Testa, and the other artists around Cassiano dal Pozzo were more learned than Pietro da Cortona or the painters of Naples and Genoa. But there arises the menacing figure of Rubens to prove that an artist can be a supreme master of the Baroque style and at the same time display an erudition in matters of ancient lore which would have shamed most members of the classical faction.

As regards the attitude of seventeenth-century artists toward the formal qualities of ancient art, a second approximation would be to suggest that the classical party tended to admire and imitate the more restrained type of Greek and Roman art, such as works of the Hellenistic School, or the Neo-Attic style favored under Hadrian, and that the supporters of the Baroque turned more naturally to schools such as the Pergamene, which had closer affinities with their own art. Poussin, for instance, seems mainly to

4

have admired works of the first category. His favorite models were the *Antinoüs*, which he imitated in his early days; the Salpion Vase, which was a source of inspiration for the *Bacchanals*; the *Aldobrandini Wedding*, which influenced him in the 1640's; the *Sleeping Ariadne*, of which he made a copy in wax; the *Farnese Seated Apollo*, which he copied in his last work, the *Apollo and Daphne*. Rubens and Bernini tended to admire the *Belvedere Torso*, the *Barberini Faun,* and the *Laocoon*.[1] On the other hand, as Rudolf Wittkower shows in his paper, this is only a part of the story, and it is also essential to examine the manner in which artists transformed their models.

The practice of the two schools in the matter of borrowing from antiquity can be seen in its clearest form in the field of architecture. To study the methods of the classical school we must turn to France, where it attained its most powerful position and found the fullest expression of its doctrine in the treatises of Fréart de Chambray, Claude Perrault, and François Blondel. These authors were primarily concerned with the correct use of the Orders, and they took their models from two sources: first, the most famous buildings of antiquity—the Pantheon, the Temple of Fortuna Virilis, or the Maison Carrée at Nîmes—and secondly, the ten books of Vitruvius, which were edited with a commentary by Perrault and were the foundation of both Fréart de Chambray's and Blondel's doctrines. It is characteristic of the attitude of Baroque artists that no new edition of Vitruvius was published in Italy during the seventeenth century;[2] indeed Italian architects were extremely free in their use of Orders, and Borromini, for instance, took the utmost liberties with them. There is, however, one illuminating instance in which he copies the Orders of

[1] One might expect to be able to draw important conclusions from a comparison of the drawings after the Antique by Rubens and Poussin, but in fact they were made for such different purposes that any deduction is likely to be misleading. Rubens made his drawings as exact records to take home with him, as we might buy an Alinari photograph. Poussin had the original always near at hand, and when he made a drawing after an ancient statue or relief, it was to record a particular impression of it rather than its actual physical appearance.

[2] Daniele Barbaro's edition was reprinted in Venice in 1629 and again in 1641, and Rusconi claimed that his *Architettura*, published in 1660, also in Venice, was in accordance with the precepts of Vitruvius. In Rome, however, no interest was manifested in Vitruvius during the seventeenth century.

antiquity. In the side panels of his great fireplace in the Sala di Ricreazione in the Oratory (Pl. i, i), Borromini copies exactly a very unusual and complicated form of fluting that is to be found on a pair of ancient columns in S. Agnese fuori le Mura (Pl. i, 2). None of the seventeenth-century writers on the monuments of ancient Rome seem to mention or illustrate columns of this type. They are first mentioned by Daviler in his *Cours d'Architecture,*[3] and he condemns their fluting as being *trop confus.*

Generally speaking, however, pure Baroque architects like Borromini were more interested in the plans and general forms of ancient buildings than in details of the Orders, and there are many buildings dating from the later Roman Empire which would undoubtedly have greatly excited their imagination, if they had known them. The Treasury at Petra, for instance, or the oval fountains in the Flavian palace on the Palatine with their curved concave bays (Pl. ii, 3), have many elements in common with the work of Borromini, and the stucco relief shown in Pl. ii, 5 might have stimulated Bernini to create the perspective effects in his Cornaro Chapel reliefs. Unfortunately Petra was not discovered until the 1840's, the Flavian palaces were only uncovered in the present century, and the relief comes from the recent excavations under St. Peter's.

It is, however, very probable that other similar buildings were known in the seventeenth century and have now disappeared. The case of the famous round temple at Baalbek is perhaps typical (Pl. ii, 4). The ruins of Baalbek had been engraved by Belon in 1555, but the engravings in his book are so small and clumsy that they would be of little use to an architect. On the other hand, there is an early seventeenth-century engraving of a tomb near Tivoli (Pl. iv, 8) which shows almost exactly the same characteristics and would certainly have been studied by the architects of the Baroque.

Certain of the more fantastic features of Roman Baroque architecture can be traced back to sources of a slightly different kind. The Romans seem to have been freer in the architectural forms that they employed in the decorative parts of their bas-reliefs

---

[3] Ed. P. J. Mariette, 1750, p. 336. Drawings of various columns of this type by Montanus can be found in the Soane Museum series.

than in their monumental architecture. So, for instance, the form of arch used by Maderna in the aisles of St. Peter's does not seem to be found in examples of ancient monumental architecture known in the seventeenth century, but it is common on sarcophagi, such as that at Melfi (Pl. III, 6) or the marriage sarcophagus formerly in the Palazzo Riccardi, Florence. These were probably the models that Maderna had in mind when he employed the motive in St. Peter's.[4]

Another source of importance for Baroque architects seems to have been the *scenae frons* of the Roman stage. In its more elaborate form, as it is now known in the theaters of Sabratha (Pl. III, 7), Leptis Magna, or Corinth, it contains many of the essential characteristics of Baroque architecture, particularly the re-entrant curves with columned rectangular blocks protruding in them. These particular examples were not known in the seventeenth century, but the theater at Orange was familiar from the fifteenth century onward, and the theaters at Lyons and Vienne, which have similar stages, were probably partly visible in the seventeenth century.[5]

The problem of what was known and what was not known in the seventeenth century in the way of ancient buildings is, of course, complex, but on the whole it seems safe to assume that, if we can now point to the existence of an ancient building related in style to Baroque architecture, there was almost certainly some other specimen of the type known in the seventeenth century and since destroyed. Sometimes, as with the round temple at Tivoli, a record of these buildings exists, but one is bound to ask how accurate such records are.

In the case of this temple, the engraving is after a drawing by Giovanni Battista Montanus, who plays a curious and impor-

---

[4] Other motives from sarcophagi seem to have been taken up by sixteenth-century architects and decorators. For instance, the idea of partly open doors, used by Veronese, is frequently to be found on sarcophagi, though more exact parallels with a figure appearing through the door are found in ancient painting. The closest of all, now in the Naples museum, comes from the Stabian Baths at Pompeii, but a similar example may have been known to Veronese.

[5] According to some reconstructions, the Septizonium of Septimius Severus had a series of curved bays (see Luigi Crema, *L'Architettura romana* [*Enciclopedia classica*], Turin, 1959, p. 547).

tant part in the story. Montanus was born in Milan in 1534, came
to Rome before 1579, and died there in 1621. At his death he
left a huge series of finished drawings, which were acquired by
Cassiano dal Pozzo and are now in Sir John Soane's Museum,
London. A large number of these were published by his pupil,
Giovanni Battista Soria, between 1624 and 1684.[6] The greater
part of the drawings and engravings show reconstructions of
ancient temples or tombs, and among them we find in embryo
a number of fundamental Baroque types of building: the contrast
of concave and convex forms characteristic of Borromini; the
curved front of Cortona's Vigna Sacchetti; the idea of setting a
domed building against a semi-circular enclosure, as in Bernini's
Sta. Maria dell'Assunta at Ariccia; a circular building with
coupled columns and curved reentrant bays, like Borromini's
lantern on S. Ivo, and even the false perspective of the Spada
Gallery (Pls. IV, 9-11; V, 12, 13).

The objection will, of course, at once be raised that these reconstructions are the product of Montanus' imagination and are
not faithful to their originals. This is no doubt true, and nothing
but a systematic comparison of Montanus' compositions with existing remains could settle the problem of how far his reconstructions were justified by what he actually found. Before condemning him utterly, however, it should be borne in mind that some
ancient monuments survive today which show a freedom of form
corresponding to many of Montanus' reconstructions. The famous
Conocchia near Capua Vetere (Pl. V, 14), for instance, which
was drawn from the fifteenth century onward, could be described
as a completely Baroque monument and may have been the
model for the drum of Borromini's dome of S. Andrea delle
Fratte,[7] and some of the tombs recently discovered at Ostia (Pl.

---

[6] The exact date of the drawings is uncertain. One is dated 1611 on the back,
and the same date appears on the portrait of Montanus, signed by Villamena,
on which the engraved frontispiece by David is based. The style of the drawings
suggests the late sixteenth century, and Montanus probably began them soon
after his arrival in Rome. The engravings in general follow his drawings accurately, but do not reproduce more than a part of them. On the other hand,
there are engravings for which drawings do not exist in the Soane Museum,
although they may be in other collections.

[7] Other examples are at Pozzuoli (see Crema, *op.cit.*, p. 329, figs. 375, 376),
Athens (*ibid.*, p. 499, fig. 646), and Aquileia (*ibid.*, p. 260, fig. 289).

VII, 18) and under St. Peter's show curved elements like the forms of the *scenae frons*. Moreover, although in most cases the elevations in Montanus' reconstructions must be almost entirely invented, he may have known from surviving ruins the plans of a great many buildings which have today completely disappeared.[8]

Irrespective of the accuracy of his reconstructions, however, the case of Montanus is of interest because the designs that he produced—and he died in 1621 and probably made his drawings some time earlier—contain ideas that had not been developed at that time by practicing architects. Montanus certainly thought that these ideas were justified by ancient examples.[9]

The problem of wrong reconstructions and their influence is one that deserves more careful study than it has received. A curious case is provided by the Piazza d'Oro at Hadrian's Villa. From the parts excavated in the sixteenth century Pirro Ligorio made a reconstruction (Pl. VI, 15) showing the principal building as an oval, the dome of which was supported by two oval colonnades, one with coupled columns. Modern excavations have shown that its form is nearer to a Greek cross with curved bounding lines (Pl. VI, 16). Ligorio died in 1583,[10] and in the next year Ottaviano Mascherino produced a plan for the church of Sto. Spirito dei Napolitani which is almost identical with Ligorio's reconstruction of the Piazza d'Oro. In this case the reconstruction no doubt inspired the church design, but, as always, the problem of the egg and the chicken is more complicated than that, because Ligorio's reconstruction was conditioned by certain tendencies in the architecture of his own time which led him to see an oval where no oval was, and these tendencies were given vigorous and original expression by Mascherino in his church plan (Pl. VI, 17). If Mascherino had not known Ligorio's reconstruction, he would no

[8] In certain cases Montanus gives a hint of the actual site of the monument that he reproduces, indicating that it is "on the via Appia," "near Albano," or "at Tivoli," but generally these indications are too vague to follow up. The drawing for pl. 28 of Book III has on it a long inscription, which is clearly corrupt but is evidence that Montanus was recording something that he saw.

[9] The last book of his engravings consists of original designs for tabernacles, and some of these are startlingly Baroque. One, for instance, displays the basic elements of Cortona's façade of Sta. Maria della Pace.

[10] His plan must, in fact, have been made before he left Rome for Ferrara in 1572.

doubt have found some other ancient monument that would have justified a similar, although no doubt not identical, form.

There is, therefore, evidence to show that Baroque architects could have known and actually studied a number of ancient models that were in conformity with their own stylistic inclinations.

It must be said again, however, that there are exceptions to the rule that Baroque architects were attracted to Baroque models and classical to classical. The tastes of Borromini at one end of the scale and Poussin at the other are in general consistent, but not absolutely so. If Borromini's works are fundamentally allied to the architecture of Baalbek and Petra, there is one instance at least in which he borrowed from a celebrated classical example of fourth-century Greek architecture, the Choragic Monument of Lysicrates, a building known in Italy through a drawing by Cyriac of Ancona and probably by later and more detailed renderings. The lower part of the Campanile of S. Andrea delle Fratte seems to be based on the monument, and the curious element topping the little church of S. Giovanni in Oleo (Pl. VII, 19) probably derives from the same source (the resemblance is even closer between Borromini's preliminary drawing and the engraving published in 1676 by Spon and Wheler [Pl. VII, 20], which shows how the seventeenth century saw the monument).[11] This instance, however, is not a real proof of Borromini's interest in classical models, because, though the monument itself is classical, the particular crowning element that he borrows is almost Baroque—certainly fantastic—in character.

Poussin on the other hand generally turned to classical models, so that it is a surprise to find him praising the *Barberini Faun* as among the finest works of ancient sculpture.[12] It is, however, worth noting that, as far as we know, he did not draw it or imitate it in any of his paintings, and, as I have already said, his taste led him to study and admire a quite different kind of ancient art, which conforms to classical standards.

An extreme example of this tendency is the fact that in some

[11] It is engraved in Spon and Wheler's *Voyage d'Italie . . . fait aux années 1675 et 1676.*

[12] *Correspondance*, ed. Jouanny, Paris, 1911, p. 278.

of his paintings he introduces figures of women wearing the peplos, based exactly on fifth century B.C. types, which he could have known from a number of copies in Roman collections. This seems to have been a unique phenomenon among seventeenth-century painters, but it was undoubtedly a conscious gesture, for Passeri records that Poussin and his friend François Duquesnoy consciously distinguished between the Greek and Roman styles, and manifested a strong preference for the Greek. The passage is of sufficient interest to quote in full: "He [Duquesnoy] wanted to prove himself a strict imitator of the Greek manner, which he called the real model for perfect work, because it combines grandeur, nobility, majesty and beauty [*grandezza, nobiltà, maestà, e leggiadria*], all qualities which it is hard to unite in a single work; and this love was strengthened by the comments of Poussin who wanted in every way to vilify the Latin manner, for reasons which will be told in his life."[13] Unfortunately Passeri does not develop this point as he promises, and we have no means of knowing exactly what Poussin and Duquesnoy meant by Greek and Roman manners,[14] but his statement is explicit enough to make it plain that these two artists deserve the distinction, usually awarded to Winckelmann a century later, of being the first to differentiate between Greek and Roman art, and to praise the former at the expense of the latter.

There is, therefore, I believe, reason to suppose that certain artists in seventeenth-century Rome made a clear distinction between different kinds of ancient art and took up a definite position, approving one kind and condemning another. Not all were probably as conscious as Poussin of the principles on which their judgments were based, but if the ancient sources used by Borromini were collected, I believe they would make a list almost as consistent as the corresponding series of models used by Poussin.

[13] Passeri, *Die Künstlerbiographien von Giovanni Battista Passeri*, ed. J. Hess, Leipzig and Vienna, 1934, p. 112.

[14] The distinction may have been partly based on the test of naturalism. Poussin would certainly have preferred the idealization of Hellenistic or Hadrianic sculpture to the naturalism of Roman portrait busts. In architecture the distinction between the Greek and Roman Orders had, of course, long been familiar from Vitruvius, but it was emphasized in the circle of Poussin. Fréart de Chambray, for instance, only includes the Greek Orders in his *Parallèle de l'architecture ancienne avec la moderne* (1650).

VAN DYCK, TASSO, AND THE ANTIQUE

RENSSELAER W. LEE

ANTHONY VAN DYCK certainly painted two subjects from Tasso's *Gerusalemme Liberata*, perhaps three; but the connection of the third with Tasso is more than debatable and will not occupy us here.[1] As preparation for a discussion of the Flemish painter's important contribution to the illustration of the famous Italian epic, a few facts are worth setting down about the fame of the poem and its early illustration by painters. Published in 1581, it took cultivated Europe by storm. By the year 1627—this was forty-six years after its appearance—when Van Dyck left Italy to return home, a veritable host of Italian editions had appeared, eleven of which had each its different set of engraved illustrations. The poem was early rendered into French, and in England, which is more our concern here, Edward Fairfax published his fine translation dedicated to Queen Elizabeth in 1600, a translation that was to have considerable influence on English taste and even on English poetry. Fairfax's Tasso was a favorite of King James I, and along with Spenser's *Faerie Queene*, itself owing much to Tasso, and Sir John Harington's translation of Ariosto, it did much to solace the imprisonment of Charles I, Van Dyck's most illustrious and most unfortunate patron.[2] In fact, it was through the painting of a romantic subject from Tasso's poem that Van Dyck in 1629 was reintroduced to England. In that year Charles I himself, nearly two decades before his death on the scaffold, bought the splendid *Armida and the Sleeping Rinaldo* which is now in the Baltimore Museum (Pl. XI, 13).[3]

The *Gerusalemme Liberata* is, as everyone knows, an epic poem

[1] The painting, now at Blenheim, was formerly called *Erminia Putting on Clorinda's Armor* (see L. Cust, *Anthony van Dyck*, London, 1900, p. 142 and p. 285, no. 214), but it is better interpreted as *Venus in the Armor of Mars*. It shows a woman half-length wearing armor, her left hand resting on a helmet, with a Cupid beside her. There is nothing specific in the picture to warrant any reference to Tasso's Clorinda; see G. Glück, *Van Dyck, des Meisters Gemälde* (Klassiker der Kunst), New York, 1931, p. 564 and fig. p. 408.

[2] See S. Stevenson, *Charles I in Captivity*, New York, 1927, pp. 91-92.

[3] See below, pp. 21ff and n. 28.

of high seriousness. Its medieval theme, the siege and final capture of Jerusalem by the crusaders under Godfrey of Boulogne, symbolic of the ultimate victory of the Church militant over its enemies, discloses the spirit of the Counter Reformation and is related to other remanifestations of medievalism during the sixteenth century. In structure the poem also reflects the classical predilections of its age; it is based mainly on the *Iliad* and the *Aeneid,* and Tasso aimed, without great success because he included much adventitious romantic material, at a single consistent action according to the canons of Aristotle. Now it is to the credit of the seventeenth-century painters, some of whom are recorded as having read Tasso *con amore,* that they paid scant attention to the highly imitative main action of the poem. With a direct instinct for genuine poetry, they cut through its arid rhetorical shell to those episodes where Tasso laid aside an often mannered style and wrote with superb ease and naturalness, episodes amorous and idyllic, like Erminia and the Shepherd, Erminia and Tancred, or Rinaldo and Armida, that contain some of the finest poetry in Italian literature and became at once the inspiration of music as well as painting. Here Tasso's characteristic pathos and tender sentiment find full expression; here also his Renaissance love of sensuous beauty, even if he may morally disapprove of this beauty, breaks through the spiritual constriction of one side of his own nature and of the age in which he lived. And, as I have written elsewhere, these subjects "were immediately popular, not only for their intrinsic beauty and human interest, but because they had behind them a long tradition of pastoral art and literature extending back into antiquity, with its images of the country, its implications of escape from the weary, complex life of courts and cities, and its haunting references to the Golden Age when an idly happy life prevailed. And such current erotic mythologies among the Renaissance painters as Venus and Adonis, Aurora and Cephalus, or Diana and Endymion, and the general popularity of Ovid, helped to prepare particularly for the enthusiastic reception accorded the story of Rinaldo and Armida." In the third decade of the seventeenth century, Van Dyck, as we have just seen, elected to illustrate this story. In so doing he was following in the footsteps of such famous Early Baroque masters as Annibale Carracci,

Domenichino, and Guercino, as well as of others less renowned.[4]

Various incidents in the story of Rinaldo and Armida attracted the painters of the seventeenth century. Most popular was the scene from the sixteenth canto, set in the garden of Armida's palace, in which Rinaldo, the Christian Achilles, who has renounced his martial duty for carnal love, is discovered erotically content in the lap of his mistress by Carlo and Ubaldo, proponents of virtue, who have been sent to recover him to the Christian army. Van Dyck's painting of this famous scene is in the Louvre (Pl. XII, 16). Scarcely less popular was the scene from the fourteenth canto which represents Armida falling in love with Rinaldo as he lies asleep on the bank of the river Orontes; as she bends over, dagger in hand, to kill the Christian hero who is her mortal enemy, she suddenly finds her hate transformed into love. The following moment, when Armida binds Rinaldo with a garland of privet, lilies, and roses[5] before abducting him in her chariot to her palace in the Fortunate Isles, depicted rarely in seventeenth-century painting, is the subject of Van Dyck's *Armida and the Sleeping Rinaldo* in Baltimore, as well as of a fine drawing, formerly in the Fairfax Murray Collection (Pl. VIII, 1), which served as model for the large picture in the Los Angeles County Museum (Pl. VIII, 3).[6] A fine decorative picture, this must be regarded as

[4] For discussion of the story of Rinaldo and Armida in painting see the following articles by the present writer: "*Ut pictura poesis*: The Humanistic Theory of Painting," *Art Bulletin*, XXII, 1940, pp. 242-50; "Van Loo's *Rinaldo and Armida* in the Princeton Museum," *Record of the Art Museum, Princeton University*, XIX, 1960, pp. 44-49; "Giambattista Tiepolo's Drawing of Rinaldo and Armida," *Bulletin of the Smith College Museum of Art*, XLI, 1961, pp. 10-22; "Armida's Abandonment: A Study In Tasso Iconography Before 1700," in *De Artibus opuscula XL: Essays in Honor of Erwin Panofsky*, New York, 1961, pp. 335-49 (n. 3, p. 336 lists other articles of a more general nature dealing with Tasso's influence on the history of painting).

[5] Stanza 68: "Di ligustri, di gigli e de le rose, / Le quai fiorian per quelle piaggie amene / Con nov'arte congiunte, indi compose / Lente, ma tenacissime catene, / Queste al collo, alle braccia, ai piè gli pose, / Così l'avvinse, e così preso il tiene. . . ." For the whole episode, see stanzas 56-79.

[6] It was recorded as being on the London art market in 1954, but I do not know where it is at present (see *A Catalogue of Flemish, German, Dutch and English Paintings, XV-XVIII Century*, Los Angeles County Museum, 1954, p. 24). It was formerly in the Collection of Sir J. C. Robinson (see L. Cust, *op.cit.*, p. 70 and p. 251, no. 96).

a school piece, being uneven in execution and unattributable, as it stands, to the master himself.[7] But even in its differences from the drawing, it probably represents Van Dyck's ideas, and, not improbably, it is a copy of a lost original.

The drawing (Pl. VIII, 1) and the Los Angeles painting (Pl. VIII, 3), then, show Armida bending lovingly over the sleeping Rinaldo to bind him with flowers. In the previous moment, of Armida's falling in love, Tasso, with Ovid in mind, had beautifully compared her, bending over and looking at the sleeping warrior, to Narcissus at the fountain. What sources, pictorial or sculptural, Renaissance or antique, lie behind Van Dyck's rendering of this tender and nostalgic subject, the main motif of which is a woman leaning over her sleeping lover, while a Cupid about to extinguish a torch completes the central triangle formed by the protagonists?

Van Dyck could have found this episode illustrated in no editions of Tasso published before 1627,[8] the year in which, in all probability, he left Italy after a sojourn of six years.[9] He could, however, during one of his visits to Rome, have seen Baglione's fresco of 1614 in the Casino Rospigliosi (Pl. VIII, 2),[10] in a small room next to the *salone* containing Guido Reni's *Aurora*. Baglione's painting has the essential feature of Armida leaning over to entwine the sleeping Rinaldo with flowers, and it shares other features as well with Van Dyck's invention: various Cupids, including one flying in the air (Baglione's flying Cupid, however, shoots an arrow at Armida, whereas in Van Dyck's versions the flying putti are otherwise engaged), and the column that bore

[7] It has been accepted as a genuine Van Dyck by W. R. Valentiner (*"Rinaldo and Armida* by van Dyck," *Quarterly, Los Angeles County Museum*, VIII, 1950, pp. 8-10), and by Gerson (in H. Gerson and E. H. Ter Kuile, *Art and Architecture in Belgium*, Baltimore, 1960, p. 191, n. 47). Cust (*op.cit.*, p. 70 and p. 251, no. 96) considers it "probably a school picture. . . ." It was also listed as a school work in the catalogue of the Van Dyck exhibition at Genoa in 1955 (*100 opere di van Dyck*, Genoa, 1955, p. 40, no. 81).

[8] The illustrations for Canto XIV in editions before 1627 are martial, religious, and didactic in character.

[9] For a reasonable account of Van Dyck's Italian itinerary, see Gerson and Ter Kuile, *op.cit.*, pp. 116-19.

[10] See C. Guglielmi, "Intorno all'opera pittorica di Giovanni Baglione," *Bollettino d'Arte*, XXXIX, 1954, p. 318.

the legend enjoining Rinaldo to discover the hidden marvels in the midst of the river which appears at the left in the Los Angeles painting. But it is perfectly clear that if Van Dyck got the suggestion for his subject from the fresco painted eight years before he first arrived in Rome in 1622, he was not inspired either by its composition or its cumbersome style. And although Sandrart says of Van Dyck in Rome: ". . . weil ihn aber die Romanische Reglen und Academien der Antichen, auch Raphaels und anderer dergleichen seriose Studien nicht gefällig, blieb er nicht lang allda . . . ,"[11] and although Bellori, unimpressed with Van Dyck as an historical painter, remarks that he was deficient in *perfetta idea*,[12] we must certainly look to antique models for nearly all the elements that make up Van Dyck's composition. Many of them, in fact, are found together in antiquity, in the representations of Selene approaching the sleeping Endymion whom she loves, an episode alike in content to that which Van Dyck portrays in his *Armida and the Sleeping Rinaldo* (Pl. VIII, 1, 3). And, indeed, in this composition, Van Dyck, anticipating Poussin in the next decade of the century,[13] employs features of the Endymion story as he could have seen it reproduced on antique sarcophagi during his sojourns in Rome, for instance on a sarcophagus set in the outer wall of the Casino Rospigliosi, which was built in 1613[14] and contained within the fresco by Baglione which we have already discussed. On this sarcophagus (Pl. VIII, 4) are several of the elements of Van Dyck's composition. The sleeping figure of Endymion which in all essentials of pose, notably in the position of bent and outstretched arms and legs, is particularly com-

---

[11] *Joachim von Sandrarts Academie der Bau- Bild- und Mahlerey-Kunst von 1675. . .* , ed. A. R. Peltzer, Munich, 1925, p. 174.

[12] Giovanni Pietro Bellori, *Le vite de' pittori, scultori et architetti moderni*, Rome, 1672, p. 264.

[13] For a discussion of Poussin's beautiful *Armida and the Sleeping Rinaldo*, now in Moscow, in its relation to the Endymion story in ancient art, see Lee, "*Ut pictura poesis. . .* ," pp. 243-45 and fig. 1. Poussin portrays the moment prior to that portrayed by Van Dyck, when Armida, bending over to kill Rinaldo, falls in love with him.

[14] See C. Robert, *Die antiken Sarcophag-Reliefs*, Berlin, 1890-1919, III, part 1 (1897), p. 59 and pl. XII, fig. 39. The Casino was built by Vasanzio (Jan van Santen) 1612-13 (see R. Wittkower, *Art and Architecture in Italy*, Baltimore, 1958, p. 12).

parable to Rinaldo in Van Dyck's drawing; the typical oval form of Selene's flying veil and her intent gaze toward Endymion recalling Van Dyck's Armida; and the Cupid moving between Selene and Endymion with the flaming torch, which, however, unlike Van Dyck's Cupid, he holds aloft instead of inverted. Only one Cupid with a torch appears in Van Dyck's composition; on the sarcophagus, however, the Endymion story is enclosed by two other Cupids who, with eyes closed, lean on inverted but still burning torches.

It is clear, then, that a number of features in Van Dyck's composition are derived from the single source in which they all appear together: the ancient representations on sarcophagi of the story of Selene and Endymion. Van Dyck's Cupid is particularly interesting. Holding his torch inverted (Pl. VIII, 1), like the flanking Cupids on the sarcophagus (Pl. VIII, 4), he strides forward, in a manner resembling its striding Cupid, to quench the flame in the river waves. Van Dyck thus remembered both the striding and the flanking Cupids, and there can be no doubt that the change from the torch held aloft by the striding Cupid on the sarcophagus to the torch that he holds inverted in the drawing (Pl. VIII, 1) and the Los Angeles painting (Pl. VIII, 3) has a particular and appropriate significance. Its quenching, and one may compare for like import the inverted torch carried by the Cupid who walks with downcast eyes in Rubens' *Triumph of Heavenly Love* in Madrid,[15] means the quelling of the base affections. In Van Dyck's case, the action of the Cupid prophesies the conclusion of the story of Rinaldo and Armida, when carnal love between them is extinguished. Amor extinguishing the affections was also Bellori's interpretation later in the century of the scene which he found on an ancient sarcophagus of a Cupid quenching an inverted torch on the breast of a dead man (Pl. IX, 5).[16] And it was not until 1769, well past the middle of the eighteenth century, that

[15] *P. P. Rubens, des Meisters Gemälde* (Klassiker der Kunst), ed. R. Oldenbourg, Stuttgart, etc., n.d., fig. p. 296.

[16] See *Admiranda romanarum antiquitatum ac veteris sculpturae vestigia . . .* (with engravings by Pietro Santi Bartoli and notes by G. P. Bellori), Rome, 1693, pl. 67. Bellori's note on the detail of the engraving reproduced in Pl. IX, 5 is as follows: "Amor facem et affectus in pectore de mortui hominis extinguit corollā funebrē tenet. Papilio anima est a corpore seiuncta. . . ." For the torch as a

Lessing, in his wonderful essay, "Wie die Alten den Tod gebildet," proved, disputing Bellori, that for the ancients the figure on the sarcophagus represented not Amor quenching the affections, but Death which extinguishes all life. We also owe to Lessing the knowledge that a pair of Cupids with inverted torches, such as we saw on the Endymion sarcophagus (Pl. VIII, 4), represent Sleep and Death. Actually, however, Van Dyck must have known, as Rubens did,[17] more than a century before Lessing wrote his essay, that the inverted torch could have funerary implications. In his *Crucified Christ between St. Dominic and St. Catherine of Siena*, painted at Antwerp soon after his Italian sojourn, a winged boy, pointing to the dead Christ, sits on a stone at the foot of the cross, between his legs an inverted torch which thrusts its flame against the ground (Pl. IX, 6).[18]

Ancient representations of the Endymion story are probably not the only classical source for Van Dyck's drawing and for the Los Angeles picture. Indeed, there are other elements in Van Dyck's composition which may recall his experience of ancient art in Italy. The nymph singing the voluptuous lullaby that charmed Rinaldo into slumber, with her curved back, bent right arm, and head in profile, clearly belongs to the race of Nereids who appear on many antique sarcophagi (Pl. IX, 7),[19] although it is possible that Van Dyck might have got her indirectly from antiquity through such a figure as Paolo Veronese's marvelous *Autumn* at Maser, which he had seen,[20] or perhaps through a

---

symbol of *amor carnalis* in the Middle Ages, see E. Panofsky, *Renaissance and Renascences in Western Art*, Stockholm, 1960, pp. 94ff.

[17] An engraving by P. Clouwet after a design by Rubens for the tomb of a married couple shows a pair of inverted torches (see Julius Held, "Rubens Designs for Sepulchral Monuments," *Art Quarterly*, XXIII, 1960, p. 256 and fig. 4).

[18] See Glück, *op.cit.*, p. 544.

[19] See Andreas Rumpf, *Die Meerwesen auf den Antiken Sarkophagreliefs*, Berlin, 1939, for examples already known by the beginning of the seventeenth century, e.g., p. 32, no. 81, pl. 24 (Rome, Palazzo Altieri); pp. 45-46, no. 116, pl. 40 (Vatican), our Pl. IX, 7; pp. 56-57, no. 132, pl. 40 (Louvre).

[20] Reproduced in R. Pallucchini, *Veronese*, Bergamo, 1943, pl. 53. Van Dyck's visit to Maser is proved by his drawing of Veronese's famous fresco depicting Natural Love in his Italian Sketchbook, now at Chatsworth (see *Anton van Dyck, Italienisches Skizzenbuch*, ed. G. Adriani, Vienna, 1940, p. 46, fol. 37).

drawing by Rubens of the Nereids, in the famous *Arrival of Marie de Médicis at Marseilles* in the Luxembourg series, which he might have seen before leaving Antwerp for Italy. Rubens' Nereid at the right, seen in back view (Pl. ix, 8),[21] is obviously derived from the Antique, and there is a strong resemblance between her and Van Dyck's nymph of the river. Again, the Cupid with his finger on his lips enjoining silence might recall representations common in ancient Rome of the boy Harpocrates, son of Isis, a statuette of whom Bellori owned (Pl. x, 9),[22] although here Van Dyck may very appropriately have had in mind another intermediary between himself and antiquity: the Cupid making the same gesture in Annibale Carracci's *Diana and Endymion* in the Farnese Gallery,[23] a subject that, as we have just seen, is close in content to his own invention. Finally, the inclination of the head, the movement of the arms, and the drooping left hand of the graceful figure of Armida also evoke memories of the Antique, of a figure like the *Victory* of Brescia, now considered to have been originally a Venus gazing into the shield of Mars (Pl. x, 10).[24] Here, however, it is not unlikely that the painter also sees

[21] Peiresc refers to the Luxembourg commission in a letter of December 1621. If, then, as Dumont maintains, Van Dyck arrived in Genoa on November 20, 1621, after a journey of a month and a half from Antwerp, he might well have seen a sketch for the Nereids in Rubens' famous painting before he began his journey south. See Gerson and Ter Kuile, *op.cit.*, pp. 90, 116.

[22] For Harpocrates, see F. Cumont, *Les religions orientales dans le paganisme romain*, Paris, 1929, p. 73 and pl. vi. Cf. *Le grand cabinet romain ou recueil d'antiquitez romaines . . . qu'ils ont trouvé a Rome avec les explications de Michel Ange de la Chausse*, Amsterdam, 1706, pp. 54-55, figs. 26 and 27; also Gisb. Cuperi, *Harpocrates et monumenta antiqua*, Traiecta ad Rhenum, 1687, for many illustrations.

[23] See H. Voss, *Die Malerei des Barock in Rom*, Berlin, 1925, fig. p. 170.

[24] Pl. x, 10 shows the reconstruction of the Brescia *Victory* shorn of her recently held shield and of the helmet under her raised foot, both of which were discovered to have been added in 1838. She was originally a self-admiring Venus of the Tiberio-Claudian period, gazing, like her predecessors the *Aphrodite* of Corinth and the *Venus* of Capua, into the shield of Mars. It was under Vespasian that she was transformed into a Victory by the addition of wings, and thus became a forerunner of the figures of Victory on the Columns of Trajan and Marcus Aurelius, and of the Victories that appear later on strigillate and Christian sarcophagi. For the history of the Brescia *Victory*, see L. Borelli, "Il restauro della Vittoria di Brescia," *Bollettino dell'Istituto centrale del Restauro*, 1, 1950, pp. 29-35; for the development of the Victory type, see K. Lehmann-Hartleben,

the Antique through Titian, for whose art he had high admiration. A page in the Chatsworth Sketchbook has at the top a nude woman drawing a garment over her head, which is after a composition of Titian's (Pl. x, 12); the bending movement of head and torso, the position of the left arm, and the movement of the drapery which conceals the curving right arm might suggest the pose and movement of Armida in Van Dyck's composition (Pl. VIII, 1, 3).[25]

Van Dyck probably made the drawing (Pl. VIII, 1) in Italy before he returned to Antwerp in 1627 when his mind was steeped in memories of the Antique and of Italian art. The composition, and this is seen even more clearly in the Los Angeles picture (Pl. VIII, 3), is Venetian and more specifically Titianesque, recalling such a painting as the *Bacchus and Ariadne* which Van Dyck had surely seen in Rome.[26] And if we look at his nostalgic *Vertumnus and Pomona* in the collection of the Marchese Gustavo Doria in Genoa (Pl. x, 11) and belonging to his Italian period, to which and to the immediately succeeding period in Antwerp we owe his finest poesies, the Venetian composition, the Titianesque poses of the main figures and their formal relationship to each other, the Cupid on the right which is the Cupid of the drawing seen in reverse, in short, the whole language of form is very close to that of the drawing and painting of *Armida and the Sleeping Rinaldo*. And the nostalgia of the *Vertumnus and Pomona*, which is something very personal yet at the same time profoundly evocative of the sentiment of Giorgione and early Titian,[27] also in some measure informs Van Dyck's drawing of Rinaldo and

"Ein Siegesdenkmal Domitians," *Römische Mitteilungen*, XXXVIII-XXXIX, 1923-24, pp. 185-92 with plate. Cf. also P. Ducati, *L'arte in Roma dalle origini al secolo VIII*, Bologna, 1938, p. 299. Our Pl. x, 10, is taken from *Fasti-Archaeologia*, III, 1950, fig. 12.

[25] See Adriani, *op.cit.*, p. 75, fol. 111, and cf. E. Tietze-Conrat, "Das 'Skizzenbuch' des Van Dyck als Quelle für die Tizians Forschung," *Critica d'Arte*, XXXII, 1950, p. 433.

[26] Titian's great mythologies, painted for Alfonso d'Este, arrived in Rome in 1598 and were all in the possession of the Aldobrandini during Van Dyck's visits to Rome in the early 1620's (see J. Walker, *Bellini and Titian at Ferrara*, London, 1956, pp. 77-78).

[27] See Oliver Millar, "Van Dyck at Genoa," *Burlington Magazine*, XCVII, 1955, p. 314.

Armida and is unquestionably felt beneath the studio mask of the Los Angeles picture. Thus the basic antique elements in Van Dyck's poesy of Armida and Rinaldo asleep have undergone a sea-change into something warmly Venetian and Titianesque.

On March 23, 1629, more than a year after Van Dyck had returned to Antwerp, an interesting order was issued to the British Exchequer. This was to pay to a confidential agent of Charles I—who was also a connoisseur of art and, curiously enough in the context of this article, rejoiced in the name of Endymion Porter—the sum of seventy-eight pounds for a picture of Rinaldo and Armida which he had bought for the King from "Monsieur Vandick of Antwerpe."[28] This is the famous Baltimore picture (Pl. XI, 13) which, as we saw earlier, served as Van Dyck's reintroduction to England. It was also his first introduction to Charles and is therefore important as the happy prologue to the imperial theme of his splendid portraits of the English royal family.

The Baltimore *Armida and the Sleeping Rinaldo* is a stately and magnificent variation on the theme of Van Dyck's original invention in the earlier drawing (Pl. VIII, 1). It is the prospect, to use Poussin's language, of which the drawing and the Los Angeles picture are the aspect, more carefully managed, more rhetorical, more Baroque, than the earlier invention, but with all its greater splendor, rather less intimate, less Tassesque in sentiment. The relationship of the figures in the main group is essentially the same in the two pictures, the later group having evolved into something more elegant and grandiose. The Cupid enjoining silence in the drawing is seen in reverse in the Baltimore picture, at the right of Armida directly under her flying drapery. The Cupid extinguishing the torch in the earlier version—and one should also include the Cupid breaking an arrow in the Los Angeles picture—prophetically signifying the end of passionate love between Rinaldo and Armida, does not appear in the Baltimore version where we have instead, as in Baglione's painting (Pl. VIII, 2), a flying Cupid shooting his dart at Armida and thus heralding the beginning of love. There are reminiscences of the

[28] See Cust, *op.cit.*, p. 85; and G. Rosenthal, "The Van Dyck of the Epstein Collection," *Baltimore Museum of Art News*, March, 1946, pp. 3-7; Gerson and Ter Kuile, *op.cit.*, p. 122.

Antique in the Baltimore picture, but they are more sublimated than in the earlier version. Thus we no longer find a rather clear quotation from the Antique which we saw earlier (Pl. VIII, 1, 3) in the pose of Rinaldo, the oval of Armida's flying veil, the Cupid advancing with inverted torch, and the back and profile of the river nymph. Instead, although the Antique is still present, it is seen through Titian's eyes or through the eyes of some other Italian painter. The pose of the sleeping Rinaldo was one that continued to fascinate Van Dyck.[29] It had its forebears in ancient sculpture,[30] and in the case of the Baltimore picture, even in ancient painting,[31] but Van Dyck also found it plenteously in his beloved Venetians, for instance, in a lost painting of Mars and Venus by Titian, an amatory subject like Rinaldo and Armida, which he drew in his sketchbook (Pl. XI, 14),[32] and which provided in the figure of Venus a good model, if he needed one, for the sleeping Rinaldo in Baltimore. Interesting also in the Baltimore picture is Van Dyck's recollection of Titian's *Education of Cupid* in the Borghese Gallery, a sketch of which he made when he was in Rome (Pl. XI, 15).[33] Armida's neck and bare shoulder as she bends forward, with the shoulder band and the contour of her flying drapery, are closely modeled on the female figure holding the bow at the right in Titian's painting, while the Cupid leaning against Rinaldo recalls the Cupid with his hands on the shoulder of Venus. Other probable borrowings from Titian are the Cupid with upraised arms and the shooting Cupid, both of

[29] In the Rinaldo and Armida drawing (Pl. VIII, 1) it recalls, as we have seen, the pose of the sleeping Endymion in ancient art. In the Los Angeles picture (Pl. VIII, 3) it is the exact pose of the shepherd in Titian's *Nymph and Shepherd* now in Vienna, which Van Dyck might have seen in Venice before it began its history in other collections (see V. Oberhammer, *Die Gemäldegalerie des Kunsthistorischen Museums in Wien*, II, 1960, plate 7 and accompanying text).

[30] On the Endymion sarcophagi and in such a figure as the *Barberini Faun* in Munich (see M. Bieber, *The Sculpture of the Hellenistic Age*, New York, 1955, p. 112 and figs. 450-51).

[31] The pose of the bridegroom in the *Aldobrandini Wedding* is, in the position of legs and arms, remarkably close to that of Rinaldo in the Baltimore picture. Van Dyck, it is interesting to note, had devoted two pages of his sketchbook to the famous ancient painting. See Adriani, *op.cit.*, pp. 51-52, fol. 50v and 51.

[32] *Ibid.*, p. 68, fol. 106; cf. Tietze-Conrat, *op.cit.*, p. 433.

[33] Adriani, *op.cit.*, p. 75, fol. 113v.

whom have excellent ancestors in the *Worship of Venus*,[34] which Van Dyck must have known in Rome. As for the dramatically singing river nymph with slanting body, outthrust left arm, and head foreshortened as she gazes upward toward the sleeping Rinaldo, she, too, ultimately has antique ancestry among the Nereids, but her pose is strongly reminiscent of another figure that Van Dyck saw in Rome, the dramatically posed Andromeda chained to the rock in Annibale Carracci's fresco in the Palazzo Farnese.[35]

Van Dyck's portrayals of Armida and the sleeping Rinaldo which we have just considered have always appeared under their true colors. No one has ever mistaken the subject for anything else. But the *Rinaldo and Armida* in the Louvre (Pl. xii, 16), probably painted in 1632 for Frederick Hendrik of Orange-Nassau and his wife Amalia van Solms, was first described in an inventory of their possessions, dated 1632-34, as a "Mars, resting his head in the lap of Venus; nearby is a Cupid with a red velvet slipper on his foot and a garter on his leg...."[36] This error is corrected in a later Dutch inventory of 1708[37] where the picture is called Rinaldo and Armida, but the inventories of the Empire and Restoration in France reverted to the title of Mars and Venus and it was only in the mid-nineteenth century that the picture resumed its proper title.[38]

It is interesting to compare Van Dyck's version of the famous scene in the garden of Armida's palace from Tasso's sixteenth

[34] See n. 26 above.

[35] See Voss, *op.cit.*, fig. p. 174. Annibale's *Andromeda* is a closer parallel to Van Dyck's nymph than is the nude figure in Titian's *Sacred and Profane Love*, which, as has been demonstrated, is related in pose and in the way in which she sits on the edge of the marble fountain to the ancient Nereids seated on the backs of sea monsters on Roman sarcophagi (see O. J. Brendel, "Borrowings from Ancient Art in Titian," *Art Bulletin*, xxxvii, 1955, p. 117). It is worth noting, however, that Van Dyck drew the main figures from the *Sacred and Profane Love* in his sketchbook (Adriani, *op.cit.*, p. 75, fol. 113).

[36] See S. W. A. Drossaers, "Inventaris van de Meubelen van het Stadhouderlijk Kwartier met het Speelhuis en van het Huis in het Noordeinde te 's-Gravenhage," *Oud-Holland*, xlvii, 1930, p. 204, no. 57.

[37] *Ibid.*

[38] See Both de Tanzia, *Notice des tableaux exposés dans les galeries du Musée National du Louvre*, Paris, 1878, p. 72, no. 141.

canto (Pl. XII, 16) with the earlier, simpler versions, which are based more squarely than Van Dyck's on Tasso's text. In Annibale Carracci's painting in Naples, for instance (Pl. XII, 18),[39] the arrangement of the group of lovers might in most essentials have been the model for their arrangement in Van Dyck's picture. Also, in both pictures, Carlo and Ubaldo spy on the lovers, as they should, from a covert at the upper left. Where Van Dyck differs from Annibale, aside from his failure to include a view of Armida's palace in the background, is in the matter of eclectic embellishment, in the use of imagery not found in Tasso's text but supplied him by antiquity, or by antiquity seen through the Renaissance or the Early Baroque. Certainly, it was this imagery that caused the picture, clearly intended by Van Dyck to be an amorous scene from Tasso, to be mistaken for another amorous subject, Mars and Venus, which had been popular in antiquity and the Renaissance.

At the left in Van Dyck's *Rinaldo and Armida* (Pl. XII, 16), two Cupids, whose arrangement as a group recalls Bernini's *Apollo and Daphne*, ride Rinaldo's sword, now fallen into ignoble disuse; their mock-heroics might call to mind a Cupid playing with the arms of an unwarlike Mars in a Pompeian fresco of Mars and Venus (Pl. XII, 17).[40] In the right foreground of Van Dyck's pictures two Cupids sit beside a jewel box while another behind them waves a feathered fan. This imagery again recalls a scene in Pompeian painting which shows several Cupids busying themselves with the attributes of Venus. One, for instance, who holds a small jewel box in his lap, plays with an armlet and another, standing, admires a long necklace (Pl. XIII, 19).[41] The Cupids, lower right, in the *Rinaldo and Armida* with the open jewel box and the bottles of cosmetics nearby—one Cupid has amused himself by thrusting his foot into a red slipper and by adorning his

[39] This, the earliest known example of this subject, dates from the early years of the seventeenth century.

[40] From the House of Mars and Venus. For this theme in Pompeian painting, see L. Curtius, *Die Wandmalerei Pompejis*, Leipzig, 1929, pp. 250ff.

[41] From the Casa dei Bronzi. See *ibid.*, pp. 396ff, for Cupids in ancient painting. Van Dyck probably knew Annibale Carracci's painting *Sleeping Venus with Cupids*, based on the Elder Philostratus (Book 1, 6), which is now at Chantilly (Voss, *op.cit.*, fig. p. 184), but there is less emphasis here than in Van Dyck's picture on the adornment of the lady concerned.

leg with a scarf[42]—adumbrate the theme depicted above them, of the Toilet of Armida—Armida admiring herself in a mirror held by another Cupid as she arranges her hair.

Now in Annibale Carracci's painting in Naples (Pl. XII, 18), Rinaldo holds the mirror into which Armida looks as she makes her coiffure, and this accords with Tasso's text. But Van Dyck was evidently so much interested in the Renaissance theme of the Toilet of Venus, a theme also having its roots in antiquity, that he has in his rendering of Armida's Toilet failed to follow Tasso's poetry. He has instead portrayed it as a Toilet of Venus in the general manner of Titian. In the Chatsworth Sketchbook there is a drawing after a Toilet of Venus by Titian (Pl. XIII, 20).[43] This is not after the famous painting now in the National Gallery in Washington, but after a somewhat different, lost version, a copy of which exists in the Hermitage in Leningrad.[44] Van Dyck's sketch after the lost Titian shows the seated Venus, a *Venus pudica* in type, looking into a mirror held by two Cupids. Another version, attributed to Paolo Veronese after Titian, which is in the Lee Collection of the Courtauld Institute of Art, is actually closer to Van Dyck. It shows a seated Venus, of the type of *Venus genetrix*, arranging a veil on her hair and looking into a mirror held, as in the *Rinaldo and Armida*, by only one Cupid (Pl. XIII, 21).[45] Still another version, suggestive for Van Dyck, which has also been attributed to Veronese, shows a seated Venus in back view, nude to the waist; as she arranges her hair, she regards herself at arm's length in a mirror held by a single Cupid and which she also helps to support with her right hand (Pl. XIII, 22),[46] much

[42] The inventory of 1632-34 (see above, p. 23 and n. 36) misinterprets this scarf, calling it a garter.

[43] See Adriani, *op.cit.*, pp. 79-80, fol. 119v. Although both his paintings and the Chatsworth Sketchbook give ample evidence of Van Dyck's veneration for Titian and the Venetians, it is noteworthy that his own collection contained many examples of Venetian art, including no fewer than nineteen pictures either by Titian or copied by himself after Titian. See Tietze-Conrat, *op.cit.*, and J. Müller-Rostock, "Ein Verzeichnis von Bildern aus dem Besitze des van Dyck," *Zeitschrift für bildenden Kunst*, LVII, 1922, pp. 22-24.

[44] See Stephan Poglayen-Neuwall, "Titian's Pictures of the Toilet of Venus and Their Copies," *Art Bulletin*, XVI, 1934, p. 363.

[45] *Ibid.*, p. 372. Cf. catalogue of the Lee Collection, Courtauld Institute of Art, University of London, 1962, p. 26, No. 54.

[46] Poglayen-Neuwall, *op.cit.*, p. 378. One may also note the similarity of this

as Armida stretches out her left arm to support the mirror held by a single Cupid in Van Dyck's picture. But in any case, whatever Venetian painting or paintings he had in mind, Van Dyck's account of Armida's coiffure has taken on the semblance of a Toilet of Venus in the Venetian manner. This fact and the playful activity of the Cupids, recalling the Antique, which Van Dyck might have known through antique paintings now lost to us, are quite enough to account for the mistaken title of Mars and Venus which the painting earlier possessed.

Thus the Antique plays a significant role in these works of Van Dyck that illustrate episodes from Tasso's *Gerusalemme Liberata,* episodes having their own amatory ancestry in ancient mythology and ancient art. It plays a role in these paintings, and probably in others by Van Dyck, that neither Sandrart nor indeed Bellori, who also failed to detect Rubens' fundamental debt to ancient art, were in the least aware of. Bellori, of course, understood Van Dyck's great indebtedness to Titian's color and pictorial invention, but he did not know that part, at least, of the formal language that the Flemish painter learned from the great Venetian ultimately involved the Antique. The nature and the appropriateness of Van Dyck's debt to antiquity, whether direct or indirect, are thus the *raison d'être* of this paper. It is also pertinent to remark here how handsomely Van Dyck, through the forms of antiquity and of the great Venetians, has interpreted the vital poetry of two of Tasso's finest passages.[47]

Venus with her curved back and head in profile to the Nereids seen from behind on Roman sarcophagi. See above p. 18.

[47] In preparing this article I have been indebted to Erwin Panofsky, Eric Sjöqvist, Gertrude Coor, Julius Held, John R. Martin, and Charles G. Dempsey for valuable advice.

THE FINDING OF ERICHTHONIUS:
AN ANCIENT THEME IN BAROQUE ART

WOLFGANG STECHOW

IT IS dangerous in both iconographical and stylistic research to draw conclusions from scanty material. But sometimes such scarcity may be excusable and even welcome, and I can only hope that this may be true of the subject of this paper. For one thing, I have reason to believe that the material at my disposal, though indeed scanty, is virtually complete so far as it has been preserved at all; and secondly, just as a small musical score facilitates perception of each individual part without detriment to the whole, a restricted number of representations of a theme may permit significant contrasts within the fabric of a style to stand out clearly without slighting the properties that bind them together.

Like Erechtheus, Erichthonius[1] is intimately connected with the earliest myths concerning the gods and the first rulers of Attica, and of Athens in particular. From a bewildering variety of forms of the story, some basic features emerge. Erichthonius was the son of Gaea, who was impregnated when Hephaestus tried, in vain, to ravish Athena. The child, guarded by one or two snakes, shaped like a snake, or (most frequently) cursed with a serpent tail instead of feet, is hidden by Athena in a basket which she hands to Aglauros, Pandrosos, and Herse, the three daughters of Cecrops, with the stern command not to uncover it. Overwhelmed by curiosity, Aglauros, though warned by one (or both) of her sisters, opens the basket. The crow (Coronis) who watches the proceedings reports them to Athena and is punished for her tattling. The Cecropides are either pursued and killed by the guardian snake(s) or become insane and perish by hurling themselves from the Acropolis or by throwing themselves into the sea.

[1] Engelmann in Roscher, *Ausführliches Lexikon . . .*, I, col. 1303ff; Escher in Pauly-Wissowa, *Real-Encyclopaedie*, VI, 1, col. 439ff; Benjamin Powell, *Erichthonius and the Three Daughters of Cecrops* (Cornell Studies in Classical Philology, XVII), Ithaca, New York, 1906; Murray Fowler, "The Myth of Erichthonius," *Classical Philology*, XXXVIII, 1943, pp. 28ff; A. Pigler, *Barockthemen*, Budapest, 1956, II, pp. 77f. In press: my article "Erichthonius" in *Reallexikon zur deutschen Kunstgeschichte*.

These are the basic elements of the myth as reported at length, or merely alluded to, by Euripides (who specifically mentions pictorial representations; *Ion*, 20ff and 265ff), Antigonos of Karystos (*Historia Mirabilis*, 12), Ovid (*Metamorphoses*, 2, 552ff and 748f), Hyginus (*Fabulae*, 166; *Poetica astronomica*, 2, 13), and many others. In ancient art, particularly on vases, the favorite moment is the handing of Erichthonius to Athena by Gaea; the opening of the basket is rarely found; Erichthonius is rendered in purely human form. The only scene from the myth represented in the Middle Ages is that in which Athena entrusts the baby to the Cecropides, as illustration to a profusely allegorizing passage in the *Ovide moralisé*.[2] There are but few representations from the Renaissance; Raphael's (or Penni's) much-damaged fresco of 1516 in Cardinal Bibbiena's bathroom in the Vatican shows, as Goethe informed Schiller in 1797, "the importunity of Vulcan toward Minerva";[3] Sebastiano del Piombo's somewhat earlier fresco in the Farnesina (1511) represents only two daughters of Cecrops about to open the basket, with an unusually strong emphasis on the indiscretion of the crow.[4] Manneristic artists restricted themselves largely to illustrations of Ovid's version of the story; to two of these I shall return presently.

There would be little sense in investigating the Baroque image of this story but for the interest Rubens and Rembrandt took in it. All their representations of it concern the opening of the basket, and this is also true of all other Baroque versions. The precise mo-

[2] Paris, Bibl. de l'Arsénal, ms 5069, fol. 19, early fourteenth century; see *Ovide moralisé*, ed. C. de Boer, Amsterdam, 1915, I, pp. 217ff, v. 2121ff. The Middle Ages were, however, quite familiar with the ancient concept of Erichthonius as inventor of the quadriga, and as such he is depicted (crowned half figure with wheel) in a woodcut on fol. 34 of Hartmann Schedel's *Buch der Chroniken und Geschichten*, Nuremberg, 1493. The idea that he made this invention—which also caused astrologers to identify him with Heniochus-Auriga—in order to hide his misshapen legs occurs in Servius' Commentary on Vergil and was later taken up by Rabelais (see J. Seznec, *La survivance des dieux antiques* [Studies of the Warburg Institute, XI], 1940, p. 278) and Ariosto (*Orlando furioso*, XXXVII, 27).

[3] Letter to Schiller, Oct. 25, 1797; H. Dollmayr, *Archivio storico dell'arte*, III, 1890, pp. 272ff; Frederick Hartt, *Giulio Romano*, New Haven, 1958, I, p. 31, n. 35.

[4] Luitpold Dussler, *Sebastiano del Piombo*, Basel, 1942, pp. 30ff and fig. 15. The program of this cycle has not been adequately studied.

ment is almost invariably that of the full discovery; only in exceptional cases, as, for example, in a late painting by Jan Lievens (Pl. xiv, 1),[5] is emphasis placed on an attempt on the part of one of the other sisters to keep Aglauros from opening the basket.

Rembrandt treated the subject in three drawings; two of these can be dated around 1637, the other about 1648.[6] The fragment in Göttingen (B.149) already concentrates on the shock experienced by at least one of the Cecropides as the basket is opened by her sister; this element is intensified tremendously in another sheet (B.150; now in an American private collection; Pl. xiv, 3)[7] where terror reigns supreme. It is hardly doubtful that Rembrandt was here influenced by the print from Antonio Tempesta's hugely popular Ovid series of ca. 1580-90 (Pl. xiv, 2),[8] to which he may have owed his knowledge of the story. It is well known that this is not the only example of Rembrandt having been impressed by the vastly inferior but highly imaginative Italian etcher.[9] The impact of this—*sit venia verbo*—tempestuous rendering of the fright and flight of the maidens is not entirely nullified by the infinitely more funny than gruesome baby, who almost seems to mimic the

[5] Ostfriesisches Landesmuseum, Emden, No. 55 (Hans Schneider, *Jan Lievens*, Haarlem, 1932, p. 111, no. 85). Also in a composition in the round by Gerard de Lairesse, which exists in two almost identical versions: in the Wightman Memorial Gallery at the University of Notre Dame, Indiana (published by Dwight C. Miller, *Seventeenth- and Eighteenth-Century Paintings from the University of Notre Dame* (exhibition catalogue), University of Illinois, Urbana, 1962, no. 1), and in the National Gallery, Oslo.

[6] Otto Benesch, *The Drawings of Rembrandt*, London, 1954ff, I, nos. 149, 150; III, no. 622.

[7] *Rembrandt Drawings from American Collections. Exhibited at the Pierpont Morgan Library . . . the Fogg Art Museum*, 1960, no. 12.

[8] No. 14 of the series B.638-787. On the date see M. D. Henkel in *Vorträge der Bibliothek Warburg, 1926-27*, Leipzig-Berlin, 1930, p. 102; however, E. K. J. Reznicek (*Die Zeichnungen von Hendrick Goltzius*, Utrecht, 1961, p. 194) dates the series after Goltzius' of 1590, on which see below. The wild gesticulation with two arms by one of the Cecropides is prefigured in a drawing by Pirro Ligorio, in which another daughter hides her face in terror and Erichthonius sports two large serpent tails (vol. xxx, fol. 12v of the notebooks in Turin, Archivio di Stato). Tempesta's print was clearly influenced by sixteenth-century book illustrations of the *Metamorphoses* such as the one by Virgil Solis in the Frankfurt edition of 1569, p. 28.

[9] N. Beets, "Herscheppingen," *Feestbundel Abraham Bredius*, Amsterdam, 1915, pp. 1ff; Ludwig Münz, *Rembrandt's Etchings*, London, 1952, I, pp. 15ff.

fleeing daughter, and Rembrandt was captivated by it—not so much by any specific details as by the general characteristics, which include the fluency of movements and gesticulations, the slenderness of bodies and heads, and the weird, somewhat ballet-like mood. There is less violence but greater dramatic force in the drawing of about 1648, in Groningen (B.622; Pl. xiv, 4) [10] in which Rembrandt introduced several other witnesses of the event, a rare feature in post-antique art. Some echoes of Tempesta can still be heard, but the menacingly pointed serpent tail of Erichthonius and the gesture of the daughter in the center connect this drawing with Hendrick Goltzius' otherwise much more sedate composition engraved by a pupil in 1590 (Pl. xv, 5), [11] in which the sisters presage Bellange's *Marys at the Tomb* as perfect embodiments of manneristic fashion; the dog—and only the dog—comes from Rubens' first picture of the subject (Pl. xv, 6), which Rembrandt could have known from Pieter van Sompel's engraving. [12] None of these borrowings is very important; the almost Poussinesque compositional firmness of this design, which recalls a stage setting, has nothing derivative about it.

The emphasis on terror and the allusion to dire consequences embodied in Tempesta's print and Rembrandt's drawings is, so far as I can see, matched by only two other Baroque works. One is a painting by Paulus Bor, probably done about 1650, which I know only from a very poor reproduction (Pl. xvi, 8); [13] here the spectator is cleverly denied a full view of the content of the basket and is, instead, squarely and almost exclusively faced with the stark terror on the countenances of the maidens, whose ample

[10] W. R. Valentiner (*Rembrandt, Des Meisters Handzeichnungen*, ii, p. 164, no. 597) erroneously lists this drawing as being in Amsterdam.

[11] B. III, p. 104, no. 62 (no. 12 of the series).

[12] See below, p. 32.

[13] In the Rijksbureau, The Hague; once in the Brussels art trade. A drawing of 1663 by Salomon de Bray (see J. W. von Moltke in *Marburger Jahrbuch für Kunstwissenschaft*, xi-xii, 1938-39, p. 352, fig. 41, and p. 403, no. Z. 67) is a classicistic variation on Rembrandt's drawing B.150. By misnaming it "Pandora," the author joins the ranks of those who confused the name of one of the Cecropides, Pandrosos, with that of another indiscreet opener of a container; a "korfken van Bandora" is mentioned in 1702 (J. Denucé, *Art-Export in the 17th Century in Antwerp, The Firm Forchoudt*, Antwerp, 1931, p. 259); see also Dora and Erwin Panofsky, *Pandora's Box*, New York, 1956, pp. 9f and 20.

bodies are struck by a violent light. Rembrandt's straightforward drama is here turned into a sophisticated fantasy. The other such work is by Salvator Rosa (Christ Church, Oxford; Pl. xvi, 9);[14] here the terror of the Cecropides—clearly derived from Tempesta (Pl. xiv, 2), as is the weirdly curving snake—is somewhat diluted rather than strengthened by increasing their number to six, but the wind-swept trees and threatening sky are impressive enough.

Rubens' two great paintings of this subject have been well analyzed, and their complicated history brilliantly clarified, by the late Ludwig Burchard.[15] At the risk of disturbing the balance, I shall repeat only a few details of his essay and concentrate on some additional observations. The Liechtenstein picture of about 1615 (Pl. xv, 6) is fully characteristic of that perfect blend of mythological reality with "active" allegory which had been initiated by the master after his return from Italy and was to culminate in the Medici cycle of the early twenties. The grouping of the three nudes had first been attempted in a drawing by Anthonie van Blocklandt, now in Chicago (Pl. xv, 7);[16] but this work not only lacks all elements of the classical story except the basket with the little monster, but is also of rather schematic design. The beautiful nude forms of the Cecropides in Rubens' work, enlivened by the contrast with the old nurse (who does not belong in the story), the felicitous grouping and serene setting were deeply appreciated and eloquently praised by Jacob Burckhardt,[17] whose judgment of Rembrandt's drawings can readily be imagined; they convey none of the drama and foreboding embodied in the latter. But they do tell the story, and tell it well, with the help of various devices that undoubtedly were immediately

[14] L. Ozzola in *Burlington Magazine*, xvi, 1909-10, p. 150: "Hercules Leaving the Cradle"; Tancred Borenius, *Pictures by the Old Masters in the Library of Christ Church, Oxford*, Oxford, 1916, no. 171: "Erichthonius delivered to the Daughter of Cecrops to be educated."

[15] Ludwig Burchard, "Rubens' 'Daughters of Cecrops,'" *Allen Memorial Art Museum Bulletin, Oberlin College*, xi, 1953-54, pp. 4ff.

[16] Ingrid Jost (*Studien zu Anthonis Blocklandt* [Diss.], Cologne, 1960, pp. 153f), considers the Chicago drawing an original of ca. 1577-78, the one in the British Museum (Cat. Popham, v, 1932, p. 172, pl. 64), a copy.

[17] *Erinnerungen aus Rubens*, 3rd ed., Basel, 1918, p. 70 (*Recollections of Rubens*, tr. M. Hottinger, ed. H. Gerson, London, 1950, p. 38, and quoted by Burchard, *op.cit.*, p. 8).

understood by Rubens' well-read friends and admirers. One of these is the role played by the putto who helps Aglauros open the basket and at the same time turns with a mischievous glance to the sister standing on the left. Patterned upon an antique prototype, probably from the Beatrix sarcophagus in the Campo Santo in Pisa,[18] he is nevertheless a most lively creature, full of action, and fulfills exactly the same function as the cupids who help the Dioskuroi carry off the daughters of Leucippus (Munich) and the little putti who play around wintry Boreas as he abducts Oreithyia (Vienna, Akademie) :[19] the function of allegorical figures actively and decisively participating in a story from antiquity. In an earlier state of the Liechtenstein picture, preserved in Van Sompel's engraving,[20] there was another putto who flew up over the old nurse and trumpeted the event; this was obliterated by Rubens himself and—more correctly—replaced with the crow of the ancient tale. A similar device is the fountain figure. Far from being just a nymph,[21] she allegorically indicates the presence of Gaea, the mother of the little monster, in the form of the *Artemis Ephesia*,

[18] As suggested by E. Kieser (*Münchner Jahrbuch der bildenden Kunst*, N.S., x, 1933, p. 120, n. 26), who also considers the *Judgment of Paris* of the Villa Medici in Rome a possible source (Robert II, pl. 5). The imaginative use of this figure in Rubens' work is dramatically pointed up by the thoughtlessness of the torch-bearing putto in Jordaens' picture of 1617 in Brussels, which is an altogether poor paraphrase of the Liechtenstein picture (Leo van Puyvelde, "Jordaens's First Dated Work," *Burlington Magazine*, LXIX, 1936, pp. 225f). A painting attributed to G. de Lairesse (on the London art market, reproduced in *The Museums Journal*, LIX, January 1960, p. v; see Miller, *op.cit.*) is likewise patently derived from the Liechtenstein picture and shows no connection with the Oslo-Notre Dame composition by de Lairesse referred to above in n. 5. A painting sold as "Lastman" in Vienna (*Dorotheum*, March 21, 1932, no. 28, pl. IX) combines two daughters inspired by the Liechtenstein canvas with one based on a common Lastman pattern. The painting is tentatively given to Cornelis Holsteyn in the Rijksbureau, The Hague.

[19] See Wernicke, s.v. Boreas, *Pauly-Wissowa*, III, col. 728, and Eva Frank s.v. Oreithyia, *ibid.*, XVIII, 1, col. 954ff, also on the identification of Oreithyia as a sister or an aunt of the Cecropides. The iconography of Rubens' painting of ca. 1615 deserves more attention than it has received so far. The story was represented on the Kypselos Chest (on which see Lippold in *Pauly-Wissowa*, XII, col. 121ff); this was carefully described by Pausanias, whose writings Rubens knew (at least in 1630, see Ruth Magurn, *The Letters of Peter Paul Rubens*, Cambridge, Massachusetts, 1955, p. 497).

[20] Burchard, *op.cit.*, fig. 2.

[21] Burckhardt, *op.cit.*, p. 8.

so dear to Rubens[22] and quite often interpreted as *Terra* in his time;[23] in J. Sambucus' *Emblemata* (Leiden, 1599; Pl. XVI, 11), which Rubens surely knew, she already appears as a fountain statue.[24] The Liechtenstein painting was preceded by the brilliant sketch in Count Seilern's collection (Pl. XVI, 10);[25] here at the Gaea-Fountain is already present, and even the crow is there (though inactively perched on the pilaster), but the putti are missing, and instead of the nurse one discovers a strange female figure with wild hair and a rather dramatically and invitingly gesticulating right arm, which I think must be identified as a personification of *Curiositas*: Ripa specifically mentions hair standing on end and raised hands as her attributes.[26]

The replacement of this allegorical figure with the old nurse foreshadows a prominent characteristic of the second Erichthonius picture by Rubens, the large canvas of about 1633 once in the collection of the Duc de Richelieu, of which a large fragment has survived (now in the Oberlin museum; Pl. XVII, 12), and which is known in its entirety through a number of copies that preserve even two different states of the final version (Pl. XVII, 13).[27] While the oil sketch in Stockholm still lacks the nurse, she is again incorporated in the *modello* at Belvoir Castle which closely corresponds to the first state of the large canvas. And in this, Rubens

[22] Painting in Glasgow: *L'art flamand dans les collections britanniques* (exhibition catalogue), Bruges, Musée de l'Art, 1956, no. 64 and pl. 46; book illustrations: H. G. Evers, *Rubens und sein Werk*, Brussels, 1943, figs. 80, 109.

[23] Guy de Tervarent, *Attributs et symboles dans l'art profane, 1450-1600*, Geneva, 1958, I, col. 170: "Femme aux nombreuses mamelles," II: "La nature ou la terre." He illustrates a painting by Jan Brueghel and Hendrick de Clerck in Madrid (fig. 36) which contains this figure in a decidedly chthonic context, as indicated by Macrobius. The profusion of large shells which Rubens inserted in the Liechtenstein picture after covering up the trumpeting putto expresses the same thought.

[24] Hermann Thiersch, *Artemis Ephesia* (Abhandlungen der Gesellschaft der Wissenschaften zu Göttingen, Phil.-hist. Klasse, 3rd series, no. 12), Berlin, 1935, p. 106 and pl. LXII, 3.

[25] [Count A. Seilern] *Flemish Paintings and Drawings at 56 Princes Gate*, London, 1955, pp. 41ff and pl. 52.

[26] *Iconologia*, Venice, ed. 1645, p. 129: ". . . .haverà i capelli dritti, con le mani alte." It is true that the other features of Ripa's figure are missing (wings; ears and frogs strewn over her garment).

[27] On the following, see Burchard, *op.cit.*, pp. 11ff.

has significantly altered the mood of the earlier work. There is now no putto (or *Curiositas*) egging the sisters on, no excited dog, no crow tattling, no allusion to the mother of the monster; not even a hesitation remains. Behind the intimate, relaxed group stretches a garden architecture with two quiet herms;[28] the fountain, now of equally "neutral" design, permits a glimpse of a serene, very Titianesque landscape. This is an idyl, not a story; but it is a thoroughly antique idyl.[29]

If Rembrandt's interpretations stand for an antiquity seen in terms of drama and foreboding—not unlike Mantegna's—those of Rubens stand for an antiquity seen first in terms of learned allegory revitalized by an inexhaustible visual imagination—not unlike Raphael's—and later of a serene idyl—not unlike Bellini's. But all of these are Baroque possibilities and results: related to the Renaissance spirit (as so vividly felt and expressed by Jacob Burckhardt) yet none of them quite like it. Although generalizations do become dangerous here, one may perhaps say that the antiquarian aspects of antiquity have more completely disappeared from the Baroque works, and so have the demonic aspects. Even

[28] The ominous-looking faces of these herms as shown on one of the copies (Burchard, *op.cit.*, fig. 7) do not seem to have occurred on the original at all (*ibid.*, figs. 6, 8, 9; here, Pl. xvii, 13).

[29] If one looks for continued allegorical play here, one may perhaps wonder whether the fact that the foolishly curious Aglauros is rather fully clothed while her sisters are not, conveys a specific meaning; the contrast between the clothed "profane love" and the nude "divine love" in Titian's Borghese picture comes to mind.

The paintings by Rubens' pupil Samuel Hoffmann in the Historisches Museum, Frankfurt (dated 1645), by Jordaens in Vienna (late work, no. 1087 a), by an unknown Flemish painter, whose work is included in G. Coques' *Picture Gallery* at Windsor (*Burlington Magazine*, xxvii, 1915, p. 155, lower right), and by Hendrick Heerschop (Amsterdam, no. 1132, with all the girls fashionably dressed) are weak variations on Rubens' second work. The paintings by Gottfried Schalcken, once in the Cavens Collection in Brussels (Hofstede de Groot, no. 75) and by B. Breenbergh (?) in the Shapiro Collection in London (see *Burlington Magazine*, lxxxxv, 1953, p. 55) are unknown to me. It may be worth mentioning that the subject of an opera entitled *Die drei Töchter Cecrops*, written by Aurora von Königsmarck and composed by Johann Wolfgang Franck for Ansbach shortly before 1680, has nothing to do with the Erichthonius story. The opera was re-edited by G. F. Schmidt and A. Beer-Walbrunn in *Das Erbe deutscher Musik*, 2nd series (*Denkmäler deutscher Tonkunst*, xxxviii), 1938.

Rembrandt's and Bor's works are conceived and visualized as more strictly human experiences than comparable ones of the Early Renaissance, and Rubens' more than those of the High Renaissance, in which the psychological distance from antiquity speaks more strongly, and which are apt to convey the impression of either a grandiose reconstruction or a nostalgic dream. In the works of its great masters, the Baroque found a more direct, more intimate approach to the wellsprings of classical mythology.[30]

[30] For help in providing material for this paper, I am greatly indebted to Dr. H. Gerson, The Hague; Sir Anthony Blunt, Dr. L. D. Ettlinger, and Count A. Seilern, London; Dr. Freiherr von Erffa and Dr. Karl-August Wirth, Munich; Miss Felice Stampfle, New York; Professor David Coffin, Princeton; Professor Dwight Miller, Urbana, Illinois; and Dr. Gustav Wilhelm in Vaduz.

MYTHOLOGY AND
SEVENTEENTH-CENTURY SPANISH PAINTERS

DIEGO ANGULO IÑIGUEZ

THE seventeenth-century Spaniard looked askance at mythological subjects in painting because they were intimately related to the nude. There are, however, some rare cases of painters who undertook such subjects in exceptional circumstances. I refer to Velázquez, Zurbarán, and Ribera.

Velázquez, and on a much smaller scale Zurbarán, painted fables for the Court, under the protection of Philip IV. Philip II had imposed his broad-mindedness in matters of art upon his courtiers, and his grandson Philip IV had inherited this liberal tradition. Ribera, although born and bred in Spain, lived most of his life in Naples, that is, outside the Peninsula. All three painted their fables in the naturalistic way proper to the Baroque style, but what I want to bring to your attention is their attitude toward the way in which these fables were to be treated.

There is a belief among students of Velázquez, particularly Spanish students, that amounts almost to a convention: the idea that Velázquez was laughing at the gods of Olympus. This belief has been current for more than a hundred years.[1]

William Stirling, writing in the middle of the nineteenth century on *The Drinkers*, mentions Hogarth.[2] By the end of the century, in an attempt to denigrate the wine god, writers found that there was material for criminologists among the ragged devotees of Bacchus. Not many years ago the philosopher Ortega y Gasset enlarged upon this idea by writing: "And here we have our Velázquez gathering up a few rascals, the dregs of the town, dirty, sly, and besotted with drink, and saying to them: 'Come on, we are going to laugh at the gods.'"

Some maintain that in order to understand the *Forge of Vulcan* and the real feelings of the artist toward his subject, the burlesque ballad by a lewd contemporary of Velázquez, Polo de Medina,

[1] Diego Angulo Iñiguez, "Velázquez y la Mitología," *III centenario de la muerte de Velázquez*, Madrid, 1961.
[2] William Stirling, *Velázquez and His Works*, London, 1855, p. 94.

must be read. In this ballad, Vulcan, Venus, and Mars are figures of fun, the butts of bawdy jokes. The poet's desire to make a laughing stock of the gods of Olympus is only too clear. What the Renaissance tradition had supposed was the laughter of the gods, when Mars and Venus were caught in Vulcan's ingenious net, has become a continuous guffaw at the horns adorning Vulcan's head.

The lack of the heroic Renaissance appearance of the god in the *Mars* has made him the target of exaggerated mockery. He is, finally, seen at the spit of Monipodio, the Sevillian robber chief, so splendidly portrayed by Cervantes in his short story "Rinconete y Cortadillo." So that even if poor Mars loses face, Velázquez is backed up by the greatest of all Spanish writers. Only a few years ago, someone opined that Argus in the *Mercury and Argus* was in a drunken sleep after too many toasts to Bacchus.

I think the time has come for a revision of opinion on the interpretation of myths as painted by Velázquez. It is obvious, of course, that he has used the sharpest realism for the followers of Bacchus. They are certainly not gentlemen. They are poor folk who, thanks to the invention of wine, are able to drown their sorrows and even to laugh awhile. The look of veneration on the face of the man kneeling next to Bacchus with lifted glass shows no less a degree of devotion than that seen in the face of Melchor in the *Adoration of the Magi*, painted ten years before. The splendid nude god is in the finest Michelangelo tradition, and I do not think that his face with its sensual lips weakens the dashing grace of his body. It is simply the result of Velázquez's love of naturalism. Caravaggio's rendering of the feet of the dead Virgin may upset the pious, and may even be out of keeping with the dignity of the subject, but there is no flicker of mockery in his treatment. The nude figure of Bacchus' drinking companion is no less noble in aspect.

It seems to me that Velázquez's attitude to this subject is not very different from that of Goltzius in his engraving *Potores ad Bacchum*, mentioned as a possible source of the composition of *The Drinkers* by the late Martin Soria. This engraving also shows some poor people, accompanied by a soldier, going humbly to beg the god to drive away care and drown their sorrows in wine. This is explained in the lettering in the engraving itself. Except for the soldier, Velázquez chose the poorest, most ragged people, and the god does not have the almost Da Vinci-like smile of the engraving. But Goltzius is still a Renaissance man working in Holland, and Caravaggio had been dead for years when Velázquez was working. It must also be borne in mind, as Charles de Tolnay points out, that the grape harvest was a lesser Dionysiac feast at which the presence of slaves was tolerated. For Velázquez, the real purpose of the myth is to show the joy wine brings to those who have nothing to laugh at, whose lives are overburdened with poverty and miseries. This is much more moving than the effect of drink on people who still have young blood in their veins.

I think that Velázquez's treatment of the fable of Mars and Venus is too elegant to admit mockery.[3] The evolution of this fable can be followed in Spanish literature, from the Renaissance version in which the gods laugh at the spectacle of the lovers caught in the net to the burlesque seventeenth-century view, in which Venus is a repulsive trollop with, as Polo de Medina says, "a belly fatter than a prior's" and hairy bow legs, and Mars "a scowling slit-eyed cutthroat with frowning eyebrows." They fall in love with each other: "he in the moon-calf, Portuguese manner; she in the bold Turkish way," and Vulcan becomes the central theme of the cuckolded husband, the butt of all jokes.

Velázquez, however, chooses the scene in the fable that does least damage to the reputations of the inhabitants of Olympus and takes no notice of the interpretation favored by the poets of the time. If he had any satirical intentions, it seems likely that some trace of mockery would be found in the faces of the blacksmith's apprentices. I have to be emphatic about this, because there has been a very recent allusion to the sarcastic expression on the faces of Vulcan's apprentices.[4] I am afraid the only expression I can find is one of astonishment at Apollo's way of breaking the news of the adultery. It is just possible, perhaps, to discern a look of pity on the face of the apprentice in the background, an expression that a faithful servant might very well

[3] Diego Angulo Iñiguez, "La fábula de Vulcano, Venus y Marte y 'La Fragua' de Velázquez," *Archivo Español de Arte*, 1960, p. 149.

[4] Francisco Javier Sánchez Cantón, *Velázquez y lo clasico*, Madrid, 1961.

have. To Velázquez this painting is a study of expression and also of the nude, as is *Joseph's Brothers Presenting his Coat to Jacob*, painted in Rome about the same time; I am sure that in neither painting is there any intention of mockery.

The *Mars* shows the god at rest, and here too there is not the least sign of anything that might be interpreted as mockery in his expression. What is more, I feel that the size of his mustache and helmet do not permit the notice of any such expression, in spite of opinions to the contrary. On another occasion I alluded to his brooding look and the general lack of enthusiasm in his attitude, even in his natural martial violence. I even remarked that the years Velázquez painted this picture were not the luckiest ones for the Spanish army. My friend De Tolnay has recently drawn attention to the melancholy character of the Mars portrayed by Velázquez, suggesting that it may be a version of the theme of vanity. In any case, I fail to perceive any intention of mockery. As for the allusion to Argus already mentioned, it seems so totally unfounded that it need not be seriously considered.

Velázquez's mind was formed with the generation of the end of the sixteenth century, and he was educated in a tradition of respect for the ancient world. On the whole, I think that he went on respecting its myths, although, as a painter, his naturalism made him transfer the myth into an everyday setting. It has been said that this transference of the heroic Renaissance tradition into the everyday world constitutes a form of mockery in itself. This may seem comic to some people, but I do not believe that Velázquez intended any comic effect. My friend Sánchez Cantón has recently put forward the opinion that a disrespectful attitude does exist in *The Geographer*, *The Drinkers*, the *Forge of Vulcan*, the *Aesop* and *Menippus*, also in the *Mars*, but that Velázquez, on his second journey to Italy, undertaken specifically to buy statues and casts after the Antique, lost this disrespect.[5] To prove this he cites the *Venus and Cupid*, *The Spinners*, *Mercury and Argus*. Confronted with this new view of the problem, I must say first of all that I do not believe that the original version of *The Geographer* is by Velázquez at all, and I even doubt that it is Spanish. The *Aesop* and *Menippus* belong to the ancient world, but not to its myths. They are, therefore, outside the controversial limits

[5] *Ibid.*

that I have set myself in this paper. As to *The Drinkers*, the *Forge of Vulcan*, and the *Mars*, I have nothing to add to what I have just said about them.

To turn now to Ribera, the smile of the young faun in the *Silenus* has recently been described as mocking. This may be due, the writer goes on, to the painter's remembering some picaresque novel read during his years in Valencia, and also to the acting of fables at the Neapolitan court of the Viceroy, Conde de Lemos, in comic versions of, for example, Orpheus and Eurydice. This interesting reminder allows us to imagine a literary background for Ribera similar to that of Velázquez. But I would not be too sure that Ribera was more sensitive to a literary background than Velázquez.

As to Zurbarán's series of the Labors of Hercules, I do not think that there has been any mention of a mocking attitude in them, nor the possibility of such an interpretation.

I shall end now by saying that this tendency to see Velázquez as an irreverent denigrator of the gods on Olympus probably has its origin in literary criticism. Many of its most prominent promulgators are not art historians but men of letters, whose allusions to Spanish painting are so frequent that they betray a wish to discover parallels between Velázquez and Cervantes, Quevedo, Polo de Medina, etc. I have already made fleeting references to some of these supposed resemblances, and these examples could easily be multiplied. I will mention only one among the many—that Velázquez mocks at mythology just as Quevedo mocks at epic poems in the *Follies and Stupidities of Orlando*, and Cervantes mocks at books of chivalry in *Don Quixote*.

I do not, of course, deny that such parallels do ordinarily occur between the art and literature of a period in history, but I do not believe that they are bound to do so. The streets are parallel on this continent, particularly in the Spanish-speaking part, yet there are a few towns with winding streets in typically medieval layouts. And it seems to me that the historian who surveys the growth of mankind from a certain altitude finds deep satisfaction in putting historic facts into neat systems, and in placing them in prefabricated pigeon-holes, although he cannot, I fear, always indulge himself in this way.

THE ROLE OF CLASSICAL MODELS IN BERNINI'S AND POUSSIN'S PREPARATORY WORK

RUDOLF WITTKOWER

WHAT I am going to discuss has interested me for over twenty-five years, from the time when I collaborated with Walter Friedlaender on his edition of the drawings of Poussin. Ever since then, I have often returned to the problems of the present paper, and have even had occasion to refer to them briefly in recent publications. Now I should like to pull together some of these ideas and give them a unified form.

Bernini and Poussin—it is hardly necessary to say—are the chief representatives of the two great seventeenth-century currents, the Baroque and the classical, and it is generally held that there is little common ground between them or their works. Yet we know that Bernini loved and revered Poussin's paintings. In his Paris diary, Chantelou recorded such reactions of Bernini's as, "I must capitulate before Poussin's greatness"; "This is what I call a great man"; and, "Truly, this man has studied ancient art"; before the Chantelou series of Poussin's *Sacraments* he exclaimed, "I could study them for six months without interruption"; and before *The Gathering of the Ashes of Phocion*, pointing a finger to his forehead, "il signor Poussin è un pittore che lavora di là." When he spoke these words during his stay in Paris in 1665, Bernini's intense, dynamic Baroque was at the farthest removed from Poussin's puritanically severe style of the middle and late periods—yet Bernini never so much as hinted at the world of difference between their artistic productions. Although we do not know what Poussin thought about Bernini, we may venture a guess that the esteem was mutual.

The truth is that both artists shared a broad range of convictions. Both held that an artist should be learned, that decorum—the appropriate and becoming—must be the basis for a discriminating approach to the subject matter, that historical subjects—

i.e., subjects from the Bible, mythology, and ancient history—are the most worthy of representation, and that art is concerned with the expression of action and emotion. Moreover, both believed that nature was never perfect but that ideal beauty had been made manifest in ancient art and in some modern interpreters of the ancients, above all in the works of Raphael. All these are well known tenets of the classical doctrine, the various elements of which had developed from Leone Battista Alberti's days on and had become the creed of thinking artists of all kinds of opinion.

Since both Bernini and Poussin aimed in their works at representing ideal beauty, it follows that ancient art played a predominant part in all their considerations. The question then arises as to why, at the same period, in the same Roman milieu, the same ideology could lead to such contrasting results.

It might be argued that Bernini, the fiery southerner, the official artist of the papacy, produced what the Catholic orthodoxy of the Restoration period needed, the dazzling imagery of ecstasies and raptures; while Poussin, the sober Frenchman, working for French merchants and bankers, civil servants and lawyers, offered in his moral subjects and judicious classicism a pictorial realization of the most cherished ideals of a public steeped as much in Descartes' rationalism as in philosophical skepticism and stoicism. This line of argument, however, begs the question, because the particular qualities of both artists were their own and were the cause rather than the result of their being chosen by their respective patrons.

Nor can it be maintained that they studied entirely different classical works: Bernini exclusively works of the ancient "Baroque," such as the *Laocoön*, the *Marforio*, the *Borghese Warrior*, and so forth, Poussin exclusively Roman sarcophagi and reliefs, perhaps as one of Cassiano dal Pozzo's draftsmen. But even if we assume that this observation contains some truth, it would not suffice to account for the contrary orientation of the two artists. In point of fact, one can prove that the two drew inspiration from the same ancient statues. Bernini remarked in his speech before the French Academy: "In my early youth I drew a great deal from classical figures; and when I was in difficulties with my first statue, I turned to the Antinoüs as to the oracle." This very statue of Mercury in the Vatican (then called Antinoüs) also enjoyed an enormous prestige with the classical circle of Poussin, Duquesnoy, and Algardi; and Bellori, the mouthpiece of the classicists, published an engraving of it with the measurements taken by Duquesnoy and Poussin (Pl. xviii, 1).[1]

Nevertheless, one might justifiably argue that although both Poussin and Bernini studied a certain number of the same ancient works, Poussin carried his researches farther afield and consequently built up an infinitely larger classical repertory. This seems to me quite incontestable, but the fact in itself is less important than the question as to why it was Poussin rather than Bernini who felt it necessary to control as large a quantity of ancient material as possible.

I believe that one can throw some light on this question as well as on the broader issue of the Baroque and the classical, epitomized in Bernini's and Poussin's work, by investigating the different uses these artists made of classical models in the course of their preparatory studies. Although we have but little material at our disposal, compared with what has disappeared forever, sufficient evidence does exist to allow some generalizations.

Poussin's procedure was fully developed as early as the late 1620's when he painted the Chantilly *Massacre of the Innocents* (Pl. xviii, 3). All the figures of the vigorous preparatory drawing at Lille (Pl. xix, 5) are free interpretations of figures in Marcantonio's engraving of the Massacre made after Raphael, but the composition is rearranged along forceful spatial diagonals: it has been turned into a Baroque composition. In Poussin's painting, emotion is expressed by means different from those of the drawing; the figures now occupy two separate planes parallel to the picture plane, evidently in analogy to ancient reliefs: a Baroque composition has been transformed into a classical one.

At the same time, Poussin toned down action and introduced gestures expressive of *affetti*. He changed the mother's left arm with its firm grip round the executioner's waist (Pl. xix, 5) into a pose whose gesture shows her half warding off the blow and half

[1] G. P. Bellori, *Le vite de' pittori, scultori et architetti moderni*, Rome, 1672, p. 457.

43

lamenting (Pl. xvɪɪɪ, 3). For this, and for her facial expression, which derives from the type of the tragic mask (Pl. xvɪɪɪ, 2),[2] classical examples are legion. Perhaps even more striking is the alteration of the figure of the mother placed farther back, in the second plane. The drawing shows her running away, her child clasped tightly in her arms and her head turned back to the scene of murder. In the painting she moves more slowly, carrying in one hand the limp body of her dead child like a bundle that needs neither care nor protection. Her head, now shown in pure profile, is thrown back; she has raised her free arm and seems to beat her head with her fist. This expression of despair and approaching madness was known to Poussin from Medea sarcophagi; in fact, he combined here the attitude of Creusa's head with the gesture of her father Creon (Pl. xɪx, 4).[3] Classical antiquity had guided him to a psychological interpretation of the scene. Instead of the transitory action of a frightened mother, he finally depicted the deeply moving condition of a frantic soul.

Similar changes from preparatory drawings to finished work recur in all those cases where the chance preservation of drawings allows us to check. My next example, Poussin's *Moses Defending the Daughters of Jethro from Unfriendly Shepherds*, dates from the 1640's. The painting is lost, but we have the evidence of some surviving preparatory drawings. A loosely constructed drawing (in a London private collection, Pl. xx, 6) probably represents the earliest rendering of the composition; the final design seems to be that in the Louvre (Pl. xx, 7a).[4] The number of figures remains the same, but confusion has been clarified, action has been reduced, and the composition in depth has been changed into a relief composition with isolated statuesque figures. Their deriva-

[2] The example shown here as Pl. xvɪɪɪ, 2 was not found until 1824.

[3] Pl. xɪx, 4 after G. P. Bellori, *Admiranda romanarum antiquitatum ac veteris sculpturae vestigia*, Rome, 1693, pl. 55. The sarcophagus, in Poussin's day in the Villa Borghese, is now in the Louvre (Robert, *Die antiken Sarkophag-Reliefs*, Berlin, 1890, ɪɪ, no. 195).

It should be recalled that Medea revenged herself for Jason's desertion by giving his new bride Creusa a poisoned garment. In the detail, Pl. xɪx, 4, we see Creusa dying in extreme pain, her father hurrying to her side with an expression of utter despair.

[4] For transitional drawings, see Walter Friedlaender, *The Drawings of Nicolas Poussin*, London, 1939, ɪ, pp. 8f.

tion from classical statues is so patently evident—a Juno served for the imposing girl with the raised arm, and Niobids for the women protecting their pitchers (Pl. xx, 7b)—that one need not labor the point.

Typologically, the daughters of Niobe were obvious models for the daughters of Jethro, but Poussin had to transform the classical exemplars in order to invest them with a new meaning. Often he carried the reinterpretation of classical models much further than in this drawing, yet he never disavowed his source of inspiration. His first painting of the Finding of Moses, of 1638 (Louvre, Pl. xxi, 8), may serve as an example. Here Pharaoh's daughter is shown leaning languidly on the shoulder of a maid-servant. This group is derived from the common ancient representations of Dionysus leaning on a young satyr (Pl. xxi, 9) and, as the illustrations show, Poussin once again combined motifs from two different sources.[5] In the preparatory drawings for the second Finding of Moses, dating from 1647, Poussin broke away from the classical model, only to return to it in the painting (Louvre), in which the group appears facing the spectator. Similar figures served him on other occasions, for instance, for the Chantilly *Theseus Finding the Sword of his Father* (Pl. xxi, 10); even the shepherdess in the Louvre *Et in Arcadia Ego* is still connected with this expressive formula of classical ancestry.

The *Judgment of Solomon* of 1649 (Louvre, Pl. xxii, 11) belongs to Poussin's most classical period and even the preparatory drawing in the École des Beaux-Arts—admittedly representing an advanced stage—looks classical enough (Pl. xxii, 12). Although the span between drawing and painting is less obvious than in the case of the *Massacre of the Innocents*, we find our previous observations confirmed. Instead of the space-creating exedra in the drawing, a straight backdrop appears in the painting, a change whereby the composition acquires a relief character.

---

[5] The youthful Bacchus and Faun (now in Florence) shown in Pl. xxi, 9a is one of many examples that might be given for the general attitude of Poussin's group. But the attitude of the arm of Pharaoh's daughter resting on her attendant's shoulder comes from a different source: it is close to that of the bearded Dionysus in the well-known relief of the British Museum (2190) which in Poussin's day was in the Villa Montalto in Rome. Our Pl. xxi, 9b is after Bellori, *op.cit.*, pl. 43.

The guards in the background have been entirely eliminated and the number of foreground figures has been reduced. The right-hand group of spectators consists now of five adults instead of eight, not counting the soldier on whom interest was focused in the drawing. An anonymous crowd has been turned into an assembly of individuals whose striking gestures mirror their reactions. Their emotive responses to the drama hold our attention, in place of the purely physical action of the soldier.

Once again, the language of gestures reveals the close study of classical models. In the drawing there was only one individualized figure among the spectators, the mother with the child, in a pose similar to that of the *Girl with the Dove* in the Capitoline Museum. In the painting her gestures have become more complex and more expressive. With her left hand raised and her right hand stretched out, she now expresses not only fear ("I cannot bear to look") but also disgust. Her attitude and gestures follow closely those of Althaea in Meleager sarcophagi (Pl. xxii, 13b). But Althaea's action has a different meaning: she, the mother of Meleager, is burning the faggot that is magically connected with the life of her son; her raised arm expresses refusal to desist from this fateful step. A gesture with a meaning similar to Poussin's is to be found in Orestes sarcophagi (Pl. xxii, 13a),[6] and I suggest that it influenced his rendering of the studied pose in the *Judgment of Solomon*.

These examples allow us to conclude that, for Poussin, antiquity was a vehicle of catharsis coming progressively into play the more the preparatory work approached the final version. It is for this reason that the pool of classical material on which he drew could never be large enough. The cathartic influence of antiquity consisted in helping to objectify and intensify subjective concepts. This state of objectivity and penetrating analysis Poussin attempted to achieve by 1) reducing the number of figures, isolating them

---

[6] The detail in Pl. xxii, 13a, reproduced in reverse, after Bellori, *op.cit.*, pl. 52, shows Orestes' nurse with gestures that reflect her reaction to Orestes' murder of his mother Clvtemnestra and her lover Aegisthus. The sarcophagus is still in the Palazzo Giustiniani, Rome (Robert, *op.cit.*, no. 156).

The detail of the Meleager sarcophagus shown in Pl. xxii, 13b is reproduced after the sixteenth-century "Coburgensis" from Robert, *op.cit.*, 1904, iii, ii, no. 278. The sarcophagus is in the Villa Albani.

and characterizing them as individuals; 2) using ancient expressive formulas for the process of individualization, such formulas also supplying the raw material for new renderings of gestures which, once established, belong thenceforth to his repertory; and 3) carefully observing a principle of external and internal order: external insofar as he settled on compositions of utmost readability in which a classical relief-like deployment of figures naturally had preference, internal insofar as he deliberately painted his pictures in a consistent key. In this the famous Greek modes, which interested him so much, served as a guide. A battle scene and a bacchanal have to be painted in different keys, and, similarly, each figure has to have its own mode of representation. This was not only a requirement of decorum but also of proportion. Thus, a heroic figure in a history painting has to have the proportions of Apollo, while peasants in everyday scenes should rather conform to statues of fauns.

It is well known that most of Bernini's early works are close to some ancient model. Until a generation ago the Borghese *Amalthea* was believed to be Hellenistic. His *Pluto* (Pl. XXIII, 14) reveals the close study of the *Hercules* in the Capitoline Museum, a statue that Algardi had restored at a slightly earlier date (Pl. XXIII, 15). The *David* refers to the *Borghese Warrior* (Pl. XXIII, 16a, b), and the Apollo of the *Apollo and Daphne* to the Apollo Belvedere (Pl. XXIII, 17a, b).

At the time of the *Longinus*, begun in 1629, the break with antiquity would seem to be complete. However, the *bozzetto* in the Fogg Art Museum (Pl. XXIV, 18), the only surviving one of a large number, shows not only a classical stance, but also an arrangement of the mantle so obviously of antique derivation that no specific prototype need be quoted. While these classical references have disappeared in the marble, Longinus' head is still dependent on a classical model, the *Borghese Centaur*, now in the Louvre (Pl. XXIV, 20a, b).

Only in one later case, the *Daniel* of 1655 (Pl. XXV, 22), does a sufficient number of drawings survive to allow us to follow the development of Bernini's conception. His starting point was the

"Father" of the Laocoön group. He drew the torso of this figure in a study now at Leipzig (Pl. xxv, 24). It is unlikely that Bernini made this copy from the Antique as a preparation for the *Daniel*, but, when he began to plan his statue, he gave his life-model the Laocoön pose in reverse (Pl. xxv, 25). In the next drawing, the position of the arms and legs approaches that of the marble statue, whereas the torso is still closely connected with the Laocoön.[7] The next two drawings show all the characteristics of the statue, the elongated proportions and the screw-like twisting of the body (Pl. xxv, 26). But a recollection of the Laocoön can still be noticed in Daniel's head (Pl. xxv, 23a, b).

Such late works as the *Angel with the Superscription* of 1667-69 (Pl. xxiv, 19) is, of course, utterly removed from classical antiquity in formal language, stance, proportion, and sentiment. Yet a preparatory drawing of a figure in the nude (Pl. xxiv, 21) demonstrates to what extent Bernini relied on the *Antinoüs*, the statue that meant so much to him in his early youth (Pl. xviii, 1). In contrast to the first drawings for the *Daniel*, however, the proportions of this study differ considerably from the ancient model: they are elongated, almost Gothic. At this late phase of Bernini's career, a process of spiritualization set in at the earliest stage of preparation despite the fact that recollections of ancient statuary remain clearly traceable.

From this brief survey we can draw certain conclusions. As a rule, Bernini begins by following a classical model. In elaborating his idea, however, he ends up with an intensely personal Baroque solution. Thus Bernini's procedure may be described as a reversal of Poussin's. Moreover, one can clearly discern a development that again may be discussed as an antithesis to that of Poussin: the paintings of the early Poussin are comparatively loose, and only as he matured did they become progressively formalized; by contrast, the works of the early Bernini are comparatively classical, and only later in his career did they become progressively free and imaginative.

[7] For the entire series of Daniel drawings, see Brauer-Wittkower, *Die Zeichnungen des Gianlorenzo Bernini*, Berlin, 1931, pls. 42-47.

Poussin's procedure was well known to French artists who had met the master in Rome or Paris. They had a better understanding of his method than is usually realized. They discussed it often and at length, particularly in lectures delivered at the Paris Academy. When Lebrun, in a famous talk, traced the ancient prototypes for the principal figures of Poussin's *Gathering of Manna*, he acted fully in the latter's spirit. Bourdon claimed that he had Poussin's personal blessing for the following teaching method: "When a student has made a drawing from the life model . . . he should make another study of the same figure . . . and try to give it the character of an ancient statue." We have no reason to doubt the truth of Bourdon's report.

The view that Poussin's approach to painting was rational and intellectual is supported by the deliberate and methodical manner in which he developed his compositions. Bernini, on the other hand, was ultimately guided by a metaphysical concept: he firmly believed that his inspiration came to him through the grace of God and that in developing a felicitous idea he was only God's tool. We have arrived at the point where Poussin's and Bernini's ways part, also theoretically, but neither Poussin's rational classicism nor Bernini's metaphysical Baroque can be divorced from the notions that the Zuccari generation built upon Renaissance tenets.

Mannerist theory suffered from the contradiction between the *disegno interno*—the doctrine, Neo-Platonic in essence, that ideal beauty, pre-existing in man's mind, was a gift from heaven—and the *disegno esterno*, i.e., the manual work, the *maniera*, the binding rules of which guaranteed professional execution. Bernini took up the Neo-Platonic concept of Mannerist theory; but for him the idea of beauty, far from being abstract, universal, vague, and speculative, became identified with the concrete spiritual requirements of each particular work. Poussin and the classicists reverted to the Aristotelian Renaissance belief that ideal beauty results from an a posteriori selective process, best characterized by the well-known and constantly repeated Zeuxis legend. Yet insofar as Poussin and the classicists were concerned with evolving a code of objective rules, they are linked with the *disegno esterno* side of Mannerist doctrine. Once again, the concrete requirements of each individual task saved Poussin from the pitfalls of the *maniera.*

Bernini's and Poussin's different approaches to ancient proto-types—the one using them at the beginning and the other at an advanced stage of the creative process—reflect their ultimate beliefs as artists. Their contrasting procedures may go a long way to account for the "Baroque" and the "classical" trends in the seventeenth century, and yet they spring from the same faith in the eternal validity of ancient art.

JAN DE BISSCHOP'S
DRAWINGS AFTER ANTIQUE SCULPTURE

J. G. VAN GELDER

IN evaluating the influence of classical antiquity on art in seventeenth-century Holland it would be simplifying matters too much to consider only the works of sculpture then available in Dutch collections. We may be able to find out to some extent what statues, reliefs, vases, inscriptions, and so on they contained (though it would be difficult); but these objects are more important for our understanding of the small world of collectors, late humanists, and scholars than for our understanding of Dutch art. It was the sculptures of classical antiquity in Rome itself which Dutch artists took as their models and their main source of inspiration.

Classical sculpture preserved in collections in Holland nevertheless did play its part, and on more than one occasion. The English ambassador at The Hague, Sir Dudley Carleton, wrote to one of his friends in 1618, when he had turned over his collection of classical sculpture to Rubens in exchange for money and paintings worth 6,000 Dutch florins: "I am blamed by the painters of this country who made ydoles of these heads and statuas."[1] "These heads" were the eighteen busts of emperors which Carleton had acquired in 1616. Again, we know from Sandrart's *Teutsche Academie* that the Stadholder Prince Frederik Hendrik had works of classical sculpture in The Hague and at his country palaces Rijswijk and Honselaarsdijk[2]—originals, or perhaps lead garden statues copied after classical originals in Rome. A third collection, described as consisting of "marble statues," was shipped to Holland from Antwerp in 1646 through the good offices of Michel le Blon.[3] We can assume that these were classical sculptures: a *Flora*

---

[1] Max Rooses, *Correspondance de Rubens . . .* , Antwerp, 1887-1909, II, p. 167. Letter of May 23, 1618, to Sir John Chamberlain.

[2] Joachim von Sandrart, *L'Academia todesca della Architectura Scultura & Pittura oder teutsche Academie der Edlen Bau- Bild- und Mahlerey-Künste . . .* , Nuremberg, 1675-79, I, i, p. 41.

[3] Jan Denucé, *Na Pieter Pauwel Rubens, documenten uit den kunsthandel te Antwerpen in de XVIIe eeuw van Matthijs Musson*, Antwerp–The Hague, 1949, pp. 55-56.

and Faustina sold for 195 florins is mentioned, three of the purchasers are known to have collected antiques, and the term "marble statues" was commonly applied to classical sculpture. The number of pieces in this collection is not known, but it was divided among no less than twenty-six leading Amsterdam citizens, and the entire consignment was valued at 6,400 florins.[4] Rembrandt bought works from this consignment to the value of 186 florins, and I think it likely that these were the antique busts of emperors mentioned in his inventory soon afterward.[5] We cannot be certain of this, however, for Rembrandt possessed other antique works as well. We know of other Dutch collectors from Jan de Bisschop's prints after the Antique, which were intended for the use of artists. In addition to works that could be seen in Rome, he illustrated statues in the collections of Gerard Wlenburgh and Hendrik Scholten in Amsterdam, among them a *Bacchus Supported by a Faun* in each collection, a *Crouching Venus* owned by Wlenburgh, and an *Actaeon* owned by Scholten (Pls. XXVI, 1-4; XXVII, 5, 6).[6]

Another Dutch collection of antique sculpture, that in the Reynst Collection in Amsterdam, is recorded in prints published by De Lairesse in 1671.[7] In this collection there were 111 classical sculptures, many of them obtained *en bloc* from

---

[4] The twenty-six purchasers were: Reynier Pauw; Balthazar, Josef, and Jan Coymans; Nataniel Geeraerdts; Adriaen Trip; [Joan] Huydecoper; Frederick Alewyn; Jan de Neufville; Burgomaster Bacquix [?]; Thomas de Kemel [?]; Pieter and Jan van den Abele; Jacques Burchgrave; Jan van Helmondt; Rembrandt van Rijn; Hendrick Scholten; Volckert Rosendael; Dr. Vogel; Willem Dobbes; Andries Ackerswen [?]; Christoffel Thysz; Gaspar van Ricquefort; Willem van de Werve; Jan Fonteyn; Thomas Broers.

[5] C. Hofstede de Groot, *Die Urkunden über Rembrandt, 1575-1721*, The Hague, 1906, Document 169. It may be taken that all or most of the following numbers in the inventory form part of a set of busts of emperors, drawings of three such busts by Rembrandt being known: nos. 147, 149, 152, 156, 160, 168-73.

[6] Johannes Episcopius, *Signorum veterum icones*, The Hague [1669]. For sculpture in Wlenburgh's collection see vol. II, pl. 63 (*Bacchus Supported by a Faun*) and pls. 79-80 (*Crouching Venus*); for those in Scholten's collection see vol. II, pls. 66 (*Bacchus*), 67 (*Bacchus Supported by a Faun*), 68 (*Victorious Athlete*), and 69 (*Actaeon*).

[7] [Gerard de Lairesse], *Signorum veterum icones per D. Gerardum Reynst . . . collectae . . .* , Amsterdam, n.d. See also Emil Jacobs, "Das Museo Vendramin und die Sammlung Reynst," *Repertorium für Kunstwissenschaft*, XLVI, 1925, pp. 15-38.

the Vendramin collection in Venice in the 1640's. In quality these statues were comparable with those in the Palais des Tuileries, published by Claude Mellan and Etienne Baudet from 1678 to 1682.[8] The best pieces from the Reynst Collection were presented to Charles II of England in 1660 as part of the "Dutch Gift"; unfortunately these have disappeared.[9] Many of the remaining pieces were transferred in the eighteenth century, via Gerard van Papenbroek's Collection (Pl. xxvII, 7; xxvIII, 8), to Leiden University. With their modern restorations removed, they may be seen there in a museum depot.[10] Among them is a *Consul*, its seventeenth-century form now scarcely recognizable (Pl. xxvIII, 9, 10).[11] Only the prints made by De Lairesse can now give us a picture of the Reynst Collection as a whole.

There is hardly a trace of the influence of all these collections on Dutch artists. The classical sculpture of Rome (and how many did not draw it?) was all-important, and it was studied both on the spot and by means of prints. We know that artists from the Low Countries made drawings of antiques in Rome from the time of Gossaert onward. Gossaert's Roman drawings were made for Philip of Burgundy in 1509,[12] and were followed by those of Marten van Heemskerck, Lambert Lombard, and countless others.

[8] Claude Mellan and Etienne Baudet, *Livre des statues du Palais des Tuileries*, Paris, 1678-82.

[9] A number of these pieces (Sabina, Caracalla, Aesculapius, Cupid, Scipio Africanus, Brutus, Commodus, Faustina, Tiberius, Vesta, Cybele, etc.) are mentioned by Knorr von Rosenroth, who visited the collection in 1663, thus, soon after their removal. See J. C. Breen, "Aus dem 'Itinerarium' des Christian Knorr von Rosenroth. . . ," *Jaarboek Amstelodamum*, xIV, 1916, p. 241.

[10] Rijksmuseum van Oudheden, Leiden.

[11] This example may serve as a warning to our own generation. This is what archaeologists did to works of art that had been completed in later times, and what scientific workers do today in our national museums and galleries, making ruins of works of art. Tourists crowd to look at the Roman Forum; they like ruins. The visitors to our museums and churches also like ruins: our modern scientific ruins, from Rubens' *Chapeau de Paille* to Giotto's frescos in Sta. Croce. The strange and dangerous combination of modern scientists and modern tourists demands not only our tears but also our serious consideration. In the seventeenth century ruins were at least made into works of art, not works of art into ruins!

[12] J. G. van Gelder, "Jan Gossaert in Rome, 1508-1509," *Oud Holland*, LIX, 1942, pp. 1-11; H. Schwarz, "Jan Gossaert's Adam and Eve Drawings," *Gazette des Beaux-Arts*, VI/XLII, 1953, ii, pp. 145-68.

If one compares the works of antiquity first published in 1567 by Giovanni Baptista de Cavalleriis[13] with the drawings that Goltzius made from the Antique in 1591, it is clear that a canon of antiques to be studied had been established. This canon was adhered to throughout the seventeenth century. The ninety-nine works that appear in the *Icones et segmenta nobilium signorum et statuarum quae Romae extant* of François Perrier, published in 1638,[14] for the most part represent the same objects that Goltzius drew. This was the repertoire that each artist was expected to know, whether from his own observation or through drawings or prints. Yet it was not so much the works of sculpture themselves as the proportions laid down by Vitruvius and others which the artists took as their starting-point. No book tells us more about seventeenth-century ideas on this subject than the much-neglected treatise by Crispijn van de Passe, *Della luce del dipingere et disegnare*, published in Amsterdam 1643-44,[15] in which the training of the young artist is described lesson by lesson. Ernst Gombrich pointed out in his *Art and Illusion*, in a chapter entitled "Formula and Experience," that such schemes of training had followed a given pattern from the late Middle Ages onward.[16] He drew attention to the fact that a form of teaching was evolved in late sixteenth-century Italy which was taken up elsewhere in the seventeenth century, though with variations. The teaching of proportion was paramount, starting with the composition of figures on the basis of the relation between the head and the total length of the body, which might amount to seven, eight, or nine heads (Pl. xxviii, 11). Thus the basis of study was not the works of art themselves, but the interpretation of antiquity in terms of mathematics—the application of Vitruvian principles to architecture and to the natural forms of men and animals. Unless this process of interpretation is taken into account, Baroque art—even Baroque art in Holland—will remain unintelligible.

[13] J. Baptista de Cavalleriis, *Antiquarum statuarum urbis Romae*, Rome, 1567.

[14] Franciscus Perrier, *Icones et segmenta nobilium signorum et statuarum quae Romae extant. . .* , Paris, 1638.

[15] Crispino del Passo, *Della luce del dipingere et disegnare. . .* , Amsterdam, 1643-44.

[16] E. H. Gombrich, *Art and Illusion, A Study in the Psychology of Pictorial Representation*, New York, 1960, pp. 146-78.

Antique works of sculpture and architecture were, of course, portrayed again and again in the seventeenth century by Dutch artists—by Poelenburg, Doudyns, Backer, Ferreris, Doncker, and Terwesten, to mention only a few. Yet, by then, an archaeological interest had taken the place of that purely artistic interest which had fired the imaginations of Gossaert, Van Scorel, Van Heemskerck, and Goltzius. The study of antiquity began to be the province of classical scholars and dilettanti, and to be centered in the universities and Latin Schools. Constantijn Huygens, living in The Hague, belonged to these circles, and he, of all Dutch humanist scholars of his time, was most closely in contact with artists—with the artists of his own country, but also with artists from Antwerp, Brussels, and London. There is ample evidence that there were points of contact in other cities, among them Amsterdam, Leiden, and Utrecht.

Perrier's second publication, an oblong folio volume of prints of bas-reliefs, furthered the archaeological interest. This was his *Icones et segmenta illustrium e marmore tabularum quae Romae adhuc extant,* published in 1645.[17] The refinement with which the well-known bas-reliefs could be dissected, however, is best illustrated by Jan de Bisschop's drawings in the Victoria and Albert Museum, in which objects of all kinds (chairs, garments, swords, and so on) are picked out from Perrier's prints and classified (Pl. XXIX, 12, 13). These drawings were made in Holland in the 1660's. De Bisschop draws details from the reliefs on the arches of Constantine and Titus, for example, and from many sarcophagi; he also made reconstructions of Roman temples (Pl. XXIV, 14, 15), gardens, and palaces. It seems that in making these compilations he drew on the work of other artists, among them Montanus,[18] but we cannot get a picture of his sources as a whole until more research is done.

[17] Franciscus Perrier, *Icones et segmenta illustrium e marmore tabularum quae Romae adhuc extant. . . ,* Paris, 1645.

[18] He appears to have drawn on some or all of the following works by Montanus, though without copying from them exactly: *Libro primo, scielte d. varii tempietti antichi con le piante et alzatte, disegnati in prospettiva,* Rome, 1624; *Architettura con diversi ornamenti cavati dall' antico,* Rome, 1636; *Raccolta de tempij et sepolchri disegnati dall' antico da Gio. Battista Montano Milanese,* Rome, 1638.

De Bisschop's style of drawing may be directly derived from that of Breenbergh, itself closely related to the style of Poussin. Yet the governing factor in De Bisschop's work, apart from his careful study of antiquity and the way in which he set down the forms of the ancient sculptures he drew, was his didactic purpose. In his *Signorum veterum icones*, published in 1669 (not 1671 as is generally stated),[19] he published many of his own drawings from the Antique, but also some derived from other artists, among them sixteen drawings by the younger De Gheyn after statues in the Arundel Collection.[20] This book shows that he, like his German contemporary Sandrart, saw classical art as providing perfect representations of the types and forms to be found in nature, rather than as exemplifying Proportion in the abstract. And De Bisschop's dedication of the first part of his *Icones* to Constantijn Huygens agrees to a surprising extent with Sandrart's text, published six years later.[21] The stress is on the portrayal of types. De Bisschop refers to the *Farnese Hercules* as a model for "joints and muscles superhumanly strong." For Sandrart, the same statue represents "the most perfect strength of body."[22] For De Bisschop, the *Laocoön* typifies "sturdy old age" and for Sandrart "the greatest perfection of an old man."[23] For De Bisschop, again, the *Antinoüs* typifies "an almost womanly weak elegance of body"; for Sandrart, "all the beauty and decorativeness of a young person."[24] According to De Bisschop, these types represent the wide variety of nature, making it clear that the ancients looked to nature for their models. This leads to the conclusion, arrived at circuitously, that nature should be followed. Since the ancients followed nature with the greatest perfection and variety, they

[19] Episcopius, *op.cit.*; the publication is dated by the letter referred to in n. 26 below.

[20] *Op.cit.*, II, pls. 88-99.

[21] For De Bisschop, see the Introduction referred to; for Sandrart see especially his own book, *op.cit.*, I, i, pp. 33-34. The quotations that follow come from these two places.

[22] De Bisschop: "Gewrichten van meer dan menschelijcke sterckte"; Sandrart: "Die volkommenste Leibes-Stärke."

[23] De Bisschop: "Een vasten ouderdom"; Sandrart: "Die grosse Vollkommenheit eines alten Mannes."

[24] De Bisschop: "Een swacke swier van lichaem bijna vrouwelijck"; Sandrart: "Alle Schönheit und Zierde eines jungen Menschen."

themselves provide the best models for the modern artist, through which he may learn to look at nature itself. In fulfilling his aim "to put the whole of nature to its use in an exalted way;"[25] the modern artist's task is to use the Antique as an indication of what he should choose from nature herself. In other words, the formal language of the late seventeenth-century Baroque results from the artist's making a choice from the forms of antiquity. If, De Bisschop tells us, the artist does not use the types provided by antiquity, he will land in difficulties and uncertainties.

We know from a letter written from Paris in November 1669 by Constantijn Huygens' son, the mathematician Christiaan Huygens,[26] that the *Icones* were highly praised by contemporaries. Christiaan Huygens reports that the prints were valued by connoisseurs for "the correctness of outline and the softness and roundness of the nudes."[27] The only criticism that he mentions had come from Jabach and some others, who complained that in some of the heads "the physiognomy of the ancients is not followed perfectly enough."[28] (It may be added that the *air des testes*, which is complained of, was a crucial matter, for not much later two series of prints, each representing a complete repertoire of the passions, were published in France: by Testelin in 1680, and by Le Brun in 1698.)[29] In spite of Jabach's complaint, De Bisschop's *Icones* were greatly in advance of Perrier's.

At the end of the seventeenth century and the beginning of the eighteenth, the accent shifted once more, this time in the direction of an idealized form based on classical prototypes. One may ask what this ideal form was. The first requirement was no longer either the perfection of the proportions or the variety and lifelikeness of the types, but was the ideal outline of the figure. The

---

[25] "'t Geheele leven loffelijk tot sijn gebruyck te brengen."

[26] *Oeuvres complètes de Christiaan Huygens*, XXII (Supplement), The Hague, 1950, pp. 658-59. Letter of November 14, 1669 to Jan de Bisschop.

[27] "De correctheijt van omtrecken, en de sachtheijt, en rondicheijt der naeckten."

[28] "Het wesen der antiquen niet perfect genoegh naegevolgt."

[29] Henry Testelin, *Sentiments des plus habiles peintres sur la pratique de la peinture et sculpture mis en table de préceptes*, Paris, 1680. Charles le Brun, *Méthode pour apprendre à dessiner les Passions proposée dans une conférence sur l'expression générale et particulière*, Amsterdam–Paris, 1698.

scholar Lambert ten Kate, the painter Hendrik van Limborgh (working in The Hague), and the inventor and engraver J. C. le Blon, all active in the first years of the eighteenth century, struggled to arrive at a form that would give the figure beauty of outline from every angle.[30] Ten Kate's aim was to find an imagined standard of beauty (*le beau ideal*) by which, within each outline, some idea would be expressed. Conversely, he thought it possible to find an outline that was expressive of each idea. With the founding of the academies of art in Holland, starting with that of The Hague in 1682, a need arose for the importation of actual plaster casts after the Antique. But Ten Kate came to the conclusion that these newly imported casts, among them casts of the *Laocoön*, ought to be altered so as to provide an ideal outline from every viewpoint. This doctrine, which accorded with the general tendency of the time toward greater simplicity, led to the final conclusion that the ideal form in an absolute sense—that which presents unlimited possibilities—can be no other than a single point. Toward the middle of the eighteenth century, however, it was no longer this single point but the soul which determined what was considered beautiful or perfect. Here, however, we are touching on another chapter—one which in Holland begins with the philosophy of Hemsterhuis.[31] Thus, I prefer to end this paper here, with the perfection of a single point.

[30] For the theories of all three see J. G. van Gelder, *"Dilettanti" en kunstwetenschap*, Wormerveer, 1936, pp. 12-15. For Le Blon, see also Jakob Christoffel le Blon, *Generale proportie voor de onderscheidene lengte der beelden van welbesnede menselijke gestalte*, Amsterdam, 1707.

[31] See L. Brummel, *Frans Hemsterhuis, een philosofenleven*, Haarlem, 1925.

REMBRANDT'S SO-CALLED PORTRAIT OF
ANNA WŸMER AS MINERVA

E. HAVERKAMP-BEGEMANN

REMBRANDT'S attitude toward antiquity is by no means characteristic of Baroque or seventeenth-century art in general, neither of Dutch art of his time nor of the comparatively small group of his pupils. As in the representation of biblical scenes, Rembrandt's interpretation of antiquity is a highly personal one, apparently unprecedented and hardly followed.

It is perhaps for this reason that our knowledge of Rembrandt's interpretation of classical antiquity is so incomplete. The questions have to be answered without the benefit of solutions for parallel problems in the case of other artists. Since 1897, when Jan Six wrote his article on Rembrandt's painting, *Homer Dictating to a Scribe*, three studies reviewing the whole question have appeared—by Valentiner, Kieser, and Saxl—and many others dealing with more specific questions.[1] Still, the gaps in our knowledge are large, even where such a comparatively simple question as the identification of a figure is at stake. For instance, does the etching *The Woman with the Arrow* indeed represent Venus, and the etching *Sleeping Negress* the same goddess, or perhaps Cleopatra? Rembrandt's choice of scenes from mythology and classical history also needs clarification, especially in the field of drawings, and so does the question of whether contemporary literature, visual tradition, or translations of the classical texts were Rembrandt's primary sources.

[1] Jan Six, "De Homerus van Rembrandt," *Oud-Holland*, xv, 1897, pp. 4ff; W. R. Valentiner, "Rembrandt auf der Lateinschule," *Jahrbuch der königlich preussischen Kunstsammlungen*, xxvii, 1906, pp. 118-28; Emil Kieser, "Über Rembrandts Verhältnis zur Antike," *Zeitschrift für Kunstgeschichte*, x, 1941-42, pp. 129-62. Of those publications dealing with more specific questions related to the theme "Rembrandt and Antiquity," I mention only the two most recent ones: Clotilde Brière-Misme, "La Danae de Rembrandt et son véritable sujet," *Gazette des Beaux-Arts*, vi/xxxix, 1952, pp. 305-18; xli, 1953, pp. 27-36; xlii, 1953, pp. 291-304; xliii, 1954, pp. 67-76; Herbert von Einem, "Rembrandt und Homer," *Wallraf-Richartz-Jahrbuch*, xiv, 1952, pp. 182-205.

We know even less about Rembrandt's interpretation of antiquity, the values he attached to classical themes, figures, and ideas. Especially the transition from classical antiquity to Christian interpretation has to be studied, or rather, the process through which, for Rembrandt, the differences between the classical and the Christian world decreased to the point of disappearing.[2]

Two recent studies on some aspects of the iconology of Rembrandt's art, one by Von Einem, the other by Bialostocki, are of great importance in this respect.[3] Bialostocki came to the conclusion that, in order to elucidate questions concerning the meaning of Rembrandt's works, an iconological method should be applied which emphasizes the specific meaning of certain formal elements within the autonomous world of Rembrandt's art. Keeping this suggestion in mind I should like to try to come to a better understanding of the meaning of one of Rembrandt's drawings of a classical subject.

In the *Liber Amicorum* of Jan Six, the Amsterdam humanist, one-time friend and Maecenas of Rembrandt and later burgomaster of the city, there is a drawing, which dates from 1652, representing an interior with a woman seated behind a table in front of a window (Pl. xxx, 1).[4] At the left a bust, apparently of a female personage, is placed on a pedestal which looks as if it could be turned on its axis. Part of the drapery at the left rests on the head of the bust. At the right a shield is hanging on a wall; above it is a helmet, just visible under the rim of the curtain; a lance stands against the wall.

It has been supposed for a long time that the drawing represents Anna Wÿmer, Jan Six's Mother, as Minerva in her Study. Otto Benesch, the latest author to discuss the drawing, accepted this title. However, it must be considered doubtful that Anna

[2] See in this respect, Von Einem, *loc.cit.*
[3] Von Einem, *loc.cit.*; Jan Bialostocki, "Ikonographische Forschungen zu Rembrandts Werk," in *Münchner Jahrbuch der bildenden Kunst*, iii/viii, 1957, pp. 195-210, especially p. 208.
[4] *Anna Wÿmer, Jan Six's Mother, as Minerva in her Study*, Six Collection, Amsterdam. Pen and brown ink, heightened with white (partly oxidized): 190 x 140 mm. Signed: *Rembrandt f. 1652*. Listed and/or reproduced by: Hofstede de Groot, no. 1237; Valentiner no. 737; Lippmann, II, no. 54; Graul no. 47; Benesch, v, no. 914, fig. 1124.

Wÿmer is actually represented, since the figure has no individual-ized features at all. Furthermore, there are no portraits painted or etched by Rembrandt in which the figure is so small in com-parison with the space and the objects surrounding it.

The reasons for this mistaken identification can easily be un-derstood. The art historian Jan Six, descendant of the seventeenth-century Jan Six, published the drawing in 1893 for the first time, and proposed the idea that the figure was the mother of Rem-brandt's friend.[5] He had reached this conclusion on the basis of a compositional affinity of the drawing to the etched portrait of Jan Six;[6] he supposed that the drawing was a sketch for an etch-ing, planned as a companion piece to the portrait of her son which Rembrandt had etched seven years previously. "In that case," said Six, "it can hardly represent anybody else but Anna Wÿmer, the mother of Jan Six." This supposed companion piece was not only never executed, but the differences in composition make it most unlikely that it was ever planned as such.

Jan Six, the art historian, failed to see the connection with Minerva.[7] This connection was established later, undoubtedly cor-rectly, as we shall see, and has been generally accepted since. Not accepted—likewise correctly—was the original reason for Six's identification of the figure, namely the assumption that the draw-ing was meant to be a study for a pendant to the portrait of Jan Six. Still, Anna Wÿmer's name wrongly remained connected with the drawing and, thus, Jan Six's mother was supposed to be represented here in the guise of the Goddess of Wisdom.

There cannot be any doubt that Rembrandt thought of Minerva when he sketched this drawing. In 1635 he had painted a Minerva, a large figure seated behind a table on which there are books and a helmet, while a shield and a lance are displayed behind her.[8]

[5] Jan Six, in *Oud-Holland*, XI, 1893, p. 157.

[6] Bartsch 285; Hind 228; Münz 70. Dated 1645.

[7] This is the more surprising since he was an archaeologist; he also added con-siderably to a better knowledge of Rembrandt's connection with antiquity by such articles as "Apelleisches" [on Rembrandt's representations of Minerva and Mars], in *Jahrbuch des kaiserlichen deutschen archäologischen Instituts*, xxv, 1910, pp. 147-50, and the article mentioned above, n. 1.

[8] Bredius 469 (Collection Dr. Axel Wenner-Gren, Stockholm). Likewise, the painting in the Mauritshuis, The Hague, representing Minerva (Cat. 1935, no.

The same attributes are found in the drawing. Only the bust has been added. That Rembrandt introduced the bust can be explained by assuming that he thought of Minerva as the protectress of handicraft, more specifically of the artisan and the artist. Busts were regular prerequisites for teaching. Rembrandt owned many similar busts and used them for instructing his pupils, as we can conclude from the etchings *Man Drawing from a Cast* and *Artist Drawing from a Model* (also called *Pygmalion*), and from the drawing by Renesse, now in Darmstadt, representing Rembrandt's studio, in which three busts are placed on a shelf.[9] The bust as an object to draw from, represented in connection with Minerva, fulfills the same function as the standing model in Elsheimer's small painting, *The Realm of Minerva*.[10] In the background, artists are making studies of a nude man who is standing with arms outstretched above his head.

The differences between Rembrandt's drawing of Minerva and Elsheimer's painting are considerable; indeed, the compositions have in common only the conspicuous placement of the lance. These differences are significant, since we may assume that Rembrandt knew the etching made by Wenzel Hollar in 1646 after Elsheimer's painting.[11] Rembrandt's interest in, or even admiration for, Elsheimer would permit this assumption, but his knowledge of another print in the set of three to which this one belongs removes any possible doubt. The second print of the set,

626), which is either by Rembrandt himself or an early copy after a painting by him (according to K. Bauch [*Der frühe Rembrandt und seine Zeit*, Berlin, 1960, fig. 180, p. 266, n. 187], perhaps by Dou after Rembrandt) includes books, a shield, a lance, and two plaster heads. The affinity of this figure to representations of Melancholy was noted by J. G. van Gelder (*Rembrandt's vroegste Ontwikkeling*, Amsterdam, 1953, pp. 21-25, fig. 25).

[9] *Man Drawing from a Cast*: B.130, H.191, M.62; *Artist Drawing from a Model*: B.192, H.231, M.339. Even if the latter were not by Rembrandt, it reflects a practice of Rembrandt's studio. The drawing is reproduced by G. Falck in *Jahrbuch der preussischen Kunstsammlungen*, XLV, 1924, p. 197, and lately in *Rembrandt, Paintings, Drawings and Etchings, with an Introduction* by Henri Focillon; *The Three Early Biographies, Catalogue and Notes* by Ludwig Goldscheider, London, etc., Phaidon Press [1960], pl. III-b.

[10] Fitzwilliam Museum, Cambridge; see, H. Weizsäcker, *Adam Elsheimer, der Maler von Frankfurt*, Berlin, 1952, II, no. 53B.

[11] Passavant no. 31; Parthey no. 270; Weizsäcker, *op.cit.*, p. 142, no. 35.

the *Realm of Juno*—the *Realm of Minerva* is the third—served as the prototype for Rembrandt's painting of Juno, now in a private collection in the U.S.A.[12] Rembrandt disregarded the background of Hollar's etching, but borrowed from it the pose of the figure, the position of the arms, of the scepter in Juno's right hand, and even the position of her resting left hand.

In his drawing of Minerva Rembrandt, by deviating from Elsheimer's composition, purposefully adopted a scheme he had often used before. A small figure in a large and dark interior, a figure seated at a table but almost disappearing in the space, the contrasts between strong, piercing light and dark corners in such an interior—these combined elements were frequently used by Rembrandt around 1630.[13] In or about 1629 he painted the *Scholar* now in the National Gallery, London, in 1633 the *Scholar* now in Louvre, and in 1631 the painting in Stockholm, traditionally supposed to represent the hermit-writer *Anastasius*.[14]

Apparently Rembrandt associated this type of large and dark interior containing a small figure with the hermit-like scholar or saint. The combination of a small figure in a large interior, be it cell or study, undoubtedly has a long tradition, from which two of the most beautiful and influential representations, Van Eyck's painting and Dürer's engraving of St. Jerome, readily come to mind. It is significant, however, that this traditional theme was transformed by Rembrandt into a new type.

Although the contrasts between light and dark in the drawing of Minerva are similar to those in the earlier representations of scholars, there is a difference in the way the light enters the interior. In this drawing, the light comes through a window behind the figure instead of to her side; the figure of Minerva is

[12] Passavant, no. 30; Parthey, no. 269; Weizsäcker, *op.cit.*, p. 142, no. 34. For the painting of Juno, see among others A. Bredius, "Ein wiedergefundener Rembrandt: Juno," *Pantheon*, XVIII, 1936, p. 277, and J.L.A.A. van Ryckevorsel, "De teruggevonden schilderÿ van Rembrandt: de Juno," *Oud-Holland*, LIII, 1936, pp. 270-74. This painting was executed thirteen years after the Minerva drawing. There is no reason, however, to suppose that Rembrandt knew the set of prints only at the end of his life.

[13] A rather isolated later example dates from 1642 (the etching *St. Jerome*, B.105, H.201, M.247).

[14] London: Br.427; Paris: Br.431; Stockholm: Br.430. According to Bauch (*op.cit.*, p. 151), the latter would represent a theologian.

almost absorbed by the light and is identified with it. This identification of light with Minerva is similar to the identification of
light with Christian holiness and Christian salvation, as in the
Holy Family, etched in 1654, where the light of Mary's halo is
fused with the light falling through the window behind her, and
where the immaterial shape of the halo can hardly be distinguished
from the oval lead strip of the window.[15]

It is also similar to the identification of light with magic inspiration or magic revelation as we find it in the *Faust* etching,
executed in the same year as the drawing.[16] Comparison of the
three almost contemporary works shows that Rembrandt identified the natural light falling through a window first with the halo
of the Virgin Mary, then with the appearance of a magic formula,
and finally with the figure of Minerva—in order to express the
idea of endowment of supranatural properties, in one case of a
Christian, in another of a magic, and in the third case of a classical
and philosophical nature.

In the drawing of Minerva as well as in the etchings of the
Holy Family and Faust, the light is the seemingly natural light
that illuminates persons or objects, and then continues its course
toward us. This light, however, by absorbing objects and persons,
has assumed a different meaning without changing its substance.
Undoubtedly it is different from that which emanates from Christ
in many of Rembrandt's representations of New Testament
scenes: Christ's radiance signifies the revelation of the Divine
to man.[17]

The fact that in 1652 Rembrandt takes up an earlier scheme,
although modifying it, is surprising and needs a few words of
comment. Emil Kieser, in reviewing Rembrandt's relation to
antiquity, showed that there is a period of about seventeen years
in Rembrandt's life in which the artist's interest in subjects from

[15] B.63, H.275, M.229.

[16] B.270, H.260, M.275. For the latest interpretation of the etching, see Wolfgang Wegner, *Die Faustdarstellungen vom 16. Jahrhundert bis zur Gegenwart*,
Amsterdam, 1962. Wegner established that the figure in the etching is engaged
in the magic art of "mirror-gazing."

[17] See, Hans-Martin Rotermund, "The Motif of Radiance in Rembrandt's
Biblical Drawings," *Journal of the Warburg and Courtauld Institutes*, xv,
1952, pp. 101-21.

antiquity is at a low point.[18] His renewed interest started in 1652 with this drawing and *Homer Dictating his Verses*, likewise in the Six *Album Amicorum*. The next year, in 1653, Rembrandt painted the *Aristotle* for Alessandro Ruffo.[19] Aristotle is represented as a large figure, not a small one, in a shallow space and cut by the frame, resting his hand upon a bust of Homer. Aristotle, for Rembrandt as for the Middle Ages, was the personification of Wisdom and, as such, close to Minerva. It is therefore significant that Rembrandt, again personifying Antique Philosophy or Wisdom after a long interval, turned in the Six drawing to the type of the scholar as he had formerly depicted it, i.e., as a small figure in a large interior. This apparently came more readily to his mind than the academic and traditional large figure, which he subsequently used for his painting of Aristotle. Undoubtedly the importance Rembrandt attached to light as the symbol of endowment of wisdom was one of the reasons for his predilection for this type of representation.

[18] Kieser, *op.cit.*, p. 135.

[19] Br.478, The Metropolitan Museum of Art, New York (formerly Collection Mrs. A. W. Erickson, New York). Here the mysterious light is strongest on the arm that is resting on the bust of Homer, thus stressing the divine bond between Philosophy and Poetry. For the costume and the proximity of the image of the antique philosopher to that of the priest or even magician, for Rembrandt and others, see Kieser, *op.cit.*

DRAWING IN THE SEVENTEENTH CENTURY

INTRODUCTION

J . Q . V A N R E G T E R E N A L T E N A

THE significance of drawings during the seventeenth century had hardly been explored when the subject was chosen for this session. We were aware of the obvious change that occurred in the position of drawings when Mannerism developed from the art of the Renaissance, as well as of the existence of an increasing number of drawings executed from that time onward. We knew, too, that occasionally artists' biographies and special studies had analyzed within the oeuvre of a single artist a range of succeeding phases or differences in manner extending from mere scraps to accomplished compositions or finished portraits of reality. The question had been raised whether—and if so, in what cases and to what extent—drawings had been considered as works of art equal in rank, for example, to paintings, or at least as *objets de collection*.

Julius Held's paper, with its broad outlook that extends beyond the years involved and with its wealth of quotations from contemporary authors, once and for all settles this main question by producing abundant proof that a widespread traffic in drawings had existed before the year 1600.

During the discussion session, Jan Bialostocki and J. G. van Gelder suggested that some of the quotations might have been meant less in praise of drawings as such than of the *disegno* in the meaning of the pre-established pattern or idea, the program, so to speak, of a work of art to be executed in one or another technique. Held replied that he had limited himself to reactions to actual drawings. This did not imply that studies for known paintings would have been excluded from consideration.

This was particularly true in the case of Claude Lorrain's drawings, which were chosen as a subject both for their variety and for the gaps in our knowledge of their dates and interrelationships. On the basis of Michael Kitson's carefully balanced appreciations, Claude proved a welcome subject for investigation. The fact that so many of Claude's drawings must have remained in the possession of the artist during his lifetime, and the particular character of the *Liber Veritatis*, led Eckhart Knab to believe that most of them were created for his private use only. Picking up a remark made by Kitson, he denied that the drawings in the *Liber Veritatis* could have been considered by the artist as "works of art in their own right."

Many members participated in the discussion on Claude's beginnings and the question of which of the Dutch draftsmen living in Rome promoted Claude's acute sense for rendering striking contrasts of light and dark with a brush only, i.e., eliminating the pen entirely, so characteristic for Claude's early manner. Prior to Herman van Swanevelt, Cornelius van Poelenburg seems to prevail. He arrived in Rome before Bartholomeus Breenbergh, and as a close observer of nature realized the most vivid advance on Adam Elsheimer's legacy. With regard to Rembrandt, the assembly found only rare proof that he used drawings for other than his own needs (e.g., the portrait in different chalks in the Payson Collection, New York, and his contributions to the "Pandora" of Jan Six. The albums which appeared at his sale, filled with studies arranged according to the different genres, demonstrate how he had cherished the idea of keeping these documents of his memory for himself. Even so, there was no difference of opinion on the fact that both Rembrandt and Claude Lorrain were constantly striving to refine their technique and to maintain the artistically high standard of those personal experiments, to treat them, as Kitson says, "as visually complete in themselves."

François-Georges Pariset's paper, very informative and distinguished by its salient descriptions, dealt with Bellange and Lagneau as draftsmen. Anthony Blunt discussed some statements, upon which Pariset showed additional slides, among them drawings from the Amsterdam Print Room and in the trade. The Chairman explained his hesitation to attribute the "Warrior on Horseback" at Amsterdam definitely to Bellange even if it seems to show the *ductus* of his pen, because it is inscribed "Cioli," by which either Valerio Cioli or Lodovico Cigoli may be intended.

Jean Adhémar's paper, not received for publication, elucidated the character of different commissions given to French artists, mainly in the sixteenth and early seventeenth centuries. He stressed the occurrence of consistent series of drawings of documentary value and, additionally, remarked to Held that some artists who had been commissioned by the King of France to execute designs, had at the end come to consider their drawings as their own property (e.g., the material sold after the death of Audran to Tessin). In addition, he drew attention to the multiplication of original series of effigies, which happened regularly during the sixteenth century but was interrupted when they were replaced by engravings about 1580, just as, in their turn, the engravings had to yield to photography about the year 1850.

THE EARLY APPRECIATION OF DRAWINGS

JULIUS S. HELD

THE question I posed myself for this paper is this: what can we learn about the development of a taste for drawings by reading some of the early authors? Relying almost entirely on written sources, I wanted to find out the fate of drawings as physical objects; how they were described and what was the nature and origin of the aesthetic distinctions applied to them; and when they first received recognition as a special category of objects. I believe this problem has not been proposed in modern literature precisely in this way, although Meder, of course, has a great deal of pertinent material in his remarkable book.[1] Much important information is scattered through the pages of Lugt's admirable *Marques de collections*.[2] The best summary of the history of the collecting of drawings is found in Charles de Tolnay's *History and Technique of Old Master Drawings*.[3] On the other hand, little attention has been paid to these questions in books dealing with the growth of collecting and the development of taste, such as F. H. Taylor's *Taste of Angels*, and N. von Holst's *Künstler, Sammler, Publikum*.[4]

Although concentrating on the seventeenth century (as the period to which this session is devoted), I found it necessary to go both backward and forward in time. Most of the attitudes that obtained during the seventeenth century had been established by the end of the sixteenth; indeed, many of the critical concepts are in Vasari. Nor did it seem useful to break off with the end of the seventeenth century, despite the fact that an important landmark in the discussion of drawings was published precisely at the turn of the century. A more logical place to stop was the middle of the eighteenth century, when the great age of the *curieux* reached its

[1] Joseph Meder, *Die Handzeichnung, Ihre Technik und Entwicklung*, Vienna, 1919; 2nd ed., 1923.
[2] Frits Lugt, *Les marques de collections de dessins et d'estampes*, Amsterdam, 1921; supplement, The Hague, 1956.
[3] Charles de Tolnay, *History and Technique of Old Master Drawings*, New York, 1943.
[4] F. H. Taylor, *The Taste of Angels*, Boston, 1948; N. von Holst, *Künstler, Sammler, Publikum*, Darmstadt, 1960.

apogee with Mariette's remarks about the drawings of the great masters in the catalogue of the Crozat sale of 1741[5] and d'Argenville's *Abrégé* of 1745-52.[6] The historians of art of the Neoclassic period introduced concepts for which appreciation of so fragile and highly personal a thing as a drawing was of minor importance.

In view of the extended chronological limits, it seemed to me wise to restrict the paper in other ways. Since I wanted to concentrate on drawings as concrete objects, I decided not to engage in the very complex history of the term *disegno*.[7] It should be obvious, however, that the prestige of *disegno*, "padre delle tre arti nostri"[8] must have contributed greatly to the appreciation of drawings whose very name (*disegni*) legitimized them as the visible tokens of the imaginative processes underlying all the arts. For the relationship of *disegno* as a creative faculty to *disegno* as a tangible object, Guercino's well-known painting in Dresden is of special interest (Pl. XXXI, 1). It combines in one composition *Disegno*, an old man, sitting behind a table at the left, and his daughter *Pittura*, a young, elegantly dressed woman, placed before an easel at the right. *Pittura's* painting, a sleeping Cupid, stands on the easel, but she is shown turning around to look at a drawing of the same subject which *Disegno* is holding. Thus, the dependence of *Pittura* on *Disegno* is here cast into an image that limits the function of painting to a mere elaboration in colors of a design furnished it in the draftsman's medium. Obviously, priority, and the esteem that goes with it, belongs to the drawing. Indeed, it must be clear to any sensitive observer that the drawing in the hands of *Disegno* (Pl. XXXI, 2) is more than a mere attribute, more than the materialized sign of his power, more than a

---

[5] I owe to Frits Lugt the information that the first auction catalogue to include descriptions of individual drawings is that of the Lambert ten Kate Collection, of 1732. The only known copy of the catalogue is in the Print Room in Amsterdam.

[6] A. Dézallier d'Argenville, *Abrégé de la vie des plus fameux peintres et la mainière de connoître les dessins et les tableaux*, Paris, 1745-52, here quoted from the 1762 edition.

[7] See E. Panofsky, *Idea*, Leipzig, 1924, *passim*; see also Matthias Winner, *Die Quellen der Pictura-Allegorien. . .* , Diss., Cologne, 1957, *passim*.

[8] Giorgio Vasari, *Le vite de' più eccellenti pittori, scultori ed architettori*, ed. G. Milanesi, Florence, 1878-85, I, p. 168. (Hereafter cited as Vasari-Milanesi.)

model to be followed by *Pittura*. Held so carefully—with both *Disegno's* hands—and studied so attentively by both draftsman and painter, the drawing has become an object of interest and worth in its own right. Thus, while he ostensibly illustrated the familiar, and familial, relationship between *Disegno* and *Pittura*, Guercino—himself a famous draftsman—also furnished an important document for the appreciation of drawing in the seventeenth century.[9]

We may begin by finding out what actually happened to drawings once they were finished and had fulfilled their immediate function. There is clear evidence that artists who were assiduous draftsmen kept the bulk of their drawings in the studio as reference material, as tools for instruction, and as an asset for their heirs. Frans Pourbus and Rubens made testamentary provisions that their drawings be kept together at least for a while. Dürer evidently kept most of his drawings, as we can tell from inscriptions he put on them at a later date, as well as from the fact that the Imhofs got their large holdings directly from Dürer's widow. Raffaelino del Garbo's son inherited his father's drawings and dispersed them (a sign that trading in drawings was then perfectly feasible) for sums that Vasari denounced as ridiculously low.[10] Fra Bartolommeo left most of his drawings to Sister Plautilla Nelli, a nun in a convent in Siena who had been his pupil.[11] Ridolfi recalls how in the summer of 1628 he spent half a day going through Farinato's drawings, then in the hands of Farinato's son;[12] to quote a still later example, I call attention to the well-known fact that after Lebrun's death, all his drawings "qui étoient en grand nombre et le fruit des études de toute la vie d'un

---

[9] Elsewhere (Rubens, *Selected Drawings*, London, 1959, p. 14, note 2) I have called attention to Rubens' use, in the *Allegory of War* in the Pitti, of a crumpled drawing to symbolize the destruction in war of all things of beauty. It is very likely that the theme of the Three Graces appearing on that sheet of paper denotes the *arti di disegno* (see Vasari-Milanesi, VIII, 530: "le tre arti, Pittura, Scoltura ed Architettura . . . a guisa delle tre Grazie. . .").

[10] Vasari-Milanesi, *op.cit.*, IV, p. 234.

[11] Lugt, *op.cit.*, I, p. 2818.

[12] Carlo Ridolfi, *Le maraviglie dell'arte*, ed. Detlev Freiherr von Hadeln, Berlin, 1914, II, p. 132.

artiste aussi habile que laborieux"[13] fell into the hands of the
King, as did those of Mignard. Nor would there have been 600
drawings for the Galleria Farnese in one single collection (Ange-
loni) had not the Carracci themselves preserved them.[14]

Yet there are several categories of drawings which by their very
nature passed into other hands soon after they had been done.
Drawings made as models for patrons, or for other artists (like the
four St. Christophers that Dürer made for Patinir) come to mind.
A more unusual case is Poussin, who wrote from Paris promising
Cassiano del Pozzo some drawings so that his Italian friend would
be informed about his Parisian projects.[15]

Drawings submitted to engravers normally, I presume, came
back to the artist with the prints. Poussin, for instance, delayed
sending the promised drawings to Del Pozzo because Claude Mellan had not yet returned two important pieces.[16] Yet it is not likely that Calvaert's drawings sent across the Alps to be engraved[17]
ever returned to Bologna; nor is Spranger likely to have seen
again the drawings Van Mander had taken along to be engraved
by Goltzius.[18] (Buchelius' brief note of 1605: "vidi apud H. Hon-
dium Lugduni manu signata Goltzii. . ." might refer to Goltzius
drawings which Hondius had engraved and kept.)[19] A rather
drastic case of the disappearance of drawings made for prints is
that of Antonio da Trento, the engraver-assistant of Parmigianino,
who disappeared one fine morning with all the prints and drawings, "andantosene col diavolo."[20] The prints were found but the
drawings were gone for good. Drawings made for the illustration

---

[13] See Frédéric Reiset, *Notice des dessins, cartons, pastels, miniatures et émaux
exposés . . . au Musée Imperial du Louvre*, Paris, 1866, I, p. xxvii.

[14] Carlo Malvasia, *Felsina pittrice*, Bologna, 1678, III, p. 467.

[15] Giovanni Bottari and Stefano Ticozzi, *Raccolta di lettere*, Milan, 1822, I, p.
384: November 21, 1641.

[16] *Ibid.*, p. 402: March 22, 1642.

[17] Malvasia, *op.cit.*, II, p. 261.

[18] Carel van Mander, *Het Leven der Doorluchtighe Nederlandtsche en Hoogh-
duytsche Schilders*, ed. Hanns Floerke, Munich, 1906, II, p. 241. All references
are to this edition.

[19] G. J. Hoogewerff and J. Q. van Regteren Altena, *Arnoldus Buchelius, "Res
Pictoriae,"* The Hague, 1928, p. 78.

[20] Vasari-Milanesi, *op.cit.*, V, p. 227.

of books became the property of the publisher, to judge from the collection of such drawings still preserved in the Musée Plantin.

In most cases portrait drawings were bought by, or given to, the sitters or related persons. The earliest reference to an individual drawing, as far as I can see, is to a portrait of Laura made (possibly at Petrarch's own request) by Simone Martini.[21] Dürer used portrait drawing as an additional source of income; during his trip to the Netherlands he drew about ninety large portraits which he gave away in expectation of a monetary reward. He recorded with indignation that in Brussels six people so portrayed had failed to give him anything in return.[22]

We must assume similar things for other portrait specialists, for instance Goltzius and Wallerant Vaillant, although some series of portraits may have been produced for special purposes (such as Van Dyck's *Iconography*). In the seventeenth century, drawn portraits were hardly considered anything else than cheap substitutes for painted ones. Witness Alessandro Tassoni's commentary to Petrarch's poems:[23] when he came to the line "ivi [that is, in Paradise] la vide, et la ritrasse in carte," he annotated drily, "poco onore le fece, ritraendola sulla carta."

From Hainhofer's early seventeenth-century correspondence with Duke Philip II of Pomerania we learn that drawings were made to order.[24] Yet artists in the seventeenth century began also to exploit the opportunities of an open market. A pupil of Ludovico Carracci, Giovanluigi Valesio (1583-1650) drew eighteen "pensieri di Madonne" in two days; they were peddled by an assistant from house to house and sold like hot cakes.[25] The charge was one, two, or three *pistole*, according to size. This antedates by more than a hundred years the commercial activities of Boucher who at breakfast time retouched copies of his draw-

---

[21] Petrarch, *Canzoniere*, 77: "Per mirar Policleto à prova fiso. . . ."

[22] W. M. Conway, *Literary Remains of Albrecht Dürer*, Cambridge [England], 1889, p. 102.

[23] *Le rime di Francesco Petrarca, con considerazioni di Alessandro Tassoni, annotazioni di Girolamo Muzio, osservazioni di Lod. Ant. Muratori*, Venice, 1727, I, p. 153 (Sonnet LVI).

[24] O. Doering, *Des Augsburger Patriciers Philipp Hainhofer Beziehungen zum Herzog Philip II von Pommern-Stettin*, Vienna, 1894, pp. 4, 14.

[25] Malvasia, *op.cit.*, IV, p. 151.

ings that students had made the day before, and then sold them as originals at two louis d'or apiece.[26]

The exchange of drawings between artists as a gesture of respect begins early in the sixteenth century, if not before. The best-known case is the somewhat unequal trade between Dürer and Raphael. Sandrart's story that Schongauer and Perugino "frequently sent drawings to each other" is probably a legend formed by analogy, and more significant for the seventeenth-century author than for the Quattrocento artists.[27]

Nor is it certain that Raphael himself wrote the famous letter to Francia in which he thanks Francia for a self-portrait and promises one in return while asking also for a drawing of Francia's *Judith*.[28] But Vasari tells that he kept "carissima, per amore suo," a drawing Primaticcio had sent him as a present.[29] Hoefnagel sent one of his miniature-like drawings to Ortelius and asked no money in return but a sample of the "art" of the great cartographer.[30] Sandrart tells of a self-portrait in red chalk that Guercino sent to him "zur Gedächtnus."[31] Mention should here be made of the drawings artists contributed so often in the late sixteenth and the seventeenth centuries to the *Alba amicorum* to give permanence to occasional encounters and visits.

We know also of drawings given away, or bequeathed to friends, in payment of debts and, in the case of Parmigianino at the Sack of Rome, as ransom.[32] Van Mander's life was saved by an Italian officer who remembered having been given an occasional drawing by the artist.[33]

It was natural enough for artists to make collections of drawings of other artists. Some of the finest collections were indeed so formed: by Viti and Vasari, Calvaert and Passarotti, Rubens,

[26] J. Christian von Mannlich, *Rokoko und Revolution*, ed. E. Stollreither, Berlin, 1913, p. 56.

[27] *Joachim von Sandrart's Academie der Bau-, Bild- und Mahlerey-Künste von 1675*, ed. A. R. Peltzer, Munich, 1925, p. 61. All references are to this edition.

[28] Malvasia, *op.cit.*, II, p. 45.

[29] Quoted *ibid.*, II, p. 154.

[30] Letter of September 20, 1593; see Joannes Henricus Hessels (ed.), *Abrahami Ortelii . . . epistola*, Cambridge [England], 1887, p. 566.

[31] Sandrart-Peltzer, *op.cit.*, p. 285.

[32] Vasari-Milanesi, *op.cit.*, V, p. 225.

[33] Van Mander, *op.cit.*, II, p. 400.

Rembrandt, Quellinus, Lely, Sandrart, and finally, this side of our chronological limits, by Reynolds and Lawrence. Yet as early as the beginning of the sixteenth century we hear of collections made by amateurs. Marcantonio Michiels, in 1530, saw volumes of drawings in the house of Gabriel Vendramin (among them drawings by Raphael);[34] in 1532 he saw drawings by Jacopo Bellini in the house of Antonio Pasqualino;[35] and in 1543 a pen-drawing by Giorgione in the house of Michiel Contarini.[36] Antonio Botta, "lawyer, poet, and antiquarian," had drawings by different masters in his house in Cremona.[37]

If we remember, in addition, Aretino's eagerness to obtain drawings by great artists, it begins to look as if amateurs of the Venetian ambience of the early sixteenth century played an important role in the development of a taste for fine drawings. In this connection it is interesting that the first reproduction of a drawing in a painting appears in a Venetian work. Before this, drawings appeared only in an attributive character, in pictures of St. Luke. The well-known painting in London of the so-called Lucretia by Lotto (Pl. xxxi, 3, 4) is a different case, since the lady holds—evidently as a reference to her own chastity—a drawing of a Lucretia in her hand. Whether the North Italian environment should also be credited with an early appreciation of children's drawings, as Caroto's painting in Verona (Pl. xxxii, 5) might suggest, I leave to others to decide.[38]

Spurred by the interest of collectors such as Vasari, Vincenzo Borghini, and especially Niccolo Gaddi of Florence, a regular traffic in drawings was established by the second half of the sixteenth century. By this time there had developed a demand for drawings by masters of the past as well as of distant regions, a

[34] T. von Frimmel, *L'anonimo Morelliano, notizia d'opere del disegno* (Quellenschriften, N.S. 1), Vienna, 1888, p. 108.

[35] *Ibid.*, p. 82.

[36] *Ibid.*, p. 114.

[37] *Ibid.*, p. 45.

[38] A special study ought perhaps to be made of the rendering of drawings in paintings. In view of the relative scarcity of this motif, it is worth noting that drawn sketches, generally of heads, appear fairly frequently in paintings by A. Brouwer (e.g., Munich, Alte Pinakothek, no. 109, and Haarlem, Frans Hals Museum, no. 47) and D. Teniers (Finch College, New York; S. van Berg Collection, New York; and Wallace Collection, London, no. 227).

demand which necessitated the use of agents and dependence on experts who could guarantee the genuineness of the merchandise. The correspondence of Niccolo Gaddi throws an interesting light on this situation. One of his agents, Ercole Basso, wrote on May 4, 1574: "Io de' disegni non ho molta intelligenza, e perciò mi sono governato, e così sempre farò, col giudizio dei periti."[39] Another one, Giulio Cesare Veli, on August 7, 1578, mentions a drawing attributed to Campagnola coming from a gentleman "che fa professione di conoscere assai in questo genere di cose."[40] On February 22, 1579, Joris Hoefnagel informs Gaddi, presumably from Munich, about opportunities for obtaining first-rate drawings by great German and Flemish artists, such as Dürer, Holbein, Lucas van Leyden, Patinir, Heemskerck, Bosch, Quentin Massys, Mabuse, and even Jan and Hubert van Eyck, "tutti diseigni d'Importancia et finiti."[41] He mentions a goldsmith Giacomo, perhaps of Antwerp, as his "contact" in the Netherlands. How drawings were sold in Paris by the *marchands d'image* in their *boutique* is described in a charming poem by Berthod (1652): "de meschants petits charbonis, / De vieux morceaux de griffonis, / Desquels il fait autant d'estime / Que d'une chose rarissime. . . ."[42]

In general, drawings were kept in portfolios, the "books" of which we hear so much. Some collectors arranged them chronologically, to illustrate the growth of art through the centuries: this was the aim of Vasari (and possibly of Vincenzo Borghini whose collection he mentions frequently); it was a method recommended later by Baldinucci and even by d'Argenville. Sandrart appreciated drawings as historical documents; he used dates on drawings to prove that engraving was first practiced in Germany.[43] Following a pattern of history proclaimed by Bel-

---

[39] Bottari-Ticozzi, *op.cit.*, iii, p. 272. Basso, like other agents, sent packs of drawings from which Gaddi would pick what he liked, returning what was not wanted. Prices varied between one and two gold *scudi*.

[40] *Ibid.*, p. 317.

[41] *Ibid.*, iii, p. 324. I quote from the original now in the collection of Frits. Lugt, which differs slightly from the text published in Bottari-Ticozzi.

[42] See J. Thullier, *Art de France*, i, 1961, p. 331; the poem was found by R.-A. Weigert. I owe the reference to F.-G. Pariset.

[43] Sandrart-Peltzer, *op.cit.*, p. 317.

lori, Padre Resta arranged his drawings so as to demonstrate in his *Anfiteatro pittorico* the perfection of art at the time of Raphael, its decline in the epoch of Zuccari, and its triumphant revival with the Carracci and their school.[44] (Actually, the grouping of the more than 2,000 drawings the loquacious Padre collected for Bishop Marchetti was as illogical and as whimsical as his commentary.)

More common, surely, was the arrangement by master (particularly where the collector had strong personal preferences) and by subject. A typical example was Rembrandt's collection.[45] He had two volumes of drawings by Lastman, one with drawings by Rubens, Van Dyck, and others, one of drawings by Brouwer, and one with Tyrolean scenes by Savery. In addition, he had two volumes with landscapes, one with Roman buildings, and four mixed portfolios. His own drawings were divided strictly by subject: three volumes with landscapes, two with studies of single figures, three with drawings from antiquity, one with nudes, and one with animals. His narrative drawings made up fifteen volumes, one of which, bound in black leather, contained "the best of his work."

Drawn or painted framing devices like those by Vasari and especially Hoefnagel (Pl. xxxii, 7) were probably relatively rare; but we know that at least by the end of the sixteenth century, highly valued drawings were framed under glass.[46] They abound in seventeenth-century inventories.

At an early date, writers began to compare drawings to precious objects. Michelangelo drawings (according to Vasari),[47] Cigoli drawings (according to Baldinucci)[48] were "kept like jewels." Junius also speaks of these "jewels of art" when he mentions the collection of the Earl of Arundel.[49] The Holbein drawings that

[44] For Resta, see A. E. Popham, "Sebastiano Resta, 1635-1714, and His Collections," *Old Master Drawings*, xi, 1936-37, pp. 1ff.

[45] See C. Hofstede de Groot, *Die Urkunden über Rembrandt*, The Hague, 1906, pp. 200ff.

[46] Bottari-Ticozzi, *op.cit.*, iii, p. 317; letter by Giulio Cesare Veli to Niccolo Gaddi, August 7, 1578.

[47] Vasari-Milanesi, *op.cit.*, vii, pp. 276-77.

[48] F. Baldinucci, *Notizie de' professori del disegno . . .*, Florence, 1702, v, p. 30.

[49] Franciscus Junius, *The Painting of the Ancients*, London, 1638, pp. 270-71.

the city of Basel bought from the Amerbach cabinet in 1661 are called a *Schatz* by Sandrart,[50] not without good reason; he himself had offered 200 guilders for a single drawing by that master.[51] The word *reliquia* for a drawing appears with Aretino;[52] Malvasia uses it again when he says that Bevilacqua, who was a cleric, venerated his Passerotti drawings as if they were religious relics.[53] We also hear of efforts made by collectors to obtain a special piece (Sandrart yielded a Dürer drawing to the insistent requests of a Dutch collector made more persuasive, I admit, by the offer of 300 guilders);[54] we also hear of drawings that could not be had for love or money (one such case reported by Malvasia).[55]

Seventeenth-century writers, especially in Italy, were convinced that every scrap of paper on which a great artist had drawn was worth saving. They deplored losses caused by carelessness and ignorance. Malvasia thinks with regret of the many lost Carracci drawings, now sought *a prezzo d'oro*. Mastelletta, a pupil of Agostino Carracci, is said to have taken a drawing from the hands of his teacher, who was about to use it for cleaning a frying pan.[56] Soprani recalls that Cambiaso's wife and servant would feed the fire with the artist's drawings.[57] Vasari has written that the nuns of St. Catherina in Siena used drawings by Fra Bartolommeo to make fire,[58] and Aretino, to be sure, asked Michelangelo only for a drawing that would otherwise go into the fire.[59]

[50] Sandrart-Peltzer, *op.cit.*, p. 322.

[51] *Ibid.*, p. 102.

[52] See *Lettere sull'arte di Pietro Aretino*, ed. E. Camesasca, Milan, 1957-60, II, pp. 15-16, CLXXVIII, letter of April 1544.

[53] Malvasia, *op.cit.*, II, pp. 241-42.

[54] Sandrart-Peltzer, *op.cit.*, p. 64.

[55] Malvasia, *op.cit.*, III, p. 548.

[56] *Ibid.*, III, p. 467. An equally dramatic rescue of a drawing is reported in Mariette's *Abecedario*, Paris, 1851-62, III, pp. 94-95. On his way home from an audience with M. Fouquet, Charles Le Brun tore up and threw into an ashcan a large drawing of his which had failed to please the powerful minister of finance. Young Girardon, who was with him when this happened, later went back, collected the pieces of paper, and pasted them together again.

[57] R. Soprani, *Le vite de' pittori, scoltori, et architetti genovesi . . .* , Genoa, 1674, p. 39.

[58] Vasari-Milanesi, *op.cit.*, IV, p. 195, n. 2.

[59] Letter of January 20, 1538; see *Lettere sull'arte . . .* , I, pp. 112-13, no. LXX.

What matters is not the reproach for feeding drawings into the fire—this may have been a conventional accusation—but the implication that drawings should be preserved, not destroyed. Concern for its preservation prompted Pieter Candid de Witte to number the pages of an old sketchbook and in an inscription to ask all future owners to keep it complete and undamaged.[60] (It is, of course, another matter if some artists, out of fear for their families or because of qualms of conscience, themselves destroyed some drawings, as is reported of Fra Bartolommeo, Lorenzo di Credi, Pieter Bruegel, Pietro Testa, and Jean-Baptiste Santerre.)

A collector then, as now, was probably happiest when he could share the contemplation of his treasures with the like-minded. Jabach's and Crozat's cabinets were particularly famous for their social gatherings.[61] Perhaps the most touching story is that of young Sandrart's visits with Uffenbach, who had acquired a large body of Grünewald drawings from Hans Grimmer (who in turn had obtained them from Grünewald's widow). "The school I went to in Frankfurt was not far from his house and I visited him often, and when he was in a good mood he showed me these noble drawings of Matthaeus of Aschaffenburg which were gathered in one book, and having studied their manner carefully he explained to me their praiseworthy qualities and beauty."[62] After fifty years, Sandrart still fondly remembered these visits, which evidently were responsible for his lifelong interest in the nearly forgotten genius.

It appears that for the writers of the late sixteenth and early seventeenth centuries, drawings in pen were preferable to those done in other techniques. Borghini explains this preference with the difficulty of drawing in pen (1584);[63] Hainhofer (1610) is more specific when he says that it is more difficult to make cor-

[60] See J. Held, "Notizen zu einem niederländischen Skizzenbuch," *Oud-Holland*, L, 1933, p. 273.

[61] See, *Description sommaire des desseins des grands maistres . . . du cabinet de feu M. Crozat. Avec des réflexions sur la manière de dessiner des principaux peintres*, Paris, 1741, p. XI; hereafter cited as *Catalogue Crozat*. Mariette credits much of his knowledge to the conversations held at the weekly meetings in Crozat's cabinet.

[62] Sandrart-Peltzer, *op.cit.*, pp. 81-82. Sandrart says *Wohlstand*, which may have associations with *decorum*.

[63] R. Borghini, *Il riposo*, Florence, 1584, II, p. 139.

rections in pen drawings than in other techniques.[64] To Van
Mander, their contemporary, the supreme masters in drawing
are, characteristically, Goltzius and Spranger. In the inventory of
the large collection of Philip van Valckenisse (1614), a group of
sixteen drawings was singled out under the heading "artful pieces
done by Jan Wiericx with the pen."[65] One of them can still be
identified; it is the drawing of Apelles and Campaspe[66] (Pl. xxxiii,
8) which later was a chief attraction in the collection of Van der
Geest (Pl. xxxiii, 9) and is today in the Musée Mayer van den
Bergh at Antwerp. In his letter of 1579 (mentioned above, see
note 41), Hoefnagel had written that the most highly priced
drawings in Antwerp were the finished ones, and this is reiterated
over and over again in Hainhofer's letters.

It is strange to realize that the purpose of such virtuoso per-
formances seems to have been to rival engraving. Indeed, drawings are occasionally praised because they resemble engravings.
Sandrart calls some Holbein drawings "fleissig geschraffiert, ob
wärens in Kupfer gestochen."[67] He admired a life-size bust
portrait of the Duke of Mecklenburg by Benjamin von Block
(1631-90) because it looked like an engraving.[68] Fialetti (d. 1638)
had made drawings for Daniel Nys which, according to Boschini,
were even superior to engravings.[69] This excessive admiration for
the pen disappears at the end of our period: De Lairesse (1711)
condemned drawing with the pen as a poor practice, proper for
schoolmasters but not for artists. Instead, he highly recommends
drawing in chalk on blue or gray paper.[70]

Van Mander's favorite expressions for drawings are *claer* and
suyverlijk, suyverheydt, reynheydt, netticheydt.[71] Hainhofer uses

---

[64] Doering, *op.cit.*, p. 32.

[65] See J. Denucé, *De Antwerpsche "Konstkamers,"* Antwerp, 1932, p. 15.

[66] Described in the inventory: "Figure van naecte vrouwe die wtgeschildert
wort met andere personagien." The identification is all the more likely since
Van der Geest acquired other items from the Van Valckenisse Collection.

[67] Sandrart-Peltzer, *op.cit.*, p. 102.

[68] *Ibid.*, p. 345.

[69] Quoted by Malvasia, *op.cit.*, ii, p. 312. Nys was of Flemish origin and
hence perhaps predisposed in favor of careful pen drawings.

[70] G. de Lairesse, *Le grand livre des peintres*, Paris, 1787, i, pp. 43-44.

[71] See R. Hoecker, *Das Lehrgedicht des Karel van Mander*, The Hague,
1916, p. 383.

sauber and *schier*, and *sauber* is found often also in Sandrart. San-drart's most typical praise is *fleissig*, used liberally for drawings by Holbein, Dürer, and Aldegrever. *Fleissig* means careful rather than industrious,[72] but Sandrart also appreciated industry; "auf das aller-emsigste und sorgfaltigste" is his characterization of a lost set of anticlerical drawings by Holbein.[73] He admonishes young artists to aim more at carefulness than speed, and he is against all that is *unausgesonnen* or *wild-durchgangen*.[74] Describing what was perhaps his proudest possession, Dürer's early Orpheus drawing (Pl. xxxii, 6), he praises the landscape for the exact rendering of every individual form, "the bark of trees, the oaks, figs, and other foliage."[75]

The descriptive nouns and adjectives used for drawings by Italian writers are very different indeed. In a drawing by a Quat-trocento artist (Verrocchio), Vasari lauds the patience, but his real admiration is conveyed by words like *fiero, fierezza, vivacità, gagliardia, capriccio. Bravura, franchezza*, and *bizzaria* are laud-able qualities for Baldinucci; *gagliardia* and *fierezza* for Ridolfi. Adjectives are *spiritoso, vivace, franco* (Baldinucci); *strepitoso, tenero, guizzante, spiritoso, bizzarro, svolazzante* (Malvasia). Mal-vasia, who hardly ever is satisfied with less than four epithets, calls a Niccolò dell'Abbate drawing that excels every other piece in his own collection "tutto spirito, tutto grazia, tutto fondamento, tutto decoro,"[76] and he points out another drawing by Niccolò as capable of absolving him from the suspicion of being a "troppo ardito e appasionato scrittore."[77]

In the vocabulary of French eighteenth-century critics, *fier* is still used freely: Mariette calls Michelangelo *fier*,[78] and he praises Annibale Carracci as "un des plus fier dessinateurs qui ait jamais été."[79] "Bizarre," however, lost its attraction; having been criti-

---

[72] "Dieser Grimer hat . . . alles, was er von ihme Können zusammen tragen, fleissig aufgehoben" (Sandrart-Peltzer, *op.cit.*, p. 81). See also Dürer: "Geht fleissig damit um . . ." (letter to Jacob Heller, August 26, 1509).

[73] Sandrart-Peltzer, *op.cit.*, p. 102.

[74] *Ibid.*, p. 356.   [75] *Ibid.*, p. 322.

[76] Malvasia, *op.cit.*, ii, p. 159.

[77] *Ibid.*, p. 160.   [78] *Catalogue Crozat*, p. 3.

[79] *Ibid.*, p. 48. This passage was literally repeated by Count Tessin in his *Catalogue de quelques desseins du cabinet de G. G. T. presentés à son Altesse*

cized long before by Zuccaro, it is now applied as a term of reproach: De Piles calls works of P. Testa "un cahos de bizareries."[80] "C'étoit une peste," Mariette says of the drawings of Flemish sixteenth-century Mannerists, the contorted attitudes of figures are "aussi fausses que bisarres."[81] Rembrandt, according to him, drew the same subject in infinitely different fashions "toutes plus bisarres les unes que les autres." Only Rembrandt's landscapes pass muster: "ce qu'il a dessiné de plus vrai, sont les Paysages."[82]

In the comments on drawings which stress their freedom, boldness, imagination, even capriciousness, we see reflected a concept of the function of drawings which, as Ernst Gombrich has shown, goes back to Leonardo.[83] If the artist, like the poet, works in a creative furor, drawings, being closest to the "hot" stages of inspiration, are apt to reveal to the beholder the thoughts (*pensieri*) of the artist more clearly than the paintings. Today this has become a common place, although it may be expressed in words as different as those of Meder, who likes to observe "das geniale Suchen und Ringen"[84] and those of Edgar Wind, who speaks of the "inspired stammer" and the "bold notations in which the master's hand vibrates and flickers."[85] Franciscus Junius, who as a member of the circle of the Earl of Arundel was in touch with discerning amateurs, as well as with artists such as Rubens and Van Dyck, included a significant passage in the English edition of his work on the painting of the ancients: "... many who have a deeper insight into these arts, delight themselves as much in the contemplation of the first, second, and third draughts which great masters made of their works as in the workes themselves ... seeing ... in these naked and undistinguished lineaments ... the very thoughts of the Studious Artificer,

---

royale *Louise Ulrique, Princesse de Suède, et de Prusse, le 24 décembre,* M.DCCXLVIII, no. 12. I am indebted to Per Bjurström for having brought this inventory to my knowledge.

[80] Roger de Piles, *Dialogue sur le coloris,* Paris, 1699, p. 63.

[81] *Catalogue Crozat,* p. 92.

[82] *Ibid.,* pp. 101-2.

[83] E. H. Gombrich, "Conseils de Léonard sur les esquisses de tableaux," *L'Art et la pensée de Léonard de Vinci,* Paris-Alger, 1954, p. 1ff.

[84] Meder, *op.cit.,* p. 30.

[85] Edgar Wind, "Critique of Connoisseurship" (The Third Reith Lecture), *The Listener,* December 1, 1960, p. 976.

and how he did bestirre his judgment before he could resolve what to like and what to dislike."[86]

It is obvious from his wording that Junius refers to an opinion held by his contemporaries. Yet this opinion was certainly shaped under the influence of a classical passage the importance of which has not been sufficiently realized: there is a sentence in Pliny, between lists of little-known painters, claiming that works left unfinished are valued more than finished works because in these we see traces of the design and the thoughts of the artists (*liniamenta reliqua ipsaeque cogitationes artificum*).[87]

Vasari appears to have been the first author to introduce the idea that drawings may be superior to the finished work because the creative furor may flag if the execution of the work requires a prolonged effort. He prefers Giulio Romano's drawings to his paintings because they were done by the artist "tutto fiero ed acceso nell'opera," while the paintings took months and years.[88] Elsewhere he speaks in general of the boldness of the first sketch done in "a sort of fire of inspiration" which vanishes when it comes to finishing the work.[89] By the seventeenth century this idea has seeped down to the level of the layman; Roger North, for instance, put it this way: "These drawings are observed to have more of the spirit and force of art than finished paintings, for they come from either flow of fancy or depth of study, whereas all this or great part is wiped out with the pencil [i.e., brush] and acquires somewhat more heavy, than is in the drawings."[90] Sandrart preferred Aldegrever's drawings to the engravings made from them;[91] De Piles thought Rembrandt's drawings (of which he owned a fair number) had more *esprit* than his etchings.[92] The Richardsons had a whole list of artists who in their opinion had been better in drawings than in paintings (such as Par-

---

[86] Junius, *loc.cit.*, pp. 170-71.

[87] K. Jex-Blake, *The Elder Pliny's Chapters on the History of Art*, London, 1896, p. 168 (35, 145).

[88] Vasari-Milanesi, *op.cit.*, v, p. 528.

[89] *Ibid.*, v, p. 260.

[90] Augustus Jessopp, *The Autobiography of the Hon. Roger North*, London, 1887, p. 202.

[91] Sandrart-Peltzer, *op.cit.*, p. 92.

[92] Roger de Piles, *Abregé de la vie des peintres* (1st ed., 1699), ed. 1715, p. 425.

migianino, Polidoro, Battista Franco, and, of course, Giulio Romano). They even included Michelangelo (none of whose paintings the elder Richardson had ever seen).[93]

It was inevitable that critics should not only compare drawings to paintings and etchings but make differentiations among drawings themselves. Italian writers were the first to aver that the less a drawing is finished, the more rewarding it may be as a work of art. Vasari had defined the different types of drawing, but he had not expressed a preference for one type or another.[94] Baldinucci, however, inserted a revealing statement in his life of Tempesta. Some artists, he says, made highly finished drawings; others, of equal or higher rank, were content with only lightly finished ones; others still made drawings that to the inexperienced eye may look careless, confused, and entirely deformed ("strappazzati, confusi, e del tutto informi") and yet may be the best to serve for study and instruction.[95] That Baldinucci had great admiration for the rough draft may be seen from his definition of *macchia*: "Done with extraordinary facility and with such harmony and freshness that it almost looks as if it had appeared all by itself on the paper or the canvas."[96] Other examples, from Malvasia to the Richardsons, could be quoted in support of the observation that by this time the concept of *sprezzatura* had infiltrated the critique of the different types of drawings.

In developing a taste for the quick first sketch, critics were probably encouraged by the age-old notion that the great artist shows his mettle in a few lines. Classical authors provided examples not only for the excellence that can be demonstrated in a single line, but also for the demerit that comes from exaggerated diligence.[97] This idea reverberates in Dürer's often-quoted

[93] J. Richardson, *An Account of the Statues, Bas-reliefs, Drawings, and Pictures in Italy, France, etc.*, 2nd ed., London, 1754, p. 272. Edgar Wind ("Aesthetic Participation" [The Second Reith Lecture], *The Listener*, November 24, 1960, p. 930) deplores that Michelangelo's drawings still receive "perhaps even more attention than his frescoes."

[94] Vasari-Milanesi, *op.cit.*, I, pp. 174ff.

[95] F. Baldinucci, *Cominciamento e progresso dell'arte dell'intagliare in rame*, Florence, 1686, p. 33.

[96] *Vocabulario toscano dell'arte del disegno*, Milan, 1809, I, p. 297.

[97] Pliny, 35, ed. Jex-Blake, pp. 80-83. Apelles' criticism of Protogenes had

words that the great artist may sketch something with the pen in one day that is superior to the result of someone else's labor of a year. Sandrart alludes to it when he says that there was more understanding in an outline in pen or chalk by Elsheimer than in the most assiduous efforts of others.[98] We meet the idea also in the anecdote about Tintoretto who, confronted with some careful Flemish drawings, made a figure in a few strokes of the brush, adding ironically: "We poor Venetians know only how to draw in this manner."[99] Annibale Carracci, according to Malvasia, could do more "in a few lines" than others in many.[100] Seen in this context, Aretino's request to Michelangelo for *due segni di carbone* was obviously meant to convey a special compliment.

With the concept of linear economy goes that of speed. Speedy execution was applauded in antiquity;[101] such praise appears again in the Renaissance, in reference to drawings: Pomponio Gaurico[102] cited the speed with which Donatello filled a sheet with sketches of figures. Soprani tells that the tribute paid to Cambiaso by the Cavaliere Marino was in recognition of the speed with which the artist in a few strokes of the pen drew single figures and even whole compositions.[103] Vasari graphically described the speed of Giulio Romano,[104] and Malvasia tells a charming story about young Elisabetta Sirana: inspired by a report about a Baptism of Christ *la spiritosa figliuola* jumped to her feet, took half a sheet of paper, and sketched the same subject so rapidly that the drawing was finished by the time the conversation about the topic had ended.[105] To substantiate the truth of the story, Malvasia ends

---

been given wide currency through Castiglione's use of it in the *Courtier* (see A. Blunt, *Artistic Theory in Italy, 1450-1600*, Oxford, 1940, p. 98). Less known is a similar observation (about the paintings of Dionysius) in Plutarch's life of Timoleon (see Junius, *op.cit.*, p. 325, and *Plutarch's Lives*, Modern Library edition, p. 318).

[98] Sandrart-Peltzer, *op.cit.*, p. 162.   [99] Ridolfi, *op.cit.*, II, p. 65.

[100] Malvasia, *op.cit.*, IV, p. 429. Lanfranco, according to Bellori (*Le vite . . .* , Rome, 1672, p. 381) "riconosceva il naturale con pochi segni di carbone. . . ."

[101] See, for instance, Pliny, 35, ed. Jex-Blake, p. 109 (Nikomachus).

[102] *De sculptura seu statuaria libellus . . .* , Antwerp, 1528, p. 64v; see also H. W. Janson, *The Sculpture of Donatello*, Princeton, 1957, II, p. 217.

[103] Soprani, *op.cit.*, p. 40.

[104] Vasari-Milanesi, *op.cit.*, V, p. 551.

[105] Malvasia, *op.cit.*, IV, p. 479.

by saying that she gave him the drawing, which later was in the collection of Valerio Polazzi. (It is only fair to add that speed alone was not enough for Malvasia; Prospero Fontana, whose speed in drawing he recognizes, *oprò più di pratica, che di scienza*.)[106]

Interest in *macchie* and *schizzi* was propagated mostly by Italian writers, just as the making of such rough sketches had been a practice developed and justified by Italian artists. Under the influence of Italian writings on art and the lingo of the studios, other languages developed terms for the same thing: *gribouillage*, or *griffonnement* in French, scrabble or scratch in English, *crabbeling* in Dutch.[107] We meet these terms in catalogues of collections; so, for instance, in the inventory of the collection of Erasmus Quellinus where a good many *crabbelinge* (many by Rubens) are listed singly or in pairs.[108] Roger North speaks of the scratches in the Lely Collection, some perhaps done by artists "half drunk," which were appreciated by the "scholars."[109]

The theoretical discussion of the relative merit of the first sketches was carried on by French and English writers. At the very end of the century (1699), Roger de Piles used a formulation that still echoes in modern art historical writing, when he says, "en faisant un Dessein, (l'artiste) s'abandonne à son génie, & *se fait voir tel qu'il est*."[110] D'Argenville paraphrased this statement, as he did so many others of De Piles: "En faisant un dessein, il jette le premier feu de sa pensée; il s'abandonne à lui même; il se montre tel qu'il est."[111] Yet what D'Argenville has in mind is

[106] *Ibid.*, II, p. 216. In his *vita* of Lanfranco, Bellori (talking about art in general) states expressly that praise of a work of art should not be affected either by the speed or the slowness of its execution (*op.cit.*, p. 365).

[107] The words *kritzeln* and *Kritzelei*, which might have become the German terms for a quickly done drawing, were, in point of fact, used only for children's work, never for that of artists. The German language adopted *Skizze* from the Italian *schizzo*, but this word, like the English "sketch," was used both for drawings and oil sketches. In the reluctance of the Germans to develop a term for the sketchy drawing, there may be reflected an aesthetic prejudice, and possibly also the fact that with the exception of Elsheimer, whose drawings were largely done in Italy, there was no first-rate German draftsman in the seventeenth century.

[108] Denucé, *op.cit.*, pp. 285ff.

[109] Jessopp, *op.cit.*, p. 202. [110] *Abregé* . . . , ed. De Piles, 1715, p. 67.

[111] *Abregé* . . . , ed. D'Argenville, 1762, p. XXXII.

different from De Piles. De Piles had spoken of the "demi-con-noisseurs" who have no appreciation of drawings in general. D'Argenville reserves the title of *demi-connoisseur* (a term prob-ably derived from Baldinucci's *occhio de' poco pratici*) for those who like finished drawings better than *griffonnements*. He adds another idea, which he must have derived from a source that I have not yet been able to locate, by warning: "Défiez-vous des desseins trop finis, rarement sont-ils originaux."[112] In their *Two Discourses on Connoisseurship*,[113] the Richardsons had attacked this notion; thus, the idea must have been expressed before 1725. D'Argenville, at any rate, saw, I think correctly, that many draw-ings then admired as works of Rubens were actually done by students or engravers and only touched up by the master.

Yet, no matter how much theoretical support there was for the appreciation of the first light sketch, the finished drawings seem to have remained the favorites of the *curieux*. It is difficult for us to determine when, in the eyes of earlier critics, little finish was considered to be too little, or much to be too much. Yet, it is interesting to see what De Piles had to say on this subject. After repeating the old formula that great masters were able to characterize their themes in a few lines, and admitting that slight sketches, provided they have "character" (a personal style), please more than the finished ones because they stimulate the beholder's imagination,[114] he ends by saying that all things being equal, the appreciation of a drawing is proportionate to the degree of fin-ish.[115] The importance of the finished drawings is attested also by the number of adjectives the language provided for their descrip-tion. D'Argenville's list includes "desseins rendus, finis, arrêtés, terminés, capitaux."[116] (*Capitaele teeckeningen* are also listed in Quellinus' inventory.)[117]

[112] *Ibid.*, p. LXII.

[113] London, 1725, p. 181: "Some have fancied the Great Masters made no Finish'd Drawings, as not having Time, or Patience sufficient, and therefore pronounce all Such to be Coppies. . . ."

[114] This idea is found again with Comte de Caylus; see E. G. Holt, *A Docu-mentary History of Art*, Garden City, New York, 1958, II, p. 323.

[115] *Abregé* . . . , ed. De Piles, 1715, p. 70.

[116] *Abregé* . . . , ed. D'Argenville, 1762, p. XXXVI.

[117] See above, n. 108.

The difference between theory and practice is well illustrated by a letter of Mariette's. "There is nothing I delight in more than drawings done in this manner," that is, one done "by a great artist solely to fix his idea (*pensiero*)," he says in a letter to Bottari; he then goes on to ask for a drawing by Giuseppe Crespi "un disegno *magistrale*, non qualche piccolo schizzo."[118] In his commentary to the Raphael drawings in the Crozat Collection, he says: "Les autres jettent sur le papier leurs premières pensées & l'on apperçoit qu'ils cherchent; Raphael au contraire . . . lors même qu'il paroit entrainé par la véhémence de son imagination, produit du premier coup des ouvrages qui sont tellement arrêtéz qu'il n'y a presque plus rien à y ajouter, pour y mettre la dernière main."[119] Obviously he prefers drawings to which the artist has put *la dernière main*.

De Piles' chapter on drawings, a milestone in the history of the appreciation of drawings, is the first coherent piece of writing that deals with them as aesthetic and historical objects. Luckily for a paper stressing the seventeenth century, it was first published in 1699. It is followed by the famous lecture of the Comte de Caylus in 1732[120] and D'Argenville's book of 1745. All earlier writings on drawings (Vasari, Armenini, Van Mander, Peacham, Hoogstraeten, Goeree, to mention a few) deal with definitions and technical advice, directed toward the young artist. De Piles' chapter was written for the educated amateur, the *curieux* interested in aesthetic distinctions and in connoisseurship, "le sujet favori de la conversation" as D'Argenville put it. Of the twenty-nine chapters in De Piles' book, only two, those on drawing and on the uses of prints, were listed on the title page—a sure sign he knew that their content was of special interest to his readers.[121] The amateurs of drawings must have been flattered by his remark that it takes a special sensibility to appreciate drawings, and that the number of *curieux* in this field was still small. The thought

---

[118] Bottari-Ticozzi, *op.cit.*, IV, pp. 508-9.

[119] *Catalogue Crozat*, p. 14.

[120] See above, n. 114.

[121] The treatise *L'idée du peintre parfait*, which contains this chapter, in 1706 was erroneously published in Amsterdam as the work of J. F. Félibien. It is still occasionally catalogued under his name but De Piles' authorship is indisputable (see A. Fontaine, *Les doctrines d'art en France*, Paris, 1909, p. 58, n. 1).

of collectors of drawings forming an *élite* among the connoisseurs recurs again with the Comte de Caylus: "One is well advanced in connoisseurship . . . when one knows how to read them well."[122]

Connoisseurship, indeed, has become the central problem for these writers. It supplies answers to three questions: Who is the author? How good is the drawing? Is it an original or a copy? As to attributions, Jonathan Richardson and D'Argenville are more specific than De Piles; D'Argenville actually sounds like a Morelli *avant la lettre* when he speaks of the peculiarities of each artist's handwriting in the rendering of eyes, hair, beard, fingers, etc., which help in the identification of the master.[123] This is surely a great advance over the rather pathetic Padre Resta who, after long thoughts (he once even spoke of "mille considerationi ondeggianti"), decided that a drawing was by Raphael because the same costume details are found in Perugino and Filippino![124]

The central problem for most of these critics was the differentiation between original and copy. It had the distinction of having been of concern to ancient writers as well: Franciscus Junius collected passages from Dionysius of Halicarnassus, Diogenes Laërtius, Cicero, Seneca, and Quintilian dealing with the distinction between original and copy.[125] Copies, he concludes, will always betray themselves by their lack of "natural force of grace." D'Argenville avers that a copy is always "un ouvrage timide, servile, qui n'a jamais ni l'esprit, ni la touche, d'un original, quoiqu'il en rende exactement la pensée." He does exempt copies by great masters like Rubens who turn them into "second originals."[126]

And yet the literature of the sixteenth and seventeenth centuries is full of examples showing how well drawings could be copied. The most amusing case is that of Calvaert who found several copies he himself had made among the Michelangelo and Raphael "originals" in the collection of Cardinal Alessandro d'Este.[127] The Earl of Arundel employed a painter, Hendrik van der Borcht,

[122] Holt, *op.cit.*, p. 323.
[123] *Abregé* . . . , ed. D'Argenville, 1762, p. XLIX.
[124] See Popham, *op.cit.*, p. 17.
[125] *Op.cit.*, p. 348.
[126] *Abregé* . . . , ed. D'Argenville, 1762, p. LVII.
[127] Malvasia, *op.cit.*, II, p. 252.

who was supposed "to have a good guess of originals from copies."[128] Both Baldinucci and Malvasia make references also to forgeries of drawings; one Sebastiano Brunetti was reckoned a skillful forger of *disegni antichi*.[129] While Baldinucci believed that first sketches were less counterfeited because the freedom of their lines was more difficult to imitate,[130] Comte de Caylus thought just the opposite—that sketchy drawings were easier to copy because there was less to them.[131]

No wonder that emphatic assertions of originality are common from the later seventeenth century on. Sandrart owned, as he says, "wahre Originalia von Dürer's eigner Hand";[132] in Nuremberg he saw "eigenhändig gemachte Handrisse" by Israel von Meckenem.[133] Gaburri inscribed his drawings with remarks such as: "originale indubitale di mano di Giov(anni) da San Giovanni."[134] A good provenance was often given as a guarantee for the originality, but Richardson was already skeptical about this argument and D'Argenville called it typical dealers' talk. "C'est à la chose même, à la valeur intrinsique de l'Ouvrage qu'il faut s'attacher," he insists with a good deal of justification.[135]

The spread of connoisseurship and antiquarianism toward the end of the seventeenth century is obvious also in the attention paid by dealers and collectors to the condition of drawings. Damaged drawings had, of course, been repaired before: Rubens probably reworked many earlier drawings because they had suffered. Yet with the growing sensitivity for, and interest in, the originality of drawings, such restorations were not uniformly approved. Mariette admired these reworkings by Rubens, but the Richardsons described such a drawing as "something damaged by time and Rubens."[136] "Admirably preserved," "all of perfect conserva-

---

[128] See D. Sutton, "Thomas Howard, Earl of Arundel and Surrey, as a Collector of Drawings," *Burlington Magazine*, LXXXIX, 1947, pp. 3-9, 32-37, 75-77.

[129] Malvasia, *op.cit.*, III, p. 561.

[130] F. Baldinucci, *Lettera . . . all'illustr. Signor Marchese e Senatore Vincenzio Capponi*, Rome, 1681, p. 7.

[131] Holt, *op.cit.*, p. 327.

[132] Sandrart-Peltzer, *op.cit.*, p. 332.

[133] *Ibid.*, p. 317.

[134] Lugt, *op.cit.* (Supplement), p. 424.

[135] *Abregé . . .* , ed. D'Argenville, 1762, p. LX.

[136] *An Account . . .* , p. 79.

tion" (Richardsons) are expressions encountered again and again in the eighteenth century. Yet we must not forget that there were men like a certain Ned Wright, "who has a peculiar knack at repairing defects in old drawings."[137]

We know today that many of the opinions of the connoisseurs of the late seventeenth and eighteenth centuries, particularly in the field of drawing, were overconfident.[138] Undoubtedly there were a good many people who remained skeptical in the face of self-assured claims. Roger North wrote with a certain dry amusement about the "masters" (i.e., connoisseurs): "Considering the multitude of painters and really great masters that have been in Italy, whose names are scarce known, but probably were the authors of very many of these drawings, it is pleasant to see the confidence of the masters in christening drawings. They have a list, as Giulio, Paulo (Veronese), Raphael, Titian, etc., and because the drawings of these men have been seen, all that have any resemblance with them are fathered accordingly, and a value is set, as their work."[139]

In our own age we are witnessing an almost disquieting expansion of interest in drawings, and the list of names which the connoisseurs manipulate is larger. We might do well to remember the words of Roger North, and perhaps also those of another clever observer of the contemporary scene, the Abbé du Bos. It was he who wrote in his *Réflexions critiques sur la poésie et sur la peinture* (1719) that connoisseurship was "le plus fautif de tous les arts après la Médecine."

[137] See C. Fairfax Murray, *Two Lombard Sketchbooks*, London, 1910, I, pl. 105, and II, pl. 69. The text on the back of a drawing by Vanni was written by an unknown collector, who quotes J. Richardson, Jr.'s statement, made "in a peevish mood."

[138] For example: A drawing that Malvasia described "il disegno inarrivabile della famosa battaglia di Costantino di Raffaele, capo sublime della mia raccolta" (III, p. 522); that, according to Richardson, "may be considered as the most Capital in the world" (*An Account . . .*, p. 11); that was accepted by Bellori and Sacchi as proving Raphael's authorship of the *Battle of Constantine*; and that passed from the Malvasia Collection into the collections of Boschi and Crozat and is now in the Louvre: this famous piece was called a "school piece" by Reiset, and has been given to Penni by Frederick Hartt, as being done after a *modello* by Giulio Romano.

[139] See Jessopp, *op.cit.*, p. 203.

Having come to the end of my report, I am very much aware that I have by no means exhausted the subject. In my reading, first of all, I have not yet covered all the sources available (I have, for instance, done nothing about the Spanish writers), and I have perused some authors less thoroughly than others. This being a "working Congress," I hope for some additional information from my audience and the discussants. I know, furthermore, that this paper could be supplemented by other studies; it would be interesting, for instance, to see whether and to what extent the personal styles of the great artists affected the judgment of drawings in general. In short, in regard to its chosen theme, this paper is hardly *arrêté*. I hope it will be regarded as no more than a first scratch, a *gribouillage*, or a *crabbeling*.

THE PLACE OF DRAWINGS IN THE
ART OF CLAUDE LORRAIN

MICHAEL KITSON

FIFTY years ago, or indeed at any time during the first half of the present century, the theme of this paper would scarcely have been considered as a subject for discussion. Claude's drawings, it was assumed, were there to be "enjoyed" rather than "understood"; they were material for critical appreciation rather than art historical analysis. Their poetry, liveliness, and charm were what chiefly attracted attention. These qualities were celebrated in much admirable writing.[1] But beyond making the basic distinction between the two main categories into which the drawings may be divided—sketches from nature and compositions executed in the studio—there was little attempt to analyze their function or to perceive their relationships either with the artist's paintings or with each other.

This paper is written in the belief that a more searching examination of these problems is essential for the understanding of Claude's drawings. It will involve both a new differentiation of the variations within each category and, at the same time, a clearer recognition of the qualities of mood and feeling which unite them. Until recently the sketches from nature have usually been separated too sharply from the rest of his work, and their importance has been overemphasized at the expense of the studio drawings and paintings. This development, which began at the end of the nineteenth century under the influence of Impressionist aesthetics, carried with it a tendency to see in the nature drawings a kind of Impressionist naturalism *avant la lettre*;[2] the qual-

---

[1] See especially Roger Fry, "Claude," in *Vision and Design*, London, 1920 (essay first published in the *Burlington Magazine*, 1907); Walter Friedlaender, *Claude Lorrain*, Munich, 1921; T. Hetzer, *Claude Lorrain*, Frankfurt a/M, 1947. The first serious treatment of the drawings from a scholarly point of view, although dealing with only a small group of them, is to be found in Anthony Blunt, *French Drawings . . . at Windsor Castle*, London, 1945.

[2] So far as I have been able to discover, the first expression of this tendency to appear in print occurs in G. Grahame, *Claude Lorrain*, London, 1895, a book that is otherwise little more than a pastiche of the book by Emilia Pattison

ities that these drawings share with the studio compositions and paintings were overlooked. In reality, Claude's achievement as a draftsman emerges as more, not less, remarkable when one views it as a whole and in relation to his paintings, than it does if one selects the nature drawings as the central expression of his genius.

It will be as well to begin by gathering together such information as we can from contemporary sources. Unfortunately, there is not much. Both Sandrart and Baldinucci—the biographers of Claude—mention his drawings, but, as is usual with seventeenth-century writers where graphic art is concerned, they say little about them in detail. Sandrart, who knew Claude as a young man man in Rome in the 1630's and often went sketching with him, even thought him rather incompetent as a draftsman. He discusses his work from nature in two separate passages. In one he does not refer to drawings but describes how Claude would spend the day in the Campagna, gazing intently at the light effects; and how, after he had "prepared his colours accordingly," he would return home and apply them to the work in hand. "This hard and burdensome way of learning," Sandrart continues, "he pursued for many years . . . , until he finally met me, with the brush in my hands, at Tivoli, in the wild rocks at the famous cascade, where he found me painting from life . . .; this pleased him so much that he applied himself eagerly to adopting the same method."[3] In the second passage Sandrart does mention drawings, but again with the object of demonstrating the superiority of painting. "I myself did this [i.e., drew landscapes from nature] for several years. Finally, however, as my closest neighbour and house-companion in Rome, the famous Claudio Gilli, called Lorraine, always wanted to go to the country with me in order to draw from nature, without being favoured in this at all by his talent, yet having on the contrary a peculiar capacity for

[Lady Dilke], *Claude Lorrain, sa vie et ses oeuvres*, Paris, 1884. It is carried to extreme lengths in A. M. Hind, *The Drawings of Claude Lorrain*, London, 1925. Only Fry, in the essay cited in the previous note, attempted to restore a more balanced view and to give due attention to the paintings.

[3] From the biography of Claude in *Der teutschen Academie*, Nuremberg, 1675, 1, 2, pp. 331ff. This and other early sources concerning the artist are given in full in English translation in Marcel Röthlisberger's new and brilliant book, *Claude Lorrain: The Paintings*, 2 vols., New Haven, 1961.

imitation in painting: [instead of drawing or working in bistre wash, black chalk and the brush] in the open country in Tivoli, Frascati, Subiaco, and other places such as S. Benedetto, we began to paint entirely from nature with colours on prepared paper and cloths (*Tücher*), the mountains, grottoes, valleys, and deserted places, the terrible cascades of the Tiber, the Temple of the Sibyl, and the like."[4] Exactly how far these accounts are to be believed is difficult to judge. In so far as Sandrart intends to suggest that Claude abandoned drawing from nature altogether, the second of the two is patently false, since large numbers of such drawings exist, many of them inscribed with the names of the very places where Sandrart states that they painted. But there is no reason to doubt that, in addition to these drawings, Claude did make some colored sketches, now lost, in the way that Sandrart describes, and also occasional paintings from nature in oils on canvas, of which at least two have survived.[5] It is interesting to notice, incidentally, how the academically-minded Sandrart, despite his enthusiasm for painting *devant le motif*, evidently regarded Claude's nature drawings, in which "he could develop neither an individual manner nor delicacy," as crude. As he left Rome in 1635, he would have had no opportunity to see the composition drawings, of which Claude had at that time made only a few.

On turning to Baldinucci,[6] we find a different approach. He is a more conscientious historian than Sandrart, and his biographies of artists are distinguished as a rule by the attention he gives to drawings; but apart from his invaluable, detailed account of the *Liber Veritatis*, he says less about Claude's work in this medium

[4] From Sandrart's chapter on landscape painting, *op.cit.*, I, I, p. 51. A third passage in which drawings are discussed (from Sandrart's autobiography) merely repeats the sense of the second.

[5] In my view the most likely are: (1) the small upright *Pastoral Landscape* in the National Gallery, London, which is a variant of *Liber Veritatis* (LV) 15 of ca. 1637 and is probably to be identified with the painting described by Baldinucci as having been painted by Claude from nature in the Vigna Madama (Röthlisberger, *op.cit.*, pp. 127-30); (2) the *Landscape with Sheep* in the Akademie at Vienna, dated 1656 (*ibid.*, p. 507, no. 240). Another possibility is the other small painting in Vienna (assuming it is by Claude, which to my mind is not quite certain) of the early 1630's (*ibid.*, p. 506, no. 239).

[6] In *Notizie de' professori del disegno*, Florence, 1728, VI, pp. 357ff; translation in Röthlisberger, *op.cit.*, pp. 53-62.

than might have been hoped. In contrast to Sandrart, he met Claude only at the very end of the artist's life, visiting him in Rome in 1681,[7] the year before his death. In his statements about the *Liber Veritatis* ("which he himself showed me in his house in Rome, to my great delight and admiration"), he is mainly concerned with the origin and purpose of the book as a record of the paintings, not with the drawings in the book themselves. It seems, moreover, unlikely that he ever saw any of Claude's other drawings. But toward the end of his biography he does mention one useful fact (which he probably obtained from the artist's nephew), namely that "five or six great books of these drawings of views from nature remained to the heirs, and some bundles of loose sheets, as also, besides these, other pictures coloured by him after nature." This is confirmed by the inventory of his estate,[8] though the reference there is given differently: "12 books of sketches," a "small book of 32 drawings entitled the Life of S. Nicolò,"[9] and a "case . . . full of engravings and drawings" of varying sizes and quality. None of these items, it is true, is explicitly said in the inventory to be the work of Claude; indeed, the "case . . . of engravings and drawings" sounds as if it probably contained at least a proportion of drawings by other artists.[10] But the rest may reasonably be assumed to have been autograph.

I believe, moreover, that this material represents the major part of Claude's output as a draftsman. The considerable number of

[7] Baldinucci, a Florentine, went to Rome that year to collect material for his *Life* of Bernini (d. 1680). He probably spent only a short time with Claude and obtained most of his information by subsequent correspondence with the artist's nephew (Baldinucci himself died in 1696). His account of the origin and purpose of the *Liber Veritatis*, however, reads as if it had been taken directly from Claude himself.

[8] First published by F. Boyer in *Bulletin de la Société de l'Histoire de l'Art français*, 1928, pp. 152ff; translation in Röthlisberger, *op.cit.*, pp. 72-76. The inventory also lists the *Liber Veritatis* (195 drawings), Claude's etching plates and various paintings, besides all kinds of household effects.

[9] Also mentioned in Claude's will of 1663, together with the *Liber Veritatis* (then containing 157 drawings) and eight drawings to be given away as bequests, two to Cardinal Giulio Rospigliosi (later Clement IX) and six to Claude's godchild, Giovanni Piomer (Röthlisberger, *op.cit.*, p. 67).

[10] If so, it would help to account for the presence of drawings by artists other than Claude in collections that can apparently be traced back to the period immediately after his death.

finished composition drawings that he made, both after his paintings and independently, might seem at first sight to contradict this, for one would naturally conclude that they were done on commission or for sale. But while this was undoubtedly true in some cases, these seem to have been the exception rather than the rule. No more than a handful can be definitely traced to collections during Claude's lifetime,[11] and when he decided to part with drawings he generally inscribed them on the backs with the name of the recipient and the date, just as he recorded the names of the patrons of his paintings on the backs of the *Liber Veritatis* drawings. About a dozen drawings inscribed in this way are known, most of them being *pensées* to be given away to friends[12] rather than the kind of highly finished drawing that would appeal to collectors. The one document that refers to Claude's making drawings for sale confirms that he did so only with reluctance. Replying in a letter dated July 22, 1662, to Cardinal Leopold de' Medici, who had requested some drawings from Claude, the Cardinal's agent in Rome, Jacopo Salviati, wrote: "M. Claude has some old drawings, but in small number, and he does not want to part with them, saying that he uses them. Now that he is old it seems too tiresome to him to make new things; he therefore offers to copy two of them and to give us the copies."[13]

In view of the large number of drawings which must in fact have been in Claude's studio, this statement about a "small number" is puzzling; Claude may simply have wanted to put the Cardinal off. But the rest of the explanation—"saying that he uses

[11] E.g., two (unspecified) appear in the inventory of Poussin's friend, Jacques Stella; two now in the Louvre come from the Jabach Collection; the small group of drawings at Chantilly are said to have once belonged to Cardinal Massimi (d. 1677); one drawing bears the mark of Sir Peter Lely (d. 1680). The only collector who can be described as a "patron" of Claude as a draftsman, and who is known to have commissioned drawings from him in any number, is Cardinal Giulio Rospigliosi, whose group of eight drawings by the artist is still in the Rospigliosi-Pallavicini Collection (see F. Zeri, *La Galleria Pallavicini in Roma*, Rome, 1959).

[12] E.g., Michel Passart, for whom Claude painted the two landscapes LV 79 and 89 and to whom he gave his *pensée* for the Pamfili *Mill* (LV 113) in 1647 (the drawing is now in Bayonne); also the painter, Jacques Courtois, to whom Claude dedicated a figure drawing now in the Louvre.

[13] See Röthlisberger, *op.cit.*, p. 193; first published by F. Boyer in *Bulletin de la Société de l'Histoire de l'Art français*, 1931, p. 238.

them"—is important. It calls attention to a fact about Claude's drawings which it is essential to bear in mind: that he made them and kept them by him because he needed them for his own work. Baldinucci is quite explicit about a painting from nature done in the Vigna Madama, saying that Claude refused to part with it because "he used it every day to see the variety of trees and foliage."[14] No doubt the same was true of his drawings, which, as we have seen, were kept for the most part in books. Some of these books may have been the sketchbooks in which the drawings were originally made; drawings made on separate sheets of paper would have been pasted into albums and arranged as far as possible according to size and category. The *Liber Veritatis* is the most conspicuous example of this type of arrangement and is the only book of drawings by Claude which has remained intact. But other drawings, now dispersed, bear numbers in Claude's hand which suggest that for some at least he attempted to evolve a method of classification as systematic as that for the *Liber Veritatis* itself.[15]

In one sense, therefore, all Claude's drawings may be said to refer, directly or indirectly, to his paintings. Even the drawings from nature, which were hardly ever made with individual paintings in mind, had an ultimate bearing on the paintings which was of the greatest importance. They served as a stimulus to his imagination. It was through making them that he fixed in his memory (to quote Baldinucci) "the various and most beautiful observations which he had made of nature, of the changing and varying of air and light,"[16] so that, when executing his paintings in the studio, the effects he needed were an integral part of his consciousness, as it were; they could be reproduced, and transformed into the idealized idiom of his pictorial style, at will. Not only drawings from nature, but composition studies at all stages of completeness, figure studies, animal studies, copies—all these, together with his small group of paintings done from nature, went to form Claude's working material. Taken together,

[14] See above, n. 5.

[15] See the present writer's article, "Claude's Books of Drawings from Nature," *Burlington Magazine*, ciii, 1961, pp. 252-57.

[16] From Baldinucci's biography of Claude in the *Notizie* . . . ; see Röthlisberger, *op.cit.*, p. 56.

this material was the foundation of his art as a painter. Few other painters, and no painters of landscape, have based their work on such an intricate program of experiment and research, or have taken such pains to record it.

It is interesting to notice how the *Liber Veritatis* plays its part in this scheme, fulfilling as important a role in the creation of further paintings as it did in the documentation of those already finished. On the one hand, as Baldinucci says, it was made as a record of the artist's pictorial output, to safeguard his reputation against the activities of "certain envious men, eager for dishonest gains" who began "from the time he made the first pictures for His Majesty the Catholic King" (i.e., in 1636) to imitate his style and pass off their works as originals.[17] The book that he kept from that moment onward, and which eventually came to include 195 drawings after his pictures, was thus his means of putting on record his own true and authorized version of his work. Seen from another point of view, however, the *Liber Veritatis* played an indispensable part in the creative process, by providing Claude with an ever-increasing repertoire of imagery from which to devise new compositions. Thus, to begin at the simplest level, there were occasional instances when he would trace through a motive, such as a group of figures, on to the back of the drawing on which they had originally occurred, and then re-use it in a different setting later.[18] On other occasions, he would repeat a whole composition at the order of a patron, who had either been shown the book by Claude, or, more probably, had seen and liked the picture.[19] Sometimes, when the patron was not of particular importance, Claude himself may have decided on a variant or a repetition in order to save effort.[20] But the most important use

[17] Baldinucci, *op.cit.*; Röthlisberger, *op.cit.*, p. 59.

[18] E.g., the man pushing a bale in the left foreground of the *Seaport*, LV 17, who reappears (in reverse) in another *Seaport* a few years later, LV 29.

[19] E.g., LV 154, *Landscape with the Rest on the Flight into Egypt* (Hermitage, Leningrad, 1663), painted for Halmale, Bishop of Ypres; repeated "en petit toile" for Claude's executor, Francesco Canser, in 1675. For full details, see Röthlisberger, *op.cit.*, p. 363.

[20] E.g., LV 129, the *Adoration of the Golden Calf* (Karlsrühe, 1653), painted for Cardelli; repeated, with variations, in 1660 and recorded in a new *Liber* drawing, No. 148 (the painting now in the collection of Simon Morrison, London; the name of the original owner is illegible on the back of the *Liber* draw-

of the *Liber Veritatis* in this connection was as a means of enabling Claude to create new designs by combining, with new effect, motives from different pictures. No great artist ever depended so constantly on his own resources as Claude: yet aesthetically he was one of the least repetitive; for the motives of which his pictures are composed—trees, buildings, water, figures, animals—being basically simple, were susceptible of an almost infinite number of variations and combinations. And the light that acts as the unifying agent in his designs, and which chiefly creates their poetic mood, is varied slightly from picture to picture and becomes ever more subtle as his art matures.

Nevertheless, to consider Claude's drawings as background material for his paintings is to present only a partial view of their role in his art. Their style, their technical variety, their whole aesthetic character, make it clear that he regarded drawing not only as a means of preparing and recording his paintings but also as an art in its own right. To some of the more rapid and summary composition sketches, as also to some of the copies, this no doubt hardly applies: drawn in pen and ink or black chalk, without wash, they were studies or copies and nothing more. But everything above a certain minimum level of technical completeness—studies for paintings and *Liber Veritatis* drawings, no less than independent compositions and studies from nature—is treated to a greater or less extent as a work of art in itself. Claude was a natural and indefatigable draftsman, who obviously delighted in the immediate effects that his pen, brush, or chalk could produce on paper. He worked fluently and readily in every sort of technique: pen and ink alone, pen and ink with wash, various shades of wash, black chalk, red chalk—all either separately or together, with or without white heightening, and on either white, blue, or (occasionally) tinted paper. It would be difficult to believe, too, that Claude's

---

ing). In practice it is obviously impossible to tell for certain in any given case whether it was the patron or the artist who decided on a replica rather than a new design. But that Claude should have sometimes wished to spare himself the effort of devising a new composition is understandable (though he never skimped their execution). That he did so is confirmed by looking at the problem the other way round, so to speak, i.e., by pointing to the fact that for virtually all his really important commissions, such as those given by the popes and their nephews, he took the utmost care to produce an original invention.

sketching expeditions into the Campagna were undertaken only for the purpose of gathering material, that he did not derive pleasure from them for their own sake as well. Nor must it be forgotten that the making of landscape drawings from nature, independent of their possible future use in paintings, had a long tradition behind it by Claude's time: a tradition reaching back through his immediate predecessors, Bril, Poelenburgh, and Breenbergh, to Leonardo and Fra Bartolommeo in the Renaissance.

But the most telling evidence in favor of the importance to Claude of drawing for its own sake is the evidence of style: the fact that again and again, whatever kind of drawing he is making—nature study, preparatory design for a picture, or copy after a picture—Claude goes beyond his ostensible objective and introduces an aesthetic element into the composition, treating it as visually complete in itself.

The meaning of this in practice can best be made clear by examples. First, a nature drawing of Tivoli, datable about 1640 (Pl. xxxiv, 1),[21] which may be compared with a photograph (Pl. xxxiv, 2) taken from the same viewpoint and at the same time of day, about an hour after sunrise. The change in proportion scarcely needs pointing out; one need only draw attention to the placing of the most famous landmark at Tivoli, the Temple of the Sibyl, on the skyline instead of slightly below it, as it really appears from this viewpoint. However, neither of these alterations is in itself remarkable, since all artists select from and alter what they see in front of them: some, for example Turner, much more radically than Claude; while even the amateur would probably tend to compress the motive somewhat as Claude has done, so accustomed is the eye to visualize hills in terms of their height rather than of their width. The important point, rather, is the way in which Claude has adapted and simplified the motive, treating it primarily as a pattern of light and shade which is sharpened here and there with a few telling accents of detail. This is the work of a subjective, contemplative observer, whose

[21] British Museum. A. M. Hind, *Catalogue of the Drawings of Claude Lorrain . . .* , London, 1926, no. 20; pen and brown ink wash tinged with pink wash, 21.5 x 31.5 cm.

main concern is not with accurate delineation but with the harmony of the design on the page. The unifying element is the light, which fills the whole composition, leaving no area "dead." In the handling of tone there is continuity as well as contrast, so that the various planes are related to one another on the surface, while the spatial intervals between them remain distinct. We see how both dark and light areas are repeated in each plane, and how on the right the eye is led from the foreground to the background without having to skip a tone. Thus the total effect is classical, balanced—at once brilliantly fresh and lively, yet also lucid, composed, and serene.

The next example is a drawing of a waterfall, dated 1635 (Pl. xxxiv, 3).[22] For obvious reasons, one cannot check the literal accuracy of the rendering in this case, but what it shows even more clearly than the previous drawing is the function of the tone scheme as the controlling factor of the design. Once again, every part of the drawing is seen as an effect of light and shade, while sharp accents—leaves, broken branches, etc.—are balanced against broader, less defined areas of tone. Within this scheme Claude is able to vary the medium and even the degree of finish without upsetting the unity of the composition. The leaves silhouetted against the sky are quite highly finished with the pen, which is hardly used elsewhere in the drawing: the central area is largely drawn in black chalk combined with a medium-toned brown wash; finally, the water of the cascade and in the stream below is rendered in white body color. This apparently arbitrary disposition of media in the same drawing, which occurs quite frequently with Claude, is, I think, unprecedented, at any rate in landscape drawings. That Claude could so vary the media he used in this way, is a measure of his freedom from the normal convention that unity of effect is dependent on consistency of technique. It means that a drawing by Claude is "finished" at every stage of its production, that he can leave it as a mere sketch or elaborate it at will. This fact also accounts for the astonishing technical variety of his drawings—a variety that is largely independent of his stylistic development. To keep to the nature drawings for

[22] British Museum. Hind, *op.cit.*, no. 59; pen and brown ink wash, black chalk, white body color, 38.7 x 25.1 cm.; signed and dated 1635 on the back.

the moment: some are mere thumbnail sketches, drawn only in pen and ink, with no apparent aesthetic intention. Others are idealized to a certain extent and presented as works of art in their own right. Others again are more idealized still, and are made richer in composition by the introduction of balanced groups of trees and sometimes also pastoral figures with animals, until the point is reached when a nature drawing becomes indistinguishable from a drawing done in the studio. A similar variety is to be found in Claude's choice of motive. Here we can, it is true, distinguish between certain basic categories: studies of trees; studies of buildings, both ancient ruins and modern villas and farmhouses; waterfalls; views of the Tiber; views across the Campagna; animals; and finally—less often—figures. It is possible that Claude, in grouping the drawings in books in his studio, attempted to preserve these categories. But the distinctions between them are never absolute, and many drawings combine motives from two or more categories.

Pl. xxxv, 4 shows a third example of Claude's method of giving completeness to a design, in this instance a figure study.[23] I choose this particular one because it also illustrates another point about Claude's drawings, a point that has been overlooked until recently, though it had been made perfectly clear by Baldinucci. This is the fact that Claude took considerable pains over his figures and made studies from casts and from paintings in order to improve his style—that is, to make it more academically correct. Even if we must admit that this was probably little more than a gesture—Claude was not deeply interested in academic drawing of this kind—he still sometimes uses such a study as the basis for a figure of his own. Thus, in the present instance, he seems to have started from a study after the figure of Diogenes in Raphael's *School of Athens* (Pl. xxxv, 5),[24] which he then transformed into a shepherd seated rather awkwardly on a bank.

[23] British Museum. Hind, *op.cit.*, no. 213r; brown ink wash and black chalk, 15.6 x 23.0 cm. There is another study of the male figure, in black chalk only and more summarily drawn, on the back.

[24] British Museum. Hind, *op.cit.*, no. 207v; pen and brown ink wash, 20.2 x 26.7 cm. The drawing on the front is of a seated shepherd (not related to the studies on the back).

Pl. xxxv, 6 shows the picture, a *Pastoral Landscape*,[25] painted 1650-51, for which the two figures were used. They are pastoral figures, designed to go into a painting, not figures drawn from nature, though whether or not they were done with this particular painting in mind is hard to tell. But Claude has drawn them in black chalk and wash with considerable care, for their own sake. He has given them a setting—tree trunks on the right and a smudge of wash for the sky—which is not at all like their setting in the picture, or like the setting of any other picture in which they could have appeared. This is not to say that all Claude's figure drawings are of this kind; many are simply pen-and-ink sketches, done for the immediate purpose in hand. But other similar examples could be cited, as could examples of the same process applied to groups of figures copied after, as well as made for, paintings.[26]

Pl. xxxvi, 7, finally, is a late *Liber Veritatis* drawing,[27] showing how Claude in his last years found in that book an ever-increasing fulfillment of his interests as an artist. Though nominally undertaken, as we have seen, merely as a record of his paintings, the *Liber Veritatis* in its later stages became, I believe, more and more, an object that Claude treated as a work of art in its own right. The last thirty or so drawings are as highly and delicately

[25] William Rockhill Nelson Gallery of Art, Kansas City; LV 123; canvas, 51 x 68.5 cm. (Röthlisberger, *op.cit.*, pp. 302-4, fig. 212).

[26] E.g., the study for the figures (Teyler Museum, Haarlem) in the *Landscape with Samuel Anointing David King of Israel*, LV 69 (Louvre, 1643). For examples of drawings after paintings, see the large drawing (26.5 x 41.2 cm.; British Museum, Hind, *op.cit.*, no. 202), which is a careful copy, with modifications to fit the size of the page, of the figure group in the *Embarkation of St. Ursula*, LV 54 (National Gallery, London, 1641). Hitherto regarded as a study, its correct relationship to the painting was first pointed out by Röthlisberger (*op.cit.*, p. 193). Another, even clearer example of the modification of the original composition to fill out the design on the page is drawing no. 37 in the *Liber Veritatis*, repeating the figures from the left side of the Louvre version (1639) of the *Fête Villageoise*, with a different background.

[27] No. 184, *Coast Scene with Perseus and the Origin of Coral*; British Museum; pen and brown ink wash, heightened with white, on blue paper, 18.4 x 26.0 cm.; dated on the front 1673(?) and on the back, 1674. The painting, executed for Cardinal Massimi, is now at Holkham.

wrought as the independent studio drawings and studies for paintings that he was making during the same years.[28]

What conclusions are to be drawn from these examples? The first is, perhaps, that just as the drawings in their various ways react on the paintings, so the paintings react in reverse on the drawings. As a painter, Claude was always searching for ideal effects. The tall trees against the sky, the fragments of classical architecture, the farms and villages, the distant hills and winding streams—all are selected and combined by the artist in such a way as to communicate more clearly than can nature herself, a feeling of enchantment and delight. At a lower level of intensity, and often in small details—single trees, single buildings, motives seen in close-up—this is also the intention of his drawings. Drawing, that is to say, provided Claude with a means of extending his range of expression, of saying what he wanted to say in the form of lyrics or couplets instead of in the form of epic poems, as he did in his paintings. Many of the motives that appear in his drawings, such as the one shown in Pl. xxxvi, 8,[29] also appear, idealized and transformed, as details of his paintings. Others, however, would have been considered by him to be too familiar, too untidy, to have their place there.

Another conclusion follows from the first. It is that while we habitually, and rightly, talk of the variety of Claude's drawings, we ought also to remember their underlying unity of mood and feeling. In a sense all his works, paintings as well as drawings, studio drawings as well as drawings from nature, contain the same combination of qualities: the quality of naturalism combined with the quality of idealization; an almost magical deftness of touch, especially in the handling of wash, combined with an element of clumsiness, even pedantry, in the outlining of forms; extreme naïveté combined with extreme sophistication; a certain vigor and directness underlying the gentleness and charm; in the treatment of form and space, great precision combined with

[28] This point is discussed at greater length in M. Kitson and M. Röthlisberger, "Claude Lorrain and the *Liber Veritatis*—ii," *Burlington Magazine*, ci, 1959, pp. 328-36.

[29] British Museum. Hind, *op.cit.*, no. 71; brown wash and black chalk on rose-tinted paper, 26.1 x 20.0 cm.

poetic evocation; in the effect of the whole, a sensation of exhilaration as well as of repose.

In this paper, I have been concerned chiefly with the problem of Claude's drawings as a whole and with their interrelationships, and have made almost no reference to chronological development. Drawings of all kinds do, in fact, occur at almost all stages of Claude's career, but it would be misleading to end without mentioning an important change of emphasis. In the early period (1630's and early 1640's) drawings from nature predominated, while composition drawings and studies for paintings were comparatively rare. At this period the drawings from nature occupied the creative center of Claude's art; it was their style that determined the style of his other drawings, and even that of his paintings. See, for example, a study used for the painting in Berlin[30] and *Liber Veritatis* drawing No. 3,[31] both datable about 1635-36 (Pl. xxxvi, 9, 10). It is clear how the style of these two has been affected by that evolved for the early nature drawings: the broad handling, the use of bold contrasts of light and shade, of dark, luminous washes and picturesque, naturalistic detail are common to all three types. The style of the paintings of this period is affected in the same way. It was not for nothing that Sandrart, who knew Claude only in the thirties, was struck most of all by the naturalism of his paintings, rather than by their ideal qualities.

After the mid-1640's, however, the center of gravity of Claude's work changes. The studies from nature ceased to develop in style, and his creative interest comes to be focused on the paintings and composition drawings. The compositions, elaborately executed in pen and ink, brown or gray wash, black chalk and white body color, often on blue paper, were in effect a new type of landscape drawing,[32] only preceded by the gouache drawings of Elsheimer

[30] British Museum. Hind, *op.cit.*, no. 229; pen and brown ink wash, 15.0 x 21.0 cm. The painting (Röthlisberger, *op.cit.*, pp. 511-13, fig. 24) represents the story of Cephalus and Procris reunited by Diana; the drawing appears to be a landscape with brigands. As Röthlisberger points out (*loc.cit.*), the drawing was probably not made directly as a study for the painting, but the relationship in composition is close enough to say that it was "used" for it.

[31] British Museum; pen and brown ink wash, 18.4 x 26.0 cm. The painting is lost.

[32] The first dated example of a very highly finished drawing of this type, made

at the beginning of the century, which Claude probably did not know. At the same time he began to execute more, and more careful, studies for his paintings; altering, adjusting, rearranging; sometimes at the end of his career making as many as a dozen, including a "trial" study for the patron's approval if the commission were a very important one.[33]

Not that the sequence is always easy to follow. Pl. xxxvii, 11 shows the famous painting in Munich, *Landscape with the Dismissal of Hagar*,[34] dated 1668; Pl. xxxvii, 12, 13 are the studies for it, drawn on either side of the same sheet, the one being traced through from the other.[35] The question is, which was drawn first? Since the composition was conceived as a pendant to another painting showing Hagar and the Angel in the desert, there can be no doubt that the picture was planned as we see it in Pl. xxxvii, 11 and not in reverse.[36] Yet the drawing shown in Pl. xxxvii, 13 (the obverse of the sheet), is the freer and more richly worked of the two, and was probably done first. Claude would then have turned the sheet over, held it against the light and drawn the reverse, altering some parts, especially in the center middle distance, as he worked. Then he would have added the diagonal pattern of lines, with which to transfer the design to the canvas.[37] Further altera-

---

independently of a painting, is the *Landscape with Mercury and Argus* (British Museum. Hind, *op.cit.*, no. 208) dated 1647.

[33] See Röthlisberger, *op.cit.*, p. 400 for information about two drawings that Claude sent Henri van Halmale, Bishop of Ypres, as "trial pieces" for the *Landscape with Jacob, Rachel and Leah at the Well*, LV 169 (Hermitage, Leningrad, 1667).

[34] Alte Pinakothek, Munich; LV 173, 1668; canvas, 107 x 140 cm.

[35] Fitzwilliam Museum, Cambridge; pen and brown ink wash, the verso (Pl. xxxvii, 12) crossed with a pattern of lines in black chalk, 14.6 x 20.6 cm.

[36] The reason for this is that, in view of the pendant (LV 174), which shows a later episode in the story (*Hagar and the Angel in the Desert*), the *Dismissal of Hagar* must always have been intended as the left half of the pair—it would not have "read" correctly otherwise. It is true that if the *Dismissal* had originally been commissioned as a separate work, this argument would fall to the ground. Röthlisberger, who suggests this possibility (*op.cit.*, p. 408), is perhaps being unduly cautious. On all counts, iconographical as well as stylistic, it seems to me virtually certain that a pair was implied from the start.

[37] So far as I know, this method of "squaring up" a design by means of crossed diagonals rather than by means of the traditional "grid" system was Claude's own discovery. One should not overlook the possibility that its purpose was

tions would still be made on the canvas itself, however, including the taking over of some parts from the obverse. Even then the possibilities of the drawing were not exhausted, for Claude made use of the rocks on the left, which he had altered in this composition, for the purposes of the other painting. He seems never to have made very highly finished preparatory drawings which he would follow exactly in his paintings. Where the correspondence between a drawing and a painting is exact, this is almost always a sign, I believe, that the drawing was a copy after the painting. (Very exact preparatory drawings were made only for the etchings.) Such copies exist after the majority of later paintings; in some cases there is more than one from the same picture. There are even exact—and perfectly authentic—copies of drawings,[38] though most show some variation from the original. Copies done several years after the paintings were usually made, for obvious reasons, from the *Liber Veritatis*.

The practical purpose of these copies is one of the most puzzling features of Claude's work. From the letter quoted at the beginning of this paper, recounting Claude's offer to make copies of his drawings for Cardinal Leopold de' Medici, one might assume that they were invariably done to order. But such evidence as we have regarding the provenance of Claude's drawings suggests that some at least remained in his studio after his death. Furthermore, no copies are known to me with inscriptions on the back indicating that they were made for or given to a particular patron. Drawings inscribed in this way are invariably either studies for the paintings or finished composition drawings, made quite independently of the paintings. We return, in fact, for an explana-

---

not solely to serve as a mechanical aid but also to serve as a stage in the creative process; that is, to enable the artist to fix the structure of the composition more clearly in his mind, so that he could, if necessary, make further modifications to it on the canvas.

[38] E.g., a drawing in the Detroit Institute of Arts (Röthlisberger, *op.cit.*, fig. 307), related to the painting of *Dido and Aeneas Leaving Carthage for the Hunt* (LV 186, 1676; Collection Captain A. Heywood-Lonsdale) and corresponding closely to a drawing in Bayonne dated 1676. The similarity in composition between the two drawings is so close that one must have been copied directly from the other. The Detroit drawing is, however, very different in feeling from the one in Bayonne, being much lighter in tone and more delicate in handling.

tion of the copies to the desire of the artist to make drawings for their own sake. This was something that lay deep in Claude's psychology and which we cannot entirely fathom. Pl. xxxvii, 14,[39] a copy with slight differences made from the *Arrival of Aeneas at Pallanteum*, dated two years after the painting, shows the care that Claude lavished on these late drawings. The rapid and brilliant sketches from nature of the 1630's seem very distant. But I hope I have been able to show that there is a continuity between them; that they stand at opposite ends of a continuous spectrum with all the intermediate stages filled in; for there were not two Claudes, as critics maintained thirty years ago—the lover of nature, and the careful composer of ideal landscape in the studio—but one fully integrated, complicated artistic personality.

[39] H. M. The Queen, Royal Library, Windsor Castle. Anthony Blunt, *French Drawings at Windsor Castle*, London, 1945, no. 48; pen and brown ink with brown and gray wash, 25.7 x 33.5 cm.; signed and dated 1677. The painting from which it is taken is LV 185 (Collection Lord Fairhaven), dated 1675.

APPRECIATION OF MICHAEL KITSON'S PAPER:

STYLISTIC PROBLEMS

OF CLAUDE'S DRAFTSMANSHIP

ECKHART KNAB

WHOEVER endeavors to date Claude's drawings, and in so doing is inclined to find a certain group of stylistic features for each period, will soon learn that Claude used very different means and forms of expression during almost all periods of his work as a draftsman, more than he did as a painter, and even more than as an etcher. We have, on the one hand, to distinguish between elaborate drawings from the early years and those from later years, and on the other hand, between slight sketches of different periods. The boundary, which is a wavering one—each group having many gradations—cuts across drawings for compositions as well as drawings from nature. Thus, a famous sentence by Vasari—"L'esperienza fa conoscere che molte volte uno stesso uomo non ha la medesima maniera"[1]— applies especially to Claude's drawings. However, Claude is not the only artist and draftsman of the seventeenth century to confirm this experience. Allow me to explain this by some examples so far as Claude is concerned.

Let us begin with drawings for compositions, which are easier to date by the evidence of dated pictures, etchings, and, last but not least, by the *Liber Veritatis*. I show the preparatory drawing for Claude's first etching, *The Tempest* (R.D. 5—Blum 1), done in 1630 (Pl. xxxviii, 1). This drawing, now in the British Museum, is very elaborate, done in red chalk, pen, and bistre wash and

---

[1] Giorgio Vasari, *Le Vite* . . . , ed. G. Milanesi, Florence, 1879, iv, p. 491 (Life of Vincenzo da San Gimignano). This problem has already been discussed somewhat in previous papers by the author: "Die Zeichnungen Claude Lorrains in der Albertina," *Alte und Neue Kunst* (Wiener kunstwissenschaftliche Blätter), ii, 1953, p. 145; *idem*, "Der heutige Bestand an Zeichnungen Claude Lorrains im Boymans Museum," *Bulletin Museum Boymans*, vii, 1956, pp. 113-15; *idem*, "Die Anfänge des Claude Lorrain," *Jahrbuch der kunsthistorischen Sammlungen in Wien*, lvi, 1960, pp. 99-101. See also, Michael Kitson, "Claude's Books of Drawings from Nature," *Burlington Magazine*, ciii, 1961, p. 252.

heightened with white.[2] As another example, somewhat different, for it is done primarily with pen, I show a drawing from the Albertina (Pl. xxxviii, 2),[3] the preparatory work for an early picture, called *The Morning*, which is known only from prints by Franz Hegi (1774-1850), done in the beginning of the last century, and from a photograph in the Cabinet d'Estampes in the Bibliothèque Nationale in Paris. Let me juxtapose these elaborate compositions with other examples of nearly the same period— both dating from about 1635—representing Claude's slight style: a sketch for the etching *Campo Vaccino* (R.D. 23—Blum 17) and four sketches for a now unfortunately lost *Flight into Egypt*, a *Riposo*, in the Teyler Museum (Pl. xxxviii, 3)[4] known only from engravings by Samuel Smith (1745-1808). In order to stress the connection between drawing from nature and sketched compositions, just as it is recorded in Claude's paintings, I shall not omit mentioning that on the other side of the Teyler Museum drawing Claude drew one of his best studies from nature, a woodland scene with a sculpture of the Three Graces.[5]

Another comparison, which proves the organic, even genetic, connection between both techniques of drawing, the slight and the elaborate: on the one hand, a preparatory sketch (Pl. xxxviii, 4), now in the Morgan Library, for the famous painting *The Temple of Apollo at Delphi* in the Doria Gallery,[6] and on the

[2] Arthur M. Hind, *British Museum, Catalogue of the Drawings of Claude Lorrain*, London, 1926, no. 192; signed and dated: *Claudio 1630*; 219 x 179 mm. See Knab, "Die Anfänge . . . ," p. 101, fig. 132.

[3] Inv. 11,507; pencil, pen, and bistre wash, heightened with white, 255 x 402 mm. See Knab, "Die Zeichnungen . . . ," pp. 138-40, no. 4, figs. 4, 5; and *idem*, "Die Anfänge . . . ," pp. 120-22, figs. 159, 160.

[4] For the Campo Vaccino sketch, see Hind, *op.cit.*, no. 193, pl. 8, and Michael Kitson, "Swanevelt, Claude Lorrain et le Campo Vaccino," *Revue des Arts*, viii, 1958, pp. 215-20, 258-66. For the Teyler drawing (pen, 184 x 272 mm.), see H. J. Scholten, *Musée Teyler à Haarlem, Catalogue raisonné des dessins des écoles française et hollandaise*, Haarlem, 1904, no. 10; A. M. Hind, *The Drawings of Claude Lorrain*, London, 1925, pl. 3; and Knab, "Die Anfänge . . . ," pp. 116-17, figs. 150, 151.

[5] Hind, *The Drawings . . .* , pl. 22.

[6] *Liber Veritatis* 119, dating from about 1648. On the *Liber Veritatis*, see Michael Kitson and Marcel Röthlisberger, "Claude Lorrain and the *Liber Veritatis*," *Burlington Magazine*, ci, 1959, pp. 14-24, 328-36, 381-86; Knab, "Die Anfänge . . . ," pp. 126-29; and Marcel Röthlisberger, *Claude Lorrain*, New Haven, 1961.

other, an elaborate drawing of the whole composition, which is now in the Cabinet des Dessins du Louvre (Pl. xxxviii, 5). Both have a special meaning in the evolution of the painting.[7]

During the fifties, when Claude's style often resembles that of Titian or the Carracci, compositions and drawings from nature frequently look very similar in manner, especially if they are done mainly with pen, and are very elaborate. This is evident when comparing a preparatory study in the Louvre for Claude's etching *Cattle in Impending Thunderstorm* (R.D. 18—Blum 36) of 1651—the group reappears in other pictures of that period too— with the *Landscape with a Stone Bridge* in the Albertina.[8] In order to illustrate also the variety of Claude's draftsmanship in this period, I ask you to look at two more drawings: a landscape of the Tiber Valley with a reclining herdsman, dated 1656, in the British Museum, partly as seen from nature, partly composed, and a vision of the Campagna with a gloomy sky and a reposing figure in Carracci-like style, in the Boymans Museum, a sketch for a composition that Claude did not carry out in painting.[9]

In order to return to our major thesis, let us look at a particularly refined drawing in the Albertina done in his old age, namely, *The Calling of Peter and Andrew* (Pl. xxxviii, 6), which is a further stage of a picture painted for Sicily in 1665 (LV 165), and compare it to a fleeting composition study in the British Museum that comes from the same years, namely, *Mary Magdalene in Penitence* (Pl. xxxix, 7) which corresponds to a highly finished drawing, dated 1670, in the Louvre.[10] Let me complete

[7] C. Fairfax Murray, *J. Pierpont Morgan Collection of Drawings*, London, 1912, III, pl. 76 (pencil, black chalk, pen and bistre wash, 201 x 267 mm.); Knab, "Die Zeichnungen. . . ," pp. 146-47, n. 33; Louis Demonts, *Musée du Louvre, Les dessins de Claude Gellée, dit Le Lorrain*, Paris, 1923, no. 19. A further drawing for this composition is in the Akademie at Venice (reproduced in *Bollettino d'Arte*, xxv, p. 81, fig. 16).

[8] Demonts, *op.cit.*, no. 20; Walter Friedlaender, *Claude Lorrain*, Berlin, 1921, fig. p. 192 (below); Knab, "Die Zeichnungen . . . ," p. 151, no. 24.

[9] Hind, *British Museum Catalogue* . . . , no. 231, pl. 29; *idem, The Drawings* . . . , pl. 58; Knab, "Der heutige Bestand . . . ," p. 116, 8, fig. 14.

[10] Albertina: Inv. 11,527; pen and bistre wash, black chalk, heightened with white, 142 x 205 mm. Knab, "Die Zeichnungen . . . ," pp. 158-59, no. 32, fig. 12. British Museum: Hind, *British Museum Catalogue* . . . ," pp. 299; pencil, pen, and bistre wash, black chalk, heightened with white, 190 x 159 mm. Louvre: Demonts, *op.cit.*, no. 47. See also Knab, *ibid.*, pp. 148-50.

this sequence of drawings for compositions by showing a preparatory drawing of a very high stage of perfection in the Boymans Museum: a study for the painting in Rome in the Pallavicini-Rospigliosi Gallery called *Templum Veneris*.[11]

With regard to the studies from nature, let us begin by glancing at a splendid and elaborate early drawing of a hill with oak trees (Pl. xxxix, 8). This drawing, which reminds us very much of Claude's first etchings, e.g., *Shepherd and Shepherdess* (R.D. 25—Blum 4, Pl. xxxix, 9), belongs to the Teyler Museum.[12] Very similar to this is a view of SS. Giovanni e Paolo in Rome (Pl. xxxix, 10), a drawing from the Windsor sketchbook, the earliest sketchbook of Claude's we can trace, which should be dated from about 1627 to 1635. In the same sketchbook we already find those slight studies, equally typical for Claude's draftsmanship, such as the drawing which shows herdsmen with cattle on the Campo Vaccino (Pl. xl, 11).[13] The same style, still more developed and vivid can be seen in a view of a town in the Campagna now in the Albertina, which probably originated in the late thirties (Pl. xl, 12).[14] To continue this series, just a few examples from the years to follow: a study in the British Museum, done on the Strada da Tivoli a Subiaco in 1642 (Pl. xl, 13), the *Vista del Sasso*, dated 1649, in the Boymans Museum (Pl. xl, 14), and, finally, one of the numerous drawings Claude did in the surroundings of the famous castle La Crescenza in the course of 1661 and 1662 (Pl. xli, 15).[15] Kitson has shown another example from this group in

[11] Knab, "Der heutige Bestand . . . ," pp. 127-32, no. 15, figs. 26-28.
[12] Scholten, *op.cit.*, no. 96 (attributed to Claude Lorrain); pen, 162 x 102 mm. See Knab, "Die Anfänge . . . ," p. 103, fig. 135.
[13] Anthony Blunt, *The French Drawings at Windsor Castle*, Oxford, 1945, no. 58; pen and bistre wash, 127 x 94 mm. *Ibid.*, no. 51; pen and bistre wash, 128 x 94 mm. For the dating of the Windsor sketchbook, see Knab, "Die Anfänge . . . ," pp. 95-103.
[14] Inv. 11,540; pen and bistre wash, 95 x 160 mm. Knab, "Die Zeichnungen . . . ," p. 142, no. 8, fig. 6.
[15] Hind, *British Museum Catalogue* . . . , no. 35, pl. 10; signed and dated: *Claudio fecit, strada da tiuoli a sobiacha l'anno 1642*; pen and bistre wash, 214 x 312 mm. Knab, "Der heutige Bestand . . . ," pp. 113-15, no. 6, figs. 10, 11. Signed and dated: *Vista del Sasso faict l'ano 1649 Claudio Gille I.V.*; pen, bistre and ink wash, 190 x 268 mm. Hind, *British Museum Catalogue* . . . , no. 166; signed and dated: *Claudio crescencio Roma 1662*; pen and bistre wash, 183 x 251 mm. For La Crescenza, see also Hind, *British Museum Catalogue* . . . , nos. 79, 164,

his paper. Let me complete this sequence of drawings from nature with a more finished drawing from the Albertina, a riverside scene of the Tiber with shepherds watering cattle (Pl. XLI, 16), which is famous for its fine evening mood, and probably inspired some of his paintings in the forties.[16] This drawing may be defined as a composition done from nature, to mark the boundary and to prove again the coherence between both disciplines in Claude's draftsmanship.

I want now to add a few remarks concerning Claude's late style. It has already been stated by Walter Friedlaender, Louis Demonts, Arthur M. Hind, and lately by Michael Kitson, that in drawing from nature, Claude attained his full variety of style as early as his thirties, that is, in the prime of life. As we have seen, this statement is also true to a certain extent with regard to his drawings of composition. Personally, I think Claude is not the only artist who reached the full scope of his artistic craftsmanship at that age. That he did so does not mean that he did not achieve additional mastery within this range. Although it has been said that some of his later works show traces of weakness—a drawing in the Teyler Museum of a herdsman with goats, dated 1662, may illustrate this (Pl. XLI, 17)[17]—yet there are many of Claude's later drawings, compositions as well as studies from nature, that manifest the characteristic concentration of sublime art. This statement is borne out in a drawing which belongs to the Boymans Museum, a woodland scene with two wanderers symbolizing, as it were, the artist's own life (Pl. XLI, 18).[18]

165; Demonts, *op.cit.*, nos. 36-39; and Scholten, *op.cit.*, no. 43 (dating from earlier years).

[16] Inv. 11,511; pen and bistre wash, 197 x 260 mm. Friedlaender, *op.cit.*, p. 191, fig. p. 193. Knab, "Die Zeichnungen . . . ," pp. 143-45, no. 15. For other examples of composing *dal naturale*, see Knab, "Der heutige Bestand . . . ," p. 111.

[17] Scholten, *op.cit.*, no. 40. Signed and dated on the reverse: *Claude IV Roma vigno madama 1662*; pencil, pen, and bistre wash, 242 x 175 mm. We know that Claude felt so ill toward the end of 1662 and in the first months of 1663 that he drew up his will. See Emilia Pattison [Lady Dilke], *Claude Lorrain, sa vie et ses oeuvres*, Paris, 1884, pp. 85-91, 202-5; Ferdinand Boyer in *Bulletin de la Société de l'Histoire de l'Art française*, 1931, p. 237; Pierre Colombier, "Essai sur les personnages de Claude Lorrain," *Société Poussin*, III, 1950, p. 56; Knab, "Der heutige Bestand . . . ," pp. 122-25.

[18] Pencil and black chalk, pen and bistre wash on yellowish paper, 260 x 380 mm. Knab, "Der heutige Bestand . . . ," pp. 125-26, no. 13, fig. 24.

BELLANGE ET LAGNEAU

OU LE MANIÉRISME ET LE RÉALISME
EN FRANCE APRÈS 1600

FRANÇOIS-GEORGES PARISET

LES dessins collectionnés en France après 1600 pourraient être divisés en plusieurs groupes. Le moins connu est formé par les oeuvres conservées pour des raisons esthétiques, à cause de leur beauté, et il s'agit de créations de maîtres étrangers, d'une tendance qu'on retrouve dans le reste de l'Europe, mais force est de reconnaître que nous sommes peu renseignés jusque vers 1640. D'autres sont conservés et utilisés par les artistes, études de motifs, préparations à des compositions décoratives ou religieuses. Les crayons de portraits enfin, sont gardés par des collectionneurs privés, de grands personnages, ou par les peintres qui les reproduisent et ils le sont moins pour leur beauté que pour leur valeur documentaire.

A ce classement, échappent, comme des anomalies, les inventions de Bellange et de Lagneau qui donnent au maniérisme et au réalisme une tonalité particulière appréciée par les collectionneurs du temps. Quels sont ces collectionneurs et quelles raisons justifient leur choix, qu'ont-ils pu trouver d'original, de significatif dans les créations de ces deux maîtres, voilà les questions que nous nous posons ici.

BELLANGE ET LE MANIÉRISME[1]

Le personnage nous est assez bien connu grâce aux archives lorraines. Il a été de 1600 à 1616, le peintre de la Cour de Lorraine, alors à son apogée, milieu cosmopolite ouvert à toutes les influences artistiques, mais tourné surtout vers la France. Il nous a laissé quelques peintures, une cinquantaine de gravures à l'eau-forte,

[1] F.-G. Pariset, "Le mariage d'Henri de Lorraine et de Marguerite de Gonzague-Mantoue (1606). Les fêtes de le témoignage de Jacques de Bellange," dans *Les fêtes de la Renaissance*, Paris, 1956, pp. 152ff avec la bibliographie. En outre, *idem*, "Jacques de Bellange, origines artistiques et évolution," *Bulletin de la Société de l'Histoire de l'Art français*, 1955, pp. 96ff; T. Kamenskaya, "Les dessins inédits de Jacques de Bellange au Musée de l'Ermitage," *Gazette des Beaux-Arts,* VI/LV, 1960, pp. 95ff.

et autant de dessins sans parler de ceux de "l'École de Bellange" dont le classement est difficile.

D'autre part, on reconstitue assez aisément les étapes de sa fortune. Il a été célèbre à la Cour de Lorraine, il s'enorgueillit du titre d'"Équès"; un sonnet de Jean de Rosières paru en 1606 chante ce portraitiste de Madame, Marguerite de Gonzague-Mantoue, épouse du futur duc Henri II. Il est copié de son vivant, par M. Merian le jeune et Crispin de Passe, puis par Bosse, imité par Saint-Igny, Vignon, Lallemand, Bendl. Tout porte à croire que les artistes ont gardé ses oeuvres, durant cette première période, sans parler des fidèles du milieu lorrain. Mais le fait intéressant, est que malgré l'apparition du classicisme, il reste en faveur. Berthod[2] publie en 1652 à Lyon sa *Ville de Paris en vers burlesques*, dont il a obtenu le privilège dès 1650 et il y fait parler Guérineau, "le vendeur d'images" qui recommande aux curieux des dessins de maîtres de toutes les écoles, ainsi "Les nuditez de Goltius, / Quatre crayons faits par Belange, / Et trois autres par Michel-Ange. . . ." Que Belange soit placé pour rimer avec Michel-Ange est possible, mais c'est la première fois que des dessins français sont recommandés à des collectionneurs français pour leur intérêt artistique. Plus tard, l'abbé de Marolles dans son *Livre des Peintres*, après avoir fait l'éloge de Callot et de la Belle, écrit: "Bellange est au-dessous de ces mains si parfaites" et sans doute établit-il une hiérarchie entre ces maîtres, mais il ne néglige pas Bellange. Bien plus, dans son Addition au Livre, il parle d'un recueil de dessins et "beaucoup d'autres crayons y sont sans nom de maître." "Mais bien d'autres aussi dans ce nombreux recueil / S'y trouvent de Belange et de François Verneuil. . . ." Marolles est donc le premier collectionneur dont nous savons qu'il possédait des Bellange. Plus tard, des dessins du maître sont entre les mains de Crozat et passeront entre celles de Catherine II ou appartiennent à d'autres collectionneurs connus et si Mariette blâme l'artiste, les érudits lorrains le louent. Plus tard, encore, autour de 1850, se réveille l'intérêt des curieux, soit pour des miniatures relevées d'or et maintenant perdues, soit pour des portraits, et ceux qui paraissent alors sont parfois des faux. Plus récemment enfin, M. Dvořák le considère comme un maître maniériste nourri de la spiritualité

---

[2] P. L. Jacob, *Paris ridicule et burlesque au 17ème siècle*, Paris, 1859, p. 157.

salésienne et L. Burchard admire la technique magistrale de ses gravures qui annonce Rembrandt, tandis que notre époque est frappée par son art sensuel, décadent, "fin de siècle" et nos plus grandes collections publiques ou privées se font gloire de posséder ses créations.

Des recherches persévérantes ont permis d'augmenter le lot de ses dessins depuis une génération, et de séparer les oeuvres originales de celles de "l'École de Bellange." Si nous repoussons des attributions anciennes ou récentes dues à l'ignorance ou à la spéculation, elles méritent l'attention: ces créations qui exagèrent la "manière" de Bellange, aident à repérer les éléments qui ont frappé les collectionneurs, mais elles peuvent mener à la méconnaissance de l'artiste même.

Le dossier dont notre époque dispose nous mène à voir Bellange autrement que les collectionneurs du passé qui ne disposaient que de pièces isolées. Certes, il est encore incomplet et il lui manque les miniatures relevées d'or, encore qu'un dessin comme le Cavalier du Musée Condé et des figures de mascarade en donnent une idée. Mais il nous permet d'affirmer que les dessins conservés sont des "variations" autour d'oeuvres presque toutes disparues (décorations pour des fêtes, décorations murales, peintures religieuses) et autour de gravures qui subsistent et où il rassemble ses motifs favoris. Ces dessins ont été exécutés pour des raisons pratiques (études pour les gravures ou les peintures) ou par pur plaisir esthétique (fixer une inspiration, partir d'oeuvres déjà exécutées, de gravures ou de peintures pour de nouvelles improvisations).

Notre dossier permet aussi d'établir une évolution de l'artiste en comparant les dessins et les gravures, et voici les grandes lignes de cette évolution. Au début, Bellange ne grave pas et il exécute des dessins à la plume et au lavis, avec des contours arrondis et déjà parfois des traits emportés. Il se met à graver à partir de 1612. Ses gravures du début sont ensoleillées et riches de notations décoratives. A l'atmosphère de fête de l'Adoration des Mages succède le sadisme du Martyre de Sainte-Lucie. A la fin, les formes simplifiées se perdent dans un sfumato inquiétant et s'alourdissent d'une tension grandissante. L'angoisse de la Résurrection a Lazare mène au Portement de Croix qui est une "somme," où Bellange rassemble ses habiletés techniques ses motifs les plus divers dans une gamme d'émotions multiples. Or, les dessins évoluent sous l'influence de la pratique de la gravure. Vers 1612, les contours sont nerveux, les hachures sont lancées par plans, le lavis est plus nuancé, des sanguines vibrantes paraissent. Vers la fin, la plume l'emporte sur le lavis et le crayon; des lignes courtes, des hachures rares et violentes, un tracé saccadé témoignent d'une in différence grandissante au "bel canto," d'une force contraignante, d'une liberté enivrante. L'évolution de l'art suit celle du créateur. Notre curiosité se tourne vers lui et voudrait comprendre les secrets de son être intime. Le passé ne pouvait saisir les nuances de l'évolution et l'originalité de Bellange comme nous essayons de le faire. Mais il a été certainement sensible au "style" de Bellange.

Ce style est celui du maniérisme, il représente sa pointe extrême à la veille de sa disparition, et il est certain qu'il en est un fruit attardé, d'arrière-saison. Il nous vaut des figures serpentines, à l'élégance alambiquée, avec un excès dans les gestes et les émotions. Il présente les déficiences caractéristiques du maniérisme: difficulté à composer, ignorances variées (anatomie, perspective, conduite de la lumière), une certaine insouciance qui permet d'escamoter les problèmes.

Mais de ses défauts, Bellange fait des qualités. Ses répétitions créent une unité. Sa personnalité, le "feu sacré" qui l'habite, le mène à des effets inédits, à des frissons nouveaux. Cette originalité paraît dans des graphismes typiques, arabesques fines, champs de stries, entrecroisements de traits pour le travail à la plume, traits incisifs ou écrasés pour le crayon; taches superposées pour le lavis et toujours de l'audace et de la liberté.

Elle paraît aussi dans des formes qui reparaissent comme des leit-motives et qui deviennent des obsessions: doigts allongés et pointus faits pour caresser ou griffer, visages étroits avec une bouche gonflée et des yeux en amande remontés vers les tempes sous le front trop vaste, nuques dégagées sous de hautes coiffures et ces figures qui répondent à l'idéal maniériste ont une vie originale par leur expression tour à tour heureuse, cynique, calme, violente. Répétition aussi des costumes, étoffes et parures, avec des détails antiquisants, exotiques ou réalistes, des tuniques gonflées et plaquées sur le corps qui caractérisent les oeuvres de la maturité ou de la fin, ou encore des costumes que Bellange donne a de nobles dames et qui sont des résurgences médiévales avec des jupes bouffantes à traîne, des corsages serrés au manches étroites à crevés, des béguins à mentonnière. Répétition enfin des procédés de composition et des attitudes: êtres dressés et cambrés, êtres penchés en mouvement, et aussi figures étrangement agenouillées ou accroupiés, les genoux très hauts, les bras ou les mains tendus, la tête penchée, de sorte que la Porcia de la gravure (Pl. XLII, 1) est la soeur de la femme nue de la sanguine conservée à l'École des Beaux-Arts de Paris, de femmes agenouillées exécutées à la plume du Musée Lorrain de Nancy (Pl. XLII, 2) et de l'Ermitage de Leningrad.

Ces graphies, ces formes qui habitent Bellange, donnent à ses dessins un style que les amateurs reconnaissent et apprécient et voilà sans doute une des raisons qui justifie les collectionneurs. Mais à examiner le dossier des dessins, nous constatons qu'ils peuvent être mis en relation très souvent avec des gravures. Les collectionneurs ne se soucient pas comme nous, de classer les dessins dans le temps, ou de connaître les causes qui ont poussé Bellange à les exécuter. Il leur suffit de retrouver les mêmes thèmes que pour les gravures, les mêmes figures, le même style; il leur plaît de noter des différences dans les détails ou l'esprit. S'il est exact qu'ils aiment à confronter gravure et dessin, on peut supposer qu'ils cherchent à rapprocher dans leurs collections les oeuvres de même sujet; une gravure d'un thème donné a mené à préserver de la destruction des dessins du même thème. Les dessins sont sauvés parce qu'ils sont les doubles d'une gravure.

Notre hypothèse se vérifie en examinant les sujets de Bellange. Et d'abord ceux qui sont religieux. Autour de la gravure de la Pietà, dont les sources sont la gravure de Dürer et celle de Beatrizet d'après Michel-Ange, se placent un dessin à la plume, où les figures sont prises dans une grande arabesque, un dessin à la plume et au lavis où l'effusion mystique se mêle à une allèterie mondaine, un autre dessin très pathétique d'une Descente de Croix, projet pour une peinture, et même un Saint-Sépulcre, d'une ferveur attendrie. Ces dessins pour être appréciés vraiment doivent être confrontés avec la gravure et on peut se demander s'ils n'étaient pas conservés avec elle. On pourrait présenter la même hypothèse pour les Saintes-Familles, en particulier la Sainte-Famille avec une sainte, pour l'Adoration des Rois Mages dont la gravure et les dessins s'expliquent mutuellement, ou encore pour l'Annonciation, les deux dessins de Leningrad prêtant à des rapprochements avec la grande gravure qui dérive elle-même sans doute d'une peinture du Caravage ou avec une autre gravure signalée par Robert-Dumesnil et dont nous ne connaissons pas d'épreuve.

Mais Bellange nous intéresse aussi par ses travestis et ses gueux. Il a pour base la réalité, mais il la truque, y ajoute des artifices qui mènent à une vision nouvelle, irréelle ou, si l'on veut, à un réalisme fantaisiste.

Certaines oeuvres de l'artiste se rattachent au théâtre. Nous connaissons par les gravures de Crispin de Passe des inventions qui devaient être l'écho de représentations lorraines, de farces proches des tabarinades et de la Commédia dell'arte, et qui étaient composées comme des épisodes de l'École de Fontainebleau, mais avec davantage d'ironie et de réalisme. Des dessins aquarellés,[8] parfois rehaussés d'argent, travestis, figures de ballets, de mascarades, de carroussels, ont été conservés d'une collection à l'autre, avant de parvenir dans la Collection Rothschild maintenant au Louvre, à cause de leur valeur documentaire, de leur précision qui fait penser à des modèles de modes, mais ils ont aussi pour nous une valeur esthétique grâce au brio de l'auteur et à sa fantaisie nourrie d'indications exotiques, antiques ou populaires. Les gravures des Jardinières et peut-être celles des Rois-Mages, sont aussi des échos des fêtes de La Cour et leur réalisme rustique ou exotique, aussi artificiel que celui des romans du temps, est adapté au style maniériste. Ces gravures ont été copiées ou démarquées au dix-septième et au dix-huitième siècles. Le genre a plu et on a conservé des dessins du même goût. Le dessin d'une Jardinière (Pl. XLII, 3) est une préparation à une gravure (Pl. XLII, 4) et il devait être tentant pour un collectionneur de réunir les deux travaux. D'autres dessins dérivent des gravures et ils sont de plus en plus libres, primesautiers, l'imagination recourant

[8] F.-G. Pariset et B. Dahlbaeck, "Dessins de costumes de théâtre de Jacques de Bellange et de l'école lorraine," *Revue de l'histoire du théâtre*, 1954, pp. 68ff.

toutefois à des détails pour donner l'illusion de la vérité: une femme portant un vase, une autre faisant la révérence, une autre qui fait penser à une cantinière, un prince paré d'une aigrette, autant de dessins qui s'expliquent par la confrontation avec des gravures.

Mais Bellange s'est aussi attaché à une réalité qui n'est plus celle du théâtre ou des fêtes. Si les peintures réalistes signalées au dix-septième siècle ont disparu, deux gravures montrent, l'une un Vielleur (Pl. xLiii, 5), l'autre deux Vielleurs qui s'affrontent, dans le style maniériste, mais avec des détails d'un réalisme outrancier. A la première de ces gravures, on rattache un dessin à la plume (Pl. xLiii, 6) qui en est la préparation; ce dessin nous montre Jehan de Laxou, un vielleur pris sur le vif, il nous apprend que Bellange superpose de sang froid son style maniériste à la vérité, mais ici encore on peut se demander si un collectionneur n'a pas réuni le croquis et la gravure pour expliquer l'un par l'autre. Le croquis, fait de hachures droites, s'inspire peut-être de gravures que Callot exécute à Florence, mais le travail est plus violent et synthétique et le même travail avec des traits rageurs, le même style où la réalité est transposée, caractérisent d'autres dessins tardifs qui se relient aux Vielleurs, cuisiniers tambour, gueux, femmes, qui rejoignent les inventions dérivées des Jardinières avec de l'humeur et de la méchanceté. Les collectionneurs ont aimé ces dessins qui apportent des suggestions pour des déguisements, et plaisent par leur pittoresque inattendu et saugrenu, mais ils les conservent aussi parce qu'ils les considèrent comme des "doublets" de Callot ou des gravures même de Bellange.

Ils ont du s'intéresser à d'autres dessins de l'artiste, parce qu'ils les rapprochent des sources qui l'ont inspiré et qui sont des gravures. Bellange qui est un autodidacte et un éclectique s'appuie volontiers sur autrui. Il est utile de retrouver ces sources, intéressant d'établir comment il a transposé ces influences, assimilé les éléments étrangers en y ajoutant son grain de sel et de sentir que ses emprunts stimulent finalement son énergie créatrice. En effet, il pille, mais il transforme son butin par sa propre vie et on pourrait même penser que ce qui l'occupe est moins le motif ou le décor qui lui sert de base que l'expression de son être intime. Les collectionneurs du passé n'allaient sans doute pas aussi loin dans cette voie, mais ici encore, ils devaient se plaire à réunir la gravure qui a servi de source à Bellange et les gravures ou les dessins dont il est l'auteur.

En voici quelques exemples. Le Portement de Croix de Schongauer est une source de la grande gravure de Bellange du même thème. Une gravure de Penni qui montre Acteon portant Diane est interpretée par Bellange quand il grave Agenor portant Diane ou un courtisan qui est aussi Agenor portant une jeune fille qui est aussi Diane. Une gravure de E. Sadeler d'après Spranger est interpretée (Pl. XLIII, 7) par le maître quand il grave les Saintes femmes allant au Saint-Sépulcre (Pl. XLIII, 8) et cette gravure et celle des Saintes femmes au tombeau avec l'ange mènent à leur tour à divers dessins. Une gravure de R. Sadeler (bon) d'après Zuccaro (Pl. XLIV, 9) a servi de base à deux dessins qui montrent des saints, l'un à Francfort (Pl. XLIV, 11) l'autre au Louvre, ce dernier identifié récemment par P. Pouncey.

Les collectionneurs aiment d'autres dessins à cause de leur beauté et de leurs sentiments mais ils s'y intéressent aussi à cause de leurs rapports, même indirects avec d'autres maîtres. Ainsi, Bellange a exécuté à la sanguine une suite de figures féminines en buste qui sont des allégories des Sens: le thème est à la mode et fait l'objet de suite de gravures néerlandaises. De même, les gravures des apôtres (Pl. XLIV, 10) s'apparentent à celles du Parmesan pour la technique et la mise en place et à ces gravures se rattachent des dessins de figures isolées: femmes debout avec des enfants, que font penser à la charité ou à la fécondité, figures inclinées qui marchent ou courent, et dont la légèreté évoque un bonheur insouciant, figures dressées, immobiles, cambrées, qui font le joint entre les apôtres et les créations du théâtre ou de la réalité populaire avec un excès dans les gestes, les expressions, et une sensualité qui devient équivoque.

Pour d'autres dessins, le lien avec des gravures de Bellange ou d'autres artistes semble disparaître. Ainsi pour les cavaliers. Deux dessins se rattachent au Cavalier de l'Adoration des Mages et à ceux du Portement de Croix, et les autres se relient vaguement à de multiples traditions, mais tous frappent par leur élan héroïque. Bellange a aussi dessiné des couples, et si l'homme qui porte une femme se rattache à la gravure et par elle indirectement à la gravure de Penni, les deux dessins qui montrent l'homme et la femme côte à côte sont des inventions pures, mais tous ces couples expriment le bonheur et la passion de l'amour.

Bellange donc, est capable de créer des dessins sans rapport ou presque avec ses gravures ou avec des créations étrangères. Dépassant le maniérisme du temps, s'exprimant librement, il atteint à la pleine originalité de son style. Ardeur de vivre, beauté, élégance, fierté, sensualité, bonheur, ces dessins disent les joies d'un Paradis perdu et annoncent les "Fêtes galantes."

LAGNEAU ET LE REALISME[4]

IL nous faut maintenant comprendre pourquoi les collectionneurs—et quels collectionneurs—ont conservé les portraits de Lagneau.

La mode du portrait devient dans la France du dix-septième siècle une manie qui atteint toutes les classes sociales. Portraits peints depuis les portraits d'apparat à la manière de Pourbus, puis de Van Dyck, mais avec des accommodements, jusqu'aux effigies en buste, aux visages isolés, dont la franchise presque brutale plaît à la bourgeoisie et à la province. Portraits gravés, de plus en plus appréciés, pour leurs nombreuses épreuves destinées aux parents et aux amis. D'abord le goût flamand, des pièces petites et minutieuses, exécutées par les Flamands ou les Français, rarement sur le vif, le plus souvent d'après des peintures ou des crayons. Mais à partir de 1620, la gravure de portrait se renouvelle sous des influences étrangères grâce à Callot, Lasne, Mellan, ou encore grâce à Morin et Edelinck qui interpréteront Champagne. Nanteuil sera le seul à partir de dessins au pastel pour établir ses gravures. En atteignant la maîtrise vers 1650, elle a contribué à ruiner la pratique du crayon.

Le crayon qui avait connu sa grande période au seizième siècle

[4] Bibliographie de Lagneau dans F. Thieme et U. Becker, *Allgemeines Lexikon der bildenden Künstler*, Leipzig, 1928, XXII, pp. 218-19. Retenir l'appendice que F. Reiset donne à sa *Notice des dessins . . . du Louvre*, 1863, II, pp. 345ff, et H. Bouchot, *Les portraits aux crayons conservés à la Bibliothèque Nationale*, Paris, 1884, p. 61. La citation de B. Dorival, *Peinture française*, Paris, 1946, I, p. 46. Hélène Notthalft, *Portraits français au crayon*, Leningrad, 1936. Agnes Mongan, *100 Master Drawings*, Cambridge, Massachusetts, 1949.

reste à la mode après 1600. Du dessin fait sur le vif, on tire des copies, on s'inspire pour des peintures et les gravures. On continue à aimer à constituer des séries qui forment des albums de même que les galeries de portraits peints ornent les châteaux. Ces crayons du dix-septième siècle représentent surtout la famille royale et les grands. Le paradoxe est que la cour de France soit restée si longtemps attaché à un genre devenu archaïque et sans même se rendre compte de sa décadence. Le succès des crayons postérieurs à 1600 s'explique d'ailleurs aisément: ressemblance garantie des visages, exactitude des coiffures et des parures, une exécution plus énergique et contrastée que par le passé et, innovation goûtée, le charme de couleurs peu nombreuses, mais franches et chantantes. Mais la vérité physique de la ressemblance n'est qu'un aspect du problème de la ressemblance. Retrouver la vie intime et l'exprimer dans la vérité des formes, ce secret du vrai portraitiste que l'Europe s'efforce alors de saisir reste étranger à nos crayons. D'autre part la monotonie de la présentation et de l'exécution trop caressée crée la lassitude.

Dans cet ensemble, cependant des réussites. Les artistes malgré tout ont leur personnalité. Daniel Dumoustier (1574-1646) qui a l'époque passait pour "le plus excellent crayonneur de l'Europe" et qui maintenant est le plus déconsidéré, connait des réussites, à preuve le portrait de sa seconde épouse (1619), une simple femme du peuple, mais avenante, robuste, avec sur les lèvres un air de bonheur. Ou bien (1640) le portrait du comte de Papenheim, visage racé, avec de lourdes paupières, de grands yeux intelligents et ironiques. Des oeuvres de ce genre sortent de la convention et nous rapprochent de Lagneau.

La fortune de ce dernier est récente. Elle est comme pour les Le Nain une conséquence de la mode du réalisme populaire lancée par Champfleury et son groupe, mais elle se recommande aussi d'érudits, tel Reiset, réunis au sein de la Société de l'Histoire de l'Art français. Pourtant des voix discordantes s'élèvent. Au dire de Bouchot, De Laborde "témoignait d'une indifférence pour ces caricatures à l'estampe et ne cherchait point à relever des mérites que nous sommes impuissants à reconnaître." "Aussi bien," poursuit Bouchot, "Lagneau n'était-il qu'un fantaisiste, exagérant à la Daumier les défauts de chacun et n'ayant guère produit de portraits au sens réel du mot." Et de nos jours, pour B. Dorival "un réalisme outrancier recherche dans le caractère et donne dans un expressionisme qui correspond toujours à un fléchissement du genre français." A ces réserves s'oppose le zèle des critiques d'art, tel Gonse qui avoue son faible et qui admire les excellents dessins de Rennes et de Lille, et l'engouement des collectionneurs, grands bourgeois du Second Empire de la Troisième République, amateurs éclairés des États-Unis de notre époque. Ils prêtent leurs oeuvres à des expositions, comme celle de 1879, ils les donnent aux musées. Les prix atteints dans les ventes attestent une vogue grandissante (malgré des fluctuations et par exemple le pseudo Acarie passe de 4.050 Fr en 1898 à 780 Fr en 1900) et de nos jours les Lagneau "font" de 100 à 300.000 Fr.

Peut-être dans cette mode, pourrait-on déceler des parti-pris. On a longtemps voulu voir dans l'artiste un contemporain des Guerres de Religion, ou du moins de la Sainte-Ligue alors que personne ne nie plus que les oeuvres datent de la première partie du dix-septième siècle ou à la rigueur du règne d'Henri IV. Surtout on a voulu reconnaître les personnages représentés comme pour donner plus de prix aux effigies. On croyait pouvoir identifier Dandelot, le Cardinal du Perron, le Cardinal de Bourbon. Fillon était fier de son Goujon daté de 1564, de son Philippe de Mornay qu'il publie dans sa galerie des Portraits de Saumur, de son Acarie, un des chefs de la Ligue. Le comte de Beurnonville possédait un portrait orné de la mention "François Rabelais" qu'il prête à l'exposition de 1876. Mme Wolff prête à l'exposition d'Angoulême en 1879 des portraits d'Henri IV et de Sully. En 1912, Frantz veut reconnaître dans le vieillard de la vente Le Moyne les traits d'un "vieil huguenot irréductible." En 1961, le Musée Condé à Chantilly continue à mettre des noms sur les crayons de Dumoustier ou de Lagneau et les portraits de ce dernier seraient ceux du Président Briçonnet en 1634, du frère du précédent en 1620, du chancelier Brulart de Sillery mort en 1624, du Président Achille de Marlay mort en 1619, de M. de Barbezières en 1609, du Chancelier d'Alyre mort en 1635, de Marie de la Chastre, dame de Loubespine en 1626, d'Estienne Pasquier.[5]

[5] A. Darcel (*Gazette des Beaux-Arts*, II/XVI, 1877, p. 280) conteste déjà les noms des personnages de la Collection de Mme Wolff; la citation de Frantz, à

Notre époque plus raisonnable, ne met plus de noms sur les têtes. Mais comprend-elle Lagneau? Le connait-elle? L'artiste et son oeuvre prêtent en effet à des difficultés graves.

L'artiste d'abord. Pour nous renseigner, une seule caution, l'abbé de Marolles. Il aurait pu nous renseigner davantage et il avait annoncé en 1672 un ouvrage tout prêt, mais les éditeurs n'en n'ont pas voulu et le manuscrit en est perdu. Du moins, dans son *Livre des Peintres*, suite de quatrains médiocres et de renseignements précieux, on trouve une "Autre addition concernant les crayons et les dessins à la main" et un recueil donne l'occasion d'énumérer des noms connus et inconnus dans des quatrains dont deux sont à retenir:

VII De Vitry le François Jean de Nojure en peinture
Avait acquis du nom avec Maistre Raimond
Lanneau n'y faisoit pas bien les choses à fond
Mais tout de fantaisie en diverses postures.

VIII Beaucoup d'autres crayons y sont sans nom de Maistre
Mais bien d'autres aussi dans ce nombreux recueil
S'y trouvent de Belange et de François Verneuil ...
Puis il est question de Le Pautre, Chauveau, Caron,
Vignon, Lallemand.

Notons d'abord que de Marolles intercale l'artiste après un peintre champenois et avant le lorrain Bellange et après avoir cité un inconnu de nous, il revient aux artistes parisiens. Sa pensée semble le placer parmi les provinciaux de l'Est. Notons d'autre part qu'il parle de Lanneau. Par contre quand il dresse en 1666 le catalogue de la collection qu'il vendra au Roi, il indique au n° 252 p. 129 un volume de crayons de Lagneau et il y en a 192. Mais il forme aussitôt une nouvelle collection beaucoup plus riche en dessins qu'en gravures; cette fois l'inventaire signale in-fine Lanneau.

Ainsi incertitude quant au nom: Lagneau ou Lanneau. Toutefois le nom de Lagneau est bien spécifié dans une mention de l'album du Cabinet des Estampes de Paris dont nous allons parler et il

propos du dessin des "huguenots" (adjugé 2.000 Fr) dans la rubrique de la Curiosité de la *Revue de l'Art décoratif*, 1, 1912, p. 163.

parait aussi sur un dessin du même Cabinet des Estampes: la mention à l'encre date certainement du dix-septième siècle. Le malheur est que ni Lagneau, ni Lanneau ne figurent dans les listes d'artistes de l'est ou de Paris, ni dans le fichier Laborde, précieux recueil établi d'après les actes d'état-civil de Paris et conservé au Département des Manuscrits de la Bibliothèque Nationale. Les noms mènent à des rapprochements dont nous savons la fragilité. Lanneau fait penser à Michel Lasne et la Collection de Rothschild du Louvre possède un petit portrait du comte de Soissons, étude préparatoire à la gravure, petit dessin, dessin très enlevé, avec des couleurs vives, du jaune, de l'orange et ce portrait expressif très différent de la manière de Dumoustier est un trait d'union entre Lagneau ou Lanneau ou le sage Nanteuil. Toutefois, impossible de donner à notre Lagneau cette étude et d'admettre que Lasne en réalité est Lanneau. D'autre part, nous ignorons si Lagneau a quelque attache avec David Lagneau, médecin ordinaire du Roi, dont le Cabinet des Estampes a le portrait, sans rapport avec notre artiste ou avec Jacques Lagniet, éditeur et graveur parisien qui vers 1660, publie des pièces de facture grossière mais d'un puissant réalisme populaire: Till Eulenspiegel, Don Quichotte et surtout le Recueil des plus illustres Proverbes et s'il démarque souvent les gueux de Callot, ou des pièces d'autres maîtres, ses figures violentes ont certes des analogies avec celles de notre Lagneau.[6]

Confessons donc, avec tous nos prédécesseurs, notre ignorance de l'artiste. Et aussi, de l'oeuvre, à cause de la quantité "inépuisable" de ses dessins. Ils sont de plus en plus nombreux, avec des répliques de date parfois récente et de qualité inégale.

Pour Guiffrey et Marcel, "le nom de cet artiste est un peu comme une rubrique sur laquelle on réunit tous les crayons de la première partie du dix-septième siècle, dont le caractère est très marqué, les traits accentués et souvent un peu caricaturaux": ils parlent de l'album du Louvre, qui vient de l'amateur Gatteaux, le seul des recueils que ce dernier avait rassemblés, à avoir échappé à un incendie lors de la Commune.

[6] Le dessin du comte de Soissons de Lasne, Collection de Rothschild, au Louvre, École française, portefeuille XXIII, no. 7905. J. Guiffrey et P. Marcel, *Inventaire . . . des dessins . . . Louvre*, Paris, 1906, VII.

Dans cet album, il est aisé de distinguer les mains différentes d'artistes tous anonymes. L'oeuvre la plus intéressante, est un portrait de format plus petit que les autres, une figure d'homme âgé et grave, qui semble prise sur le vif, avec réalisme, mais sans le désir d'exagérer. Ce dessin est tracé sur une feuille de papier plus mince et au verso, on y lit la fin d'un acte avec la mention d'un notaire Saulnier, mais sans indication suffisante pour retrouver les personnages et peut-être le modèle, et aussi la date de 1625, qui suffirait à confirmer que le genre "Lagneau," correspond bien à l'époque de Louis XIII. Seulement, ce beau portrait n'est pas de notre artiste, pas plus que celui d'une centenaire conservé au Cabinet des Estampes (Pl. XLV, 12). Sur un fond clair lavé de gris jaunâtre, le portrait est exécuté au crayon ou au lavis à l'estompe de pastel repris au crayon avec de multiples traits fins qui ne coïncident pas avec l'esquisse et ces traits rouges ou gris précisent le costume, le bonnet, le visage ridé, la bouche édentée, la moue renfrognée, les petits yeux brillants, le regard fixe, méfiant, rusé. Cette étonnante évocation d'une vieillesse indomptable porte au crayon gris, en haut, à droite, les lettres F.M.A. et au-dessous "Oct. 104," des mentions anciennes à l'encre rousse ajoutent en haut à droite "n° 123," et ne bas à droite "Lagneau." Mais nous avons affaire à un autre artiste, et il en est de même pour d'autres représentations aussi vivantes, qui ont le mérite de nous faire sentir que nous avons affaire à un genre en faveur.[7]

D'autres dessins sont différents. On pourrait distinguer ceux qui sont sommairement et brutalement traités, comme des e-squisses et peut-être des calques, ceux qui abusent de l'estompe. On pourrait opposer les figures calmes et celles qui sont excentriques. L'album Gatteaux à lui seul nous donne des directions différentes. Notre but n'est pas ici, de classer de séparer les éléments d'une école, mais d'isoler et de définir Lagneau.

Pour base, le recueil N a 21 b. du Cabinet des Estampes, celui de Marolles.[8] On y trouve, page 58, une languette de papier avec

---

[7] Le portrait de la centenaire, au Cabinet des Estampes de la Bibliothèque Nationale (B 6 a Res.), où il y a d'ailleurs des Lagneau authentiques. Le portrait daté de 1625 par l'inscription au revers ". . . Saulnier, notaris . . . ce cinq mars mil six cent vingt cinq" est le second de l'album Gatteaux, du Louvre, no. 5487.

[8] Reiset en est persuadé, voir sa notice sur les dessins du Louvre et son étude sur les Actes de baptême . . . , dans *Archives de l'Art français, Documents*, 1853-55, III,

la mention ancienne: "Portraits de Lagneau, Marolles, n° 264." Le recueil vendu au Roi portait le n° 252, mais la numérotation a pu être modifiée par la suite et il y a toutes les chances d'avoir ici l'album même de Marolles, du moins en partie car au lieu de 192 dessins de l'inventaire, nous n'avons que 73 pièces; on en a ôté une en 1881 pour la placer dans l'oeuvre de Callot, plusieurs à la fin ne sont pas de la même main, deux figures de femmes, construites à grands traits et comme décalquées, des figures de jeunes religieuses, trop estompées, des enfants ou plutôt des jeunes anges. En revanche, une bonne cinquantaine de pièces présente une évidente unité. On y rattachera quelques dessins d'un autre recueil (B 6 a Res.) qui portent des numéros à l'encre d'une graphie ancienne et aussi par exemple les dessins de l'Albertine, publiés en fac-similé par Medesqui avait d'abord attribué les premiers à Daniel Dumoustier et qui a eu le mérite de rendre le lot à Lagneau.

Ces dessins ont une unité de style frappante. Leur technique et leur conception les séparent sous plusieurs rapports des "crayons" français. Assez grands, ils montrent des figures en buste, ou à mi-corps, avec parfois des mains apparentes. Les étapes de l'exécution sont les suivantes. D'abord, l'esquisse, la silhouette et quelques lignes conductrices avec des traits minces, noirs, rougeâtres ou gris brun. Puis un travail à l'estompe au crayon noir ou rouge, à la craie de couleur ocre ou parfois bleue, qui se mêlent au noir et au rouge en donnant des bruns et des verts, pour les chairs, les barbes ou les chevelures, les fourrures ou les étoffes. Parfois, un travail estompé menu pour les veines ou les petites bouffissures de la chair, parfois, un estompage un peu mou et rapide qui dépasse les contours. L'importance des couleurs ne doit pas être exagérée. Enfin, après coup, des traits nerveux au crayon ou au fusain noir ou même à la sanguine. Traits minces, anguleux, durs pour les rides ou les poils. Traits élargis, enlevés librement pour les barbes, les détails des costumes, les plis, les franges, les boutonnières, les boutons, un zèle extrême pour les accidents de l'épi-

---

p. 154ff. "Quand même le recueil de la Bibliothèque Nationale n'existerait pas, recueil qui est indubitablement celui dont parle Marolles. . . ." Bouchot partage son opinion.

derme, rides, plis et moues, veines, cordes du cou, tavelures, taches, papules verrues, pour les lèvres dont le dessin sinueux est repris par un trait mince, pour les points brillants des yeux, et les paupières qui souvent cernées d'un trait rouge sont comme enflammées.

L'analyse du recueil décèle des sources, des influences, mais fait ressortir aussi une note française.

Certaines figures interprètent des modèles. De profil à gauche, coiffé d'un bonnet à la mode du seizième siècle, vêtu strictement, mince, austère, un personnage ressemble à un prédicateur (page 10). Portant un manteau bleu et une veste faite de sanguine estompée avec des traits pour les revers et les boutons, la chevelure modelée par le fusain, le cou gonflé estompé de pastel jaunâtre, la tête carrée, colorée de pastel gris jaune estompé relevé de petits traits rouges pour les rides et les verrues, le regard fixe, l'expression attentive, un autre personnage est une sorte de Saint-Jean au pied de la croix. Il s'inspire peut-être d'une peinture mais il la transforme et l'artiste exagère les angles du visage, les verrues (page 26). Une femme monstrueuse (Pl. xlv, 13), les mains croisées sur la poitrine, les seins débordant du corsage, a le visage bouffi, le menton en galoche, les lèvres boursouflées, le nez en pied de marmite, les yeux exorbités, et tout, la perle de l'oreille, la coiffure, nous ramène à une caricaturé d'origine italienne (page 67).

Cet exemple prouve que le présumé Lagneau s'appuie sur autrui pour construire des figures. Mais une influence plus précise peut-être suggérée à en juger d'après d'autres exemples. Ce sont des hommes murs ou âgés, coiffés de callots noirs ou gris, clercs, notaires ou médecins. Celui de la page 7 (Pl. xlv, 14) qui se distingue par la qualité du travail est de profil, la main jaunâtre posée sur le costume gris, le visage arrondi, rosé, avec des éclats jaunes vers le menton et des veines bleuâtres, l'expression attentive et méprisante. Celui de la page 22, est de face, porte un costume sobre, animé de traits fermes et un collet blanc. Entre la barbe vaste et molle et la moustache relevée fièrement, la bouche est gourmande et spirituelle, tandis que les yeux regardent avec une calme audace. Parmi les effigies de vieilles, on retiendra celle de la page 68 (Pl. xlv, 15) qui se présente de profil, un peu voûtée, tenant une canne, vêtue d'etoffes bleuâtres, portant un bonnet, le visage sillonné de rides, marqué de petits gonflements nés d'un savant travail à la Rembrandt. On pourrait ajouter des exemples du même recueil, d'autres, pris dans un autre recueil du Cabinet des Estampes, coté B 6 a Res., ainsi page 1, un homme au visage allongé, coiffé d'un callot, ou page 8, un homme avec une fraise et un callot, d'autres encore, comme le beau visage de vieille femme sortant d'un voile de la vente de la Collection Oppenheimer en 1936, et ici, comment de pas penser aux représentations par Rembrandt de vieilles femmes, comme les pseudo "Mères de Rembrandt."

Ces figures nous semblent présenter des analogies avec celles de l'École de Leyde autour de 1630, de Rembrandt ou de ses amis Lievens de Don, voire de ses disciples. Même façon de lancer la silhouette vue de bas, le buste s'effilant en montant, engoncé dans des étoffes ou des fourrures. Même curiosité pour des coiffures compliquées, bonnets ou turbans, même façon de camper des callots, de décrire des chevelures, des barbes abondantes, de scruter des visages labourés de rides entrecroisées comme des cicatrices, de vieilles peaux amollies gonflées de protubérances et de boutons, et pour étudier ces chairs tragiquement ravagées par les années, même travail fait de traits incisifs et d'estompages mous. Même effort pour donner à ces visages une expression, en éclairant ou en éteignant les regards, en accentuant les moues, les dessins des lèvres.

Que les crayons français aient été consultés par Rembrandt, voilà une hypothèse que nous ne proposons pas. Mais les études de Lagneau apportent à nos yeux un supplément à l'étude de l'influence du "Frühstil," de Rembrandt tel que K. Bauch l'a étudié.[9] Bauch indique que les têtes d'expression de Leyde, dessinées, gravées, peintes, ont été célèbres, qu'elles ont été copiées et interprétées. Jacques des Rousseaux, originaire de Tourcoing, peint des têtes d'étude, des vieillards coiffés de turban ou de bonnet, Bauch note que l'émotion intérieure devient un pathos superficiel qui nous semble correspondre à l'exagération caractéristique de Lagneau. Issac de Jondreville, originaire de Metz, apprenti de Rembrandt à Leyde en 1630, exécute aussi des têtes d'expression dans la manière de Rembrandt, mais d'un modèle

---

[9] K. Bauch, *Der frühe Rembrandt und seine Zeit*, Berlin, 1960.

incertain. Le personnage hilare du Musée Bredius, buste allongé, tête étroite, sourcils relevés, lèvres fines, est presque un Lagneau. Une comparaison entre l'École de Leyde et Lagneau mènerait peut-être à des résultats fructueux.[10]

Retenons que deux artistes venus de nos régions ont été intéressés par les effigies de l'École de Leyde. Mais elles sont aussi estimées en France même. On n'ignore pas que Vignon le "prérambranesque" subit aussi l'influence de Rembrandt. Mais on connait moins bien les gravures de Jérome David éditées par Langlois, ce dernier en relation avec Van Dyck qui a fait son portrait et Vignon dont il fait graver et vendre les oeuvres. David a exécuté une suite de Rois Orientaux et de Philosophes au nombre de 36. Nous devons à R. A. Weigert les indications les plus utiles dans cette suite, comme sur David et Langlois. Et d'abord, comme l'écrit Mariette, dans ses notes manuscrites conservées au Cabinet des Estampes, T.IX, fol. 140, "Les noms . . . qu'on y trouve y ont été mis assez mal à propos, car il n'y a aucune de ces testes qui ne soit d'invention et n'ayant par conséquent nul rapport avec ce qu'on a prétendu leur faire représenter." En second lieu, il est possible que David n'a pas été le seul graveur, certaines épreuves, par exemple le n° 10, portent parfois l'indication "I. falck fet." Mais quand Florent le Comte note dans son *Cabinet de Singularités* (1700, M p. 144) que les pièces sont "dans la manière de Van Huller" il montre qu'il a senti leur style hollandais. Or, les gravures indiquent les modèles qui ont servi de source: 21 sont faites d'après Vignon, 4 d'après "Padouanus," 11 d'après Rembrandt; en fait il s'agit de 7 pièces de Rembrandt, d'autres de Van Vliet ou d'autres. Ainsi Aristote dérive d'une pièce de Van Vliet de 1634 et Scandrebec, d'une autre de 1631. L'eunuque de la Reine de Candace, le visage juvénile, penché, caché dans l'ombre sous une tignasse hirsute rappelle l'auto-portrait de Rembrandt de Cassel ou celui de la Collection Cedat à Londres. Héraclite rappelle les "pères" de Rembrandt, Démocrite, certaines de ses fig-

---

[10] Les analogies de Lievens et Lagneau doivent être retenues et creusées, par exemple la gravure d'un homme barbu de face en buste (D. 70), dont nous devons une reproduction à J. Q. van Regteren Altena, qui a bien voulu aussi nous signaler le dessin d'un cavalier de Bellange récemment acquis par le Cabinet des Estampes du Rijksmuseum; nous lui exprimons ici notre reconnaissance.

ures âgées. En comparant les gravures Hollandaises et celles éditées par Langlois, on sent l'effort pour traduire les effets lumineux et les stigmates de la vieillesse, effort consciencieux mais maladroit qui insiste, exagère, durcit, multiplie les détails. Mais c'est ainsi qu'un artiste réussit en France à rendre les rides, et les plis d'une façon nouvelle. En comparant ensuite les gravures aux vieillards de Lagneau, on acquiert la certitude que le dessina-teur reprend les mêmes effets, soit qu'il s'inspire des gravures, soit qu'il aie d'autres modèles que les interprétations de David, oeuvres hollandaises, gravures, peintures, ou dessins. En tout cas, son style est nouveau en France, en partie parce qu'il y vulgarise les têtes d'expression de l'École de Leyde.[11]

Mais malgré cette influence, subsiste chez Lagneau un goût français. Et d'abord, par ses maladresses: les mains sont mal ren-dues, les bras trop courts, les bustes trop petits, les têtes trop grosses. Mais aussi par son inconstance dans le travail. A côté de détails minutieux, des parties à peine esquissées, de la rapidité, de l'insouciance, les figures donnent l'impression d'être impro-visées.

Il y a plus, des déformations conscientes mènent à un style dif-férent de Leyde. Les données extérieures sont accentuées, multi-pliées, déformées à la manière des caricaturistes. Il s'agit d'exagérer les traits d'un modèle réel, de maintenir la ressemblance, mais en y ajoutant une note ridicule et aussi d'inventer un être absurde, impossible, mais vraisemblable. Et parfois, pour donner à ses créations plus de vie, l'artiste invente des situations qui mènent à des jeux de scène, des évènements qui justifient des attitudes. C'est par là surtout qu'il diffère des maîtres de Leyde dont les têtes d'expression ou les personnages vivent, existent en soi, sans qu'il soit besoin de pressions extérieures.

Ainsi se vérifie la définition proposée par Marolles:

> Lanneau n'y faisoit pas bien les choses *à fond*
> Mais tout de *fantaisie* en diverses *postures*

Mais cette définition n'est pas complète et l'auteur est resté au bord du vrai problème. Lagneau s'efforce de faire ressortir les

---

[11] R.-A. Weigert, *Bibliothèque Nationale, Département des Estampes. Inven-taire du fonds français. Graveurs du XVIIe siècle*, Paris, 1939, III, Notice sur J. David avec la bibliographie.

secrets de ses personnages vrais ou inventés, calmes ou affairés. Il décrit des passions, des caractères et parfois avec une subtilité et une pénétration qui donnent à ses créations une autorité fascinante. Verve gauloise? Vulgarité? Sans doute, comme pour toute l'époque. Mais aussi une introspection qui rejoint les curiosités des écrivains français du temps, celles de Mlle de Scudery lorsqu'elle décrit les nuances les plus fines des émotions de ses héros de l'Astrée, celles de Sorel, lorsque dans son Francion, partant d'êtres vrais qu'il a pu connaître, il invente des personnages qui dépassent les normes, celles de Tallemant des Réaux, qui en quelques lignes campe un contemporain avec ses travers physiques et mentaux.

Dans son désir de creuser jusqu'au fond ses personnages, de les expliquer, Lagneau en vient à en donner des versions différentes, ou bien il oppose deux figures, ou bien encore il a tendance à créer des séries. Le Recueil de Paris nous en donne des exemples. Laissons les moines, les religieuses, les notaires. Mais nous avons trois versions (pages 27, 28, 33) de personnages vêtus à l'orientale, avec des pelisses et des toques et dont les visages glabres sont exotiques. A côté de ces "Sarmates," nous avons trois versions d'ivrognes qui tiennent des cruches (pages 51, 53, 55). L'un est engourdi par une bienheureuse ivresse, le second, tenant ferme le pot, tourne la tête et est plus agressif; le troisième, l'oeil vague, hébêté rit sans savoir pourquoi. Mais nous avons aussi deux buveurs (Pl. XLVI, 16, 17) qui tiennent des coupes et qui, tournés l'un vers l'autre, forment pendant (pages 45, 46). Celui de gauche est un être plein d'entrain et d'autorité, exigeant, dur, cassant, l'autre le visage plus mou, le sourire insinuant, est à la fois timide, obséquieux et sournois. Après cette scène de comédie, nous avons deux vieillards attentifs, dont les nez très longs rejoignent les mentons en galoche; ils sont à la fois très semblables et très différents (Pl. XLVI, 18, 19). Pour l'un, droit, maigre, desséché, jaunâtre, la prudence, le calcul; mais à ce petit vieux fragile et froid s'oppose un être puissant, tout en dehors pris dans un tournoiement accentué par les hachures et dont le visage coloré respire la force: on dirait on écho de Breugel. Nous avons aussi deux hommes barbus presque semblables (pages 35, 34) également vigilants; mais le profil du premier est tout en saillie et l'expression est perplexe et triste, le profil du second est comprimé, rentré comme sous l'effet d'une pression extérieure et l'attention se mêle ici de maladie et de cruauté. De même Lagneau s'est plu à opposer deux dignes matrones coiffées du bonnet des veuves (Pl. xlvii, 20, 21), l'une placide confortable, épanouie dans sa robe gris et brun au col blanc a un visage rose pâle étalé, élargi hors de toute mesure, elle regarde par en dessous le spectateur comme si elle savait tout de lui et elle sourit ironiquement. L'autre maigre, la poitrine plate, a un visage pâle, retréci, serré, tout ridé et les lèvres fines pincées, les petits yeux presque fermés, patiente, malveillante, elle examine et juge (pages 63, 64).

D'autres images nous aident à comprendre des intentions plus profondes. Ainsi trois bravaches (pages 17, 25, 9). Le premier (Pl. xlvii, 22), chevelure ébouriffée sous le chapeau melon, le gros visage sanguin et mou fait l'important et à l'examiner, on découvre des sentiments complexes, une amabilité souriante de façade, la gourmandise ou plutôt la concupiscence, un égoïsme froid. Puis un matamore vêtu d'une tunique orange, la poitrine barrée d'une écharpe grise, le grand chapeau bien coupé, fronce les sourcils, retrousse les moustaches et joue les croque-mitaines. Enfin, un capitaine de profil (Pl. xlvii, 23), très correct, ganté de cuir gris rose; vêtu de gris, coiffé d'un grand feutre gris et rose avec des plumes rouges, fier de sa belle chevelure brune qui tombe sur l'épaule, tourne vers nous un visage mince au nez coupant, aux moustaches effilées et le teint plus jaunâtre que rose, les lèvres trop fines, les yeux durs, il mêle la fatigue et le découragement à l'audace, à la morgue et à la méfiance.

D'autres figures sont plus inquiétantes encore. Ainsi, un vieillard (page 24) dont le costume bleu qui tire vers le lilas ou le gris et dont le vaste turban où se mêlent les gris, les roses et les bruns se détachent sur un fond verdâtre. Un visage pâle, des yeux creusés, un regard noir et éteint, de la lucidité, de la lassitude, de la tristesse de l'angoisse. Puis (page 57) une femme très droite et dont l'élan est doublé par le grand col relevé, frappe par son visage intelligent et inspiré, animé par de grands yeux, mais ici l'énergie confine à une exaltation de monomane et on pense aux folles de Géricault. Hors du recueil, on trouve d'autres exemples de mélancolie, ainsi les guerriers de l'Albertine ou à Rennes l'homme au chapeau haut de forme, dont les yeux luisants et fixes sont d'un fou (Pl. xlviii, 24).

Ces dessins de Lagneau, de quand les dater? Une indication nous est fournie par quelques philosophes, comme si le dessinateur avait voulu imiter David. Sauf dans un cas, Lagneau s'écarte d'ailleurs des représentations de ces philosophes telles que son temps les admet. Il campe deux fois Socrate (pages 41-42). "Socrate, le plus sale de corps et le plus net en esprit et vertu des Grecs." Détache sur un fond jaunâtre verdâtre ses vêtements gris bleu, son visage rond et coloré, aux yeux interrogateurs et aux lèvres ironiques. "Socrate, camus, mal proportionné," plus ridicule avec son buste étroit, son front bas, ses lèvres obstinées, donne l'impression d'un rustre malpropre et entêté, mais ses yeux pétillent d'intelligence. Hippocrate (page 44) de son côté n'est qu'entêtement. Aristote (page 39), "toujours bien peigné et fort propre selon Diogène Laerce" oppose au fond verdâtre, bleuâtre, son profil calme prolongé par une barbe lisse et un curieux bonnet conique côtelé. Sur un fond analogue Platon se présente de face, vêtu d'une blouse d'un gris jaunâtre et d'une mante bleue et brune. Longue barbe presque blanche un peu cotonneuse, teint pâle, grand front, des yeux qui fixent l'infini, de la noblesse, de la fatigue. Or, cette effigie n'ignore pas le Divinus Plato de la suite de David, qui toutefois est rendu avec plus d'animation, la barbe ondulée, le bonnet relevé enfermant deux vagues inégales.

David indique qu'il a exécuté sa gravure d'après "Padouanus," qui est sans doute Vignon; quel que soit l'artiste, il s'est inspiré de près d'un type de vieillard représenté parfois par Rembrandt vers 1630 par exemple le vieillard assis dans un fauteuil et coiffé d'un bonnet fourré à deux pointes, gravé en 1632 (B. 262). Archimède, enfin, strictement vêtu, sec, droit, tenant un compas, présente un profil sévère avec une barbe effilée et il dérive d'une autre gravure de David d'après Ludovic Carrache (?) datée de 1644. Le dessinateur connait des gravures faites par David mais il ne faut pas conclure que les deux artistes sont en relation. Du moins la suite semble se placer entre 1630 et 1645 pour prendre des dates larges.

Revenons à la question initiale. Qui, au dix-septième siècle a collectionné des dessins de Lagneau et de son école? A part

Marolles, aucun répondant connu. Des particuliers ont sans doute été amateurs de portraits même chargés, de parents ou d'amis; l'époque n'y aurait pas répugné. Tel serait le cas de la centenaire ou du portrait de 1625 de la collection Gatteaux au Louvre, mais il s'agit d'oeuvres qui ne sont pas de Lagneau et de portraits plutôt que de fantaisies.

Les inventions de Lagneau ont dû plaire aux artistes qui en ont fait provision, comme des modèles qu'ils copient pour se faire la main ou qu'ils interprètent dans leurs oeuvres.

Pour justifier l'hypothèse il suffit de rappeler que les dessins de Cranach du Musée de Reims ont servi au dix-huitième siècle de modèle aux élèves de l'Académie de cette ville, et de signaler un album qui avait appartenu à l'abbaye de Saint-Germain-des-Prés et qui, étant entré en 1919 seulement au Cabinet des Estampes de la Bibliothèque Nationale est pratiquement inconnu (N A 25 Réserve). Les portraits qu'il renferme sont d'un débutant maladroit: ses essais personnels sont les plus mauvais. Certains dessins sont des calques grossiers. Mais parfois la vie ne manque pas grâce au travail brutal et aux couleurs franches. On retient un visage épuisé et livide de dormeur ou de mort (page 12) et d'étranges figures de femmes à demi cachées par des étoffes, et des mèches de cheveux, ou un masque noir (pages 22, 24 bis, 32, 38), des nattes serrées par un lien noir qui deviennent des serpents, des boucles qui caressent la bouche d'une belle endormie (pages 15, 39). Mais on retient aussi des figures expressives, par exemple celles de deux lurons cyniques (pages 8, 27) qui rappellent à la fois Lagneau et le réalisme populaire français (Pl. XLVIII, 25).

Que les artistes aient consulté "Lagneau" explique, d'autre part, les analogies entre ses dessins et le réalisme populaire. Deaux gravures de vieilles femmes en sont la preuve. Dans l'une, la femme tient une boite et lève un bras et une main, son visage est ridé, le personnage se rapproche d'une vieille de l'album Lagneau (page 65) dont la main levée l'index tendu et le visage parcheminé disent qu'elle est à la fois sentencieuse et menaçante. Dans l'autre, la femme, une bourgeoise âgée sèche, encore avenante, tient un chapelet et elle ressemble à celle d'un dessin de l'autre recueil du Cabinet des Estampes.

Mais les Lagneau peuvent aussi être mis en relation avec les petits-bourgeois d'Antoine Le Nain, avec les paysans de Mathieu. L'homme au grand chapeau de Dresde ressemble au paysan assis au centre du Repas du Louvre. Nous savons déjà que Georges de La Tour a démarqué la vieille caricaturale d'une gravure exécutée vers 1620 par Gaspard Isac pour construire la diseuse de bonne aventure du célèbre tableau du Métropolitan Museum, exécuté vers 1625, que dans la Rixe du Musée de Chambéry (il s'agit d'une réplique, l'original vraisemblable se trouvant en Angleterre), une vieille aveugle épouvantée ressemble à une vieille femme de Dresde et que le violoniste réjoui a été copié par le jeune Maurice Quentin de la Tour dans un pastel conservé au Musée de Saint-Quentin, mais après tout l'artiste du dix-huitième siècle a pu utiliser un crayon de même que le peintre lorrain: ces deux figures illustrent le rôle probablement joué par les Lagneau d'un atelier à l'autre, d'une génération à l'autre; toujours dans la même Rixe, les autres figures, construites brutalement, ridées, hirsutes sont parentes de Lagneau, ainsi que les Apôtres du Musée d'Albi ou l'apôtre signé récemment découvert. Analogies aussi pour des oeuvres de l'école de La Tour. Ainsi dans une scène de marché parait une femme coiffée de la vaste halette lorraine et un dessin de l'école de Lagneau montre une femme coiffée de même (Pl. XLVIII, 26, 27), dont les traits ne sont pas sans rapport avec la précédente, mais avec plus de dureté. On trouve parfois dans l'école de Lagneau des vieillards dont le visage est très allongé et ridé avec des pattes d'oie autour des yeux enfoncés, brillants et parfois bienveillants. Ces vieillards paraissent dans une toile d'une collection lorraine où les participants nourrissent de bouillie un chat au maillot et dans un Concert exposé au Wawel à Cracovie. Une meilleure connaissance de Lagneau prêtera sans doute à des confrontations utiles avec le réalisme des graveurs et des peintres français.

METROPOLITAN SCHOOLS
IN LATIN AMERICAN ARCHAEOLOGY
AND COLONIAL ART

INTRODUCTION

T O my knowledge, this is the first time that any session of an international congress of the history of art has been dedicated to Latin American topics. The opportunity is nevertheless hedged about with limitations and restrictions. We cannot, like Cinquecento specialists, invest our efforts in the examination of a concept like Mannerism, when so much of our subject is still to be discovered and charted. Nor can we restrict the matter to one decade like the students of 1420-30, when we are still uncertain about the geography of the schools of painting and sculpture. I do not mean, of course, to suggest that we lack surveys of the subject, or that the surveys are not useful. Yet every time a survey is made, if it is made with care, the compiler has to spend most of his ration of words on announcing fresh groupings and discoveries. The cumulative result has an imprecise outline—we still are unsure about the main distribution of values in the history of Latin American art.

The subject of this session—Metropolitan Schools—presupposes its polar opposite, the provincial art of small towns and rural settings. Allow me to outline some notions that will enable us to consider archaeology, colonial art, folk art, and contemporary art under the terms of such a polarity.

First of all, the issue has been much beclouded in recent years by the intrusion of racial terms. We have become more and more used to speaking of mestizo (or half-breed) art, and of white or Creole art. This is regrettable in the present world, where racial discrimination is inconsistent with human dignity. Yet many art historians persist in referring to those planiform expressions of Latin America, which are typical of provincial and rural arts everywhere, as mestizo, or hybridized art. The term is abusive to nearly everyone—to the mestizo people, whom it unjustly singles out, as well as to the American-born whites—the Creoles—and to the Spaniards, to Indians, and to Negroes, whose many contributions it excludes. The art thus driven to a racial issue by this term, mestizo, actually is only another example of the flat pattern and prolixity which characterize provincial or rural designs everywhere in the world regardless of race.

If we reject this racial characterization of provincial art, how shall we generalize the differences between the arts of the center and the edge, the elite and the folk? Capital and province are also inadequate, because some capitals, like Washington or Moscow, are artistically inert, and many provincial places, like Weimar or Tours, have been hyperactive. It may well be that the differences are best described as the differences between fast and slow happening, regardless of place and race, recognizable by the rate of change among linked events, more than by their expressive burden, their social meaning, or their formal density and complexity.

What causes the difference between fast and slow time—the fast time of Athenian vase painting, contrasted to the slow time of Stone Age pottery? The fast time of the contemporary dealer's gallery, where things change at the speed of fashion, and the slow time of kitchen pottery in rural places?

It is a difference probably caused by the intervention of men who can spend all their time in the production of useless things. In tribal societies of a few hundred families, everyone must raise food most of the time, and there is never enough margin for specialized guilds of artisans who are exempted from growing food. In such tribes, the manufactures show change, of course, but that change is the change of casual drift, of cumulative habit, or routine repetition with minor variations.

Between the tiny tribe of a few families struggling to survive and the vast metropolis with its crannies and ledges sheltering the meditations of many inventive minds, there are at least two more positions: the small society, self-governing, with artisans freed from the growing of food; and the provincial society, where fashion is followed, but never originated.

Absolute demographic size is probably irrelevant. Small cities have generated the principal events of history more often than the megalopolis. Urban life alone is not enough for fast time. The provinces all have cities, yet these cities are like points which usually can only receive and relay messages, but cannot originate them.

In other words, historical life may have many gears, but there are only two significant velocities in the history of art. One is the glacier-like pace of cumulative drift in small and isolated societies. The other, swift, mode is like a forest fire in its leaping action across great distances, as when unconnected centers blaze into the same activity.

Thus, fast happening depends on favorable conditions of patronage and career, while slow happening characterizes provincial or tribal settings where neither patronage nor career assures the rapid exploration of available possibilities.

A quick review shows the diminishing number of the genuine centers of cultural elaboration since the pre-Columbian era throughout Latin America. Prior to the discovery of America, and after about A.D. 1000, at least eleven metropolitan centers can be identified as having sheltered major cultural traditions: the Valley of Mexico, the Gulf Coast, Oaxaca, Yucatan, the Guatemalan highland, Puerto Rico, the Magdalena Valley, the highland of Quito, the north coast of Peru, the south coast of Peru, and the Titicaca basin. This number was nearly halved during the colonial era and the nineteenth century to include only Mexico City, Havana, Bogota, Quito, Lima, and Rio de Janeiro. In the present century the number has been reduced again: Mexico, Buenos Aires, and Rio de Janeiro. A parallel process reappears elsewhere throughout the world. The continued leveling of modern culture by mass entertainment and by industrial monotony will perhaps eventually erase all differences of cultural order, save in only the richest cities and a few university towns.

It is unlikely that the forces compelling such uniformity can now be weakened or reversed. Yet we have before us, in the spectacle of the older art of Latin America, a proof that small, isolated human groups are the most fertile ground for cultural renovation and differentiation, rather than the great uniform society of today. Possibly the careful study of these older groups will eventually yield some renovation of our own drives toward variety and richness of expression.

In any event, it should caution us against the careless use of racial allusions in regard to events of which the declining quality has less to do with race than with the decay of the small autonomous society.

THE STYLE OF THE BORGIA GROUP
OF MEXICAN PRE-CONQUEST MANUSCRIPTS

DONALD ROBERTSON

THE historian of art still faces in pre-Conquest Mexican manuscript painting outstanding problems of dating and of attributing the works of art to specific places of origin. In most instances the pedigree cannot be traced beyond a first-recorded sixteenth- or even seventeenth-century account of the appearance of the manuscript in Europe. We can make general statements saying they are pre-Hispanic and, for instance, allocate Codex Dresden to the Maya or Codex Nuttall to the Mixtecs. Others such as the Codex Borgia, although accepted as pre-Hispanic, still elude a convincing association with even such a broad location for their provenience. However, such an attribution can be arrived at by considering their position in pre-Hispanic Mexico and by relating them to other works of art done in similar styles.

George C. Vaillant established the intellectual framework still used to describe the civilization of Mexico at the time of the Spanish Conquest of 1521 and the immediately preceding period. He called this late phase the "Mixteca-Puebla" culture.[1] For our purposes, the important traits of this Mixteca-Puebla culture were a complex pantheon, religious rites, the *tonalpohualli* or ritual calendar, the use of a 52-year cycle, and a system of pictorial "writing" or mnemonic notation. Vaillant considered the Mixteca-Puebla culture as including those parts of Oaxaca occupied by the Mixtec-speaking Indians (the present-day State of Puebla, including Cholula, and Tlaxcala, including Tizatlán). But he imagined its influence as spreading far beyond the borders of the area outlined: it thus encompassed speakers of Náhuatl other than those of Tlaxcala and Puebla, for it also included the Aztecs

---

[1] George Clapp Vaillant, *Aztecs of Mexico: Origin, Rise and Fall of the Aztec Nation*, New York, 1947. Henry B. Nicholson, "The Mixteca-Puebla Concept in Mesoamerican Archeology: a Re-Examination," *Selected Papers of the Fifth International Congress of Anthropological and Ethnological Sciences, Philadelphia, September 1-9, 1956: Men and Cultures*, Philadelphia, 1960, pp. 612-17.

of Mexico-Tenochtitlán (present-day Mexico City), in the Central Valley of Mexico. Vaillant's Mixteca-Puebla culture can be compared with the intellectual, political, technological and artistic upheaval of the Renaissance, and the Mixtecs and Aztecs as similar to the Italian and North European manifestations of this key change of direction given to European culture from the fifteenth century on. In a recent publication Philip Dark has called this period in the State of Oaxaca the "Mixtec Pictorial Horizon," a phrase first proposed by George Kubler.[2]

Traditionally the lands of the Mixtec-speaking Indians were divided into three parts. The Pacific Coast region, called the Flat Land or the Land of Maize, had as its principal city Tututepec, which ruled over a large domain. The Lower Mixteca, called the Hot Land, was seemingly of less importance. The Upper Mixteca, the heartland, was called the Venerable or the Esteemed Land. It had a series of important cities, such as Coixtlahuaca and Tlaxiaco, and others looming large in the content of the history manuscripts: Texupan, Teozacoalco, and Tilantongo.[3] The Upper Mixteca consisted of small city-states in high intramontane valleys alternately linked by alliances or divided by war until conquered by the Mexicans. Our knowledge that this part of the Mixteca was of most significance in their culture and art derives from several sources: their own traditions as preserved in their pictorial history manuscripts, outside observations recorded in accounts written in the sixteenth century and later, and archaeological discoveries made in the area.[4]

[2] Philip Dark, "Speculations on the Course of Mixtec History Prior to the Conquest," *Boletín de Estudios Oaxaqueños*, No. 10, Oaxaca, 1958, p. 10, based on conversations with George Kubler in 1957.

[3] Léon Diguet, "Contribution à l'étude géographique du Mexique précolombien: le Mixtécapan," *Journal de la Société des Américanistes de Paris*, new ser. 3, No. 1, Paris, 1906, pp. 15-43, 1 map.

[4] The Mixtec history manuscripts include codices Nuttall, Colombino (also Dorenberg), Selden, Bodley, Waecker-Götter or Egerton, Vienna, Becker I (also du Cacique), and Becker II. For later accounts see: *Papeles de Nueva España, segunda serie: Geografía y estadística,* Francisco del Paso y Troncoso, ed., Madrid, 1905-6, v; Fray Antonio de los Reyes, *Arte en lengua mixteca*, Mexico, 1593; Fray Francisco de Burgoa, *Geográfica descripción de la parte septentrional del polo ártico de América* (Publicaciones del Archivo General de la Nación, XXV-XXVI), Mexico, 1934. For archaeology of the Mixteca see: Ignacio Bernal, "Archeology of the Mixteca," *Boletín de Estudios Oaxaqueños*, No. 7, Oaxaca,

The series of pre-Conquest pictorial history manuscripts has been firmly linked with the Upper Mixteca by Alfonso Caso.[5] They preserve for us a complex and detailed account of Mixtec marriages, warfare, and religious practices. The number of examples assumed to be either pre-Conquest or in a pre-Conquest style is impressive but not large.[6] The historical tradition continued into the Colonial period, and we have a total of nearly sixty manuscripts,[7] according to Howard Cline, one of the small group of scholars currently studying them. In his key study of the history manuscripts, Caso showed that codices Nuttall (Pl. xlix, 1), Vienna, Selden, Bodley, Colombino, and Becker I and II all make reference to complex dynastic successions and refer to the kings of Tilantongo and Teozacoalco. In his recent interpretation and translation of the Codex Bodley he says that in Codex Nuttall the lineage of the city of Texupan is probably also important.[8] There

1958, and his "Exploraciones en Coixtlahuaca, Oaxaca," *Revista mexicana de estudios antropológicos*, x, Mexico, 1948-49, pp. 5-76; Gabriel de Cicco and Donald Brockington, *Reconocimiento arqueológico en el suroeste de Oaxaca* (Instituto Nacional de Antropología e Historia, Dirección de Monumentos Pre-Hispánicos, Informes 6; Mexico, 1956); *Excavations at Yagul—I*, Tom Swinson, ed., *Mesoamerican Notes*, 4, Mexico, 1955; *Excavations in the Mixteca Alta*, John Paddock, ed., *Mesoamerican Notes*, 3, Mexico, 1953; Eulalia Guzmán, "Exploración arqueológica en la Mixteca Alta," *Anales del Museo Nacional de Arqueología, Historia y Etnografía*, v, 1, Mexico, 1934, pp. 17-42; John Paddock, "Exploración en Yagul, Oaxaca," *Revista mexicana de estudios antropológicos*, 16, Mexico, 1960, pp. 91-96. See also the following archaeological reports by Alfonso Caso, *Las Exploraciones en Monte Albán, temporada 1931-1932* (Instituto Panamericano de Geografía e Historia, 7), Mexico, 1932; *Exploraciones en Oaxaca, quinta y sexta temporadas 1936-1937* (Instituto Panamericano de Geografía e Historia, 34), Tacubaya, D. F., 1938; "Resumen del informe de las exploraciones en Oaxaca, durante la 7a y la 8a temporadas 1937-38 y 1938-39," *Vigesimoseptimo congreso internacional de americanistas, actas de la primera sesión, celebrada en la ciudad de México en 1939*, Mexico, 1947, ii, pp. 159-87; and Caso and D. F. Rubín de la Borbolla, *Exploraciones en Mitla, 1934-1935* (Instituto Panamericano de Geografía e Historia, 21), Mexico, 1936. For a recent synthesizing work see: Barbro Dahlgren de Jordan, *La Mixteca, su cultura e historia prehispánicas* (Cultura mexicana, 11), Mexico, 1954.

[5] Alfonso Caso, "El Mapa de Teozacoalco," *Cuadernos americanos*, xlvii, 5 (Sobretiro al xxix Congreso internacional de Americanistas, New York, 1949), Mexico, 1949, pp. 3-40.

[6] For the list of eight manuscripts see note 4 above.

[7] Personal communication to the author.

[8] Alfonso Caso, *Interpretation of the Codex Bodley 2858* (boxed with facsimile in color), Mexico, 1960, p. 18.

is a difference of style among these manuscripts, however, that has not been studied adequately as yet. At some time in the future it may be possible on the basis of the monumental studies of Caso to relate individual styles to their places of origin. One may also be able to link them through the surviving colonial history manuscripts now being studied intensively by Caso as well as by Howard Cline and Ross Parmenter.

The history manuscripts, being small in scale and finely worked, are parallel to other examples of Mixtec art that have come down to us. The Mixtecs seem to have been excellent lapidaries working in jade and rock crystal.[9] Bernal notes that forty-eight or so of the fifty-odd pre-Hispanic small-scale mosaics that come to us with a provenience are from the Mixtec region.[10] Caso has discovered in the Mixtec tombs of Monte Albán[11] delicately carved bones and cast-gold ornaments of a virtuosity of execution. It is interesting to note, on the other hand, that the Mixtec sites so far studied show little evidence of monumental sculpture, or of the feeling for great planned cities that we find in Teotihuacán or Monte Albán.[12] It is possible that future archaeology in the Mixtec area will bring now-buried examples to light, since Mixtec archaeology has really only begun; on the basis of what is now known, however, we can say the Mixtecs worked in the small and the finely wrought rather than in the large and monumental.

Codex Borgia is the main document of the religious manuscripts known as the "Borgia Group" and conforms to this general statement of the nature of Mixtec art, for it too is small in scale and finely wrought (Pls. L, 3; LI, 5; LII, 8).[13] The Borgia Group in-

[9] Frederick A. Peterson, *Ancient Mexico*, New York, 1959, p. 276; Miguel Covarrubias, *Indian Art of Mexico and Central America*, New York, 1957, pp. 306-7.

[10] Bernal, *op.cit.*, p. 8.

[11] Caso, *Las Exploraciones en Monte Albán.*

[12] See note 4 above.

[13] *Il manoscritto messicano Borgiano del Museo etnografico della S. Congregazione di Propaganda Fide; riprodotto in fotocromografia a spese di S. E. il Duca di Loubat a cura della Biblioteca Vaticana*, Rome, 1898. *Codex Borgia: Eine altmexikanische Bilderschrift der Bibliothek der Congregatio de Propaganda Fide herausgegeben auf Kosten Seiner Excellenz des Herzogs von Loubat, erläutert von Dr. Eduard Seler*, Berlin, 1904-9, hereafter referred to as Seler Borgia Commentary.

cludes codices Borgia, Vaticanus B, Cospi, Laud and Fejérváry-Mayer. Mexican Manuscript Number 20 of the Bibliothèque Nationale, Paris, also known as the Culte Rendu à Tonatiuh, is sometimes included.[14] Their reason for being grouped together under the rubric "Borgia Group" seems to be merely that they are all ritual manuscripts, although the content is not exactly the same in all. Codices Borgia and Vaticanus B are linked by striking similarities of content demonstrated by Seler in his commentaries on them.[15] They both begin with a *tonalamatl* or table of the names of the days of the native ritual year, using a format found in no other pictorial source.[16] In subsequent pages the *tonalamatl* appears closer to the form known to us in the manuscripts from the territories of Náhuatl speakers.[17] Codices Laud, Cospi and Fejérváry-Mayer remain apart because of divergences in content from the other two (some passages are so obscure that even Seler, the great scholar of the material, was baffled[18]) and because of a distinct style. The *Culte Rendu à Tonatiuh* is also different, since it is only a single large panel with a single scene rather than being a complete book of several chapters like the others.

[14] *Il manoscritto messicano Vaticano 3773; riprodotto in fotocromografia a spese di S. E. il duca di Loubat a cura della Biblioteca Vaticana*, Rome, 1896, and *Codex Vaticanus No. 3773 (Codex Vaticanus B): An Old Mexican Pictorial Manuscript in the Vatican Library Published at the Expense of His Excellency the Duke of Loubat, Elucidated by Dr. Eduard Seler*, A. H. Keane, trans.; Berlin and London, 1902-3, hereafter referred to as Seler Vaticanus B Commentary. *Descripción del Códice Cospiano manuscrito pictórico de los antiguos Náuas que se conserva en la Biblioteca de la Universidad de Bolonia reproducido en fotocromografía a expensas de S. E. el Duque de Loubat*, Rome, 1898. Carlos Martínez Marín, *Códice Laud, introducción, selección y notas* (Instituto Nacional de Antropología e Historia, Investigaciones 5), Mexico, 1961. *Codex Fejérváry-Mayer: An Old Mexican Picture Manuscript in the Liverpool Free Public Museum, 12014/M, Published at the Expense of His Excellency the Duke of Loubat, Elucidated by Dr. Eduard Seler*, A. H. Keane, trans., Berlin and London, 1901-2. "Le culte rendu au soleil (Tonatiuh)," in Eugène Boban, *Documents pour servir à l'histoire du Mexique*, Paris, 1891, I, pp. 329-48; Atlas, pl. 20.

[15] Seler Borgia Commentary, p. 17; Seler Vaticanus B Commentary, p. 5.

[16] A similar presentation of the *tonalamatl* appears at the beginning of Codex Cospi, but with the addition of an extra figure in each of the "boxes." See Seler Borgia Commentary, p. 17; Seler Vaticanus B Commentary, p. 5.

[17] For pictorial documents see the Tonalamatl of Aubin, Codex Borbonicus, and the related codices Telleriano-Remensis and Ríos.

[18] *Codex Fejérváry-Mayer*, pp. 74 and 209.

The Codex Borgia is a strip of animal hide (probably deerskin) made up of fourteen separate pieces giving a total length of 10.34 meters and folded into thirty-nine leaves each 26.5 x 27 centimeters.[19] The smaller but related Codex Vaticanus B is composed of ten pieces of hide with a total length of 7.35 meters, folded into forty-nine leaves each 12 to 13 x 15 centimeters.[20] A comparison of page 9 of Codex Nuttall (Pl. XLIX, 1)[21] with page 21 of Codex Borgia (Pl. L, 3) and page 19 of Codex Vaticanus B (Pl. L, 4) shows the essential differences and similarities of their styles. The figures of the Vatican Codex, more coarsely done, are not so well adjusted to the areas within their frames as those of Codex Nuttall and Codex Borgia. In the Nuttall and Borgia codices the feet are drawn in profile, while the artist of the Vatican manuscript has drawn them in a more clumsy manner as though they were seen from above and at an angle. Borgia fingernails are delicate; the Nuttall and Vaticanus ones are square and blunt. The Borgia and Nuttall masters, using a projecting large nose and receding chin, create a head of greater distinction and angular precision. The Borgia page is a succession of angular and precise patterns deriving from iconographic requirements. The Nuttall page is equally angular and precise in obedience to the demands of its historical content, while the Vatican page with its lesser degree of precision makes the religious iconographic materials less clear, and less well organized into a unified over-all pattern. All three, however, can be subsumed under the term "conceptual" so far as artistic style is concerned.[22] The human figure is drawn as a series of parts—head, torso, arms, legs— united in additive fashion as though the design started with the head and the other parts of the body were added as quasi-independent units. The temples of codices Nuttall and Vaticanus B

[19] Walter Lehmann, "Les Peintures Mixtéco-Zapotèques et quelques documents apparentés," *Journal de la Société des Américanistes de Paris*, 2, Paris, 1905, p. 251.

[20] *Ibid.*, p. 253.

[21] *Codex Nuttall: Facsimile of an Ancient Mexican Codex Belonging to Lord Zouche of Harynworth, England, with an Introduction by Zelia Nuttall*, Cambridge, Massachusetts, 1902.

[22] Donald Robertson, *Mexican Manuscript Painting of the Early Colonial Period: The Metropolitan Schools*, New Haven, 1959, p. 23.

are similarly composed in a unitary fashion; the pyramids are in side elevation, but the staircase is a combination of elevation and side view. The temples proper are in elevation, but the support of their lintels on the side of the bird and the advancing figure have been elided so that they may make their offering uninterrupted by the wall of the temple.

The style of all three manuscripts is essentially one of a frame line with the areas defined by this line painted in flat washes, giving no illusion of three-dimensional form or light and shade. To a far greater extent than either the Nuttall or the Vatican manuscript, the Borgia Codex uses delicate linear patterns as enrichments over these areas of color. All three manuscripts are essentially two-dimensional and seem to avoid as much as possible representing extensions backward or forward into space. Representation of three-dimensional space is avoided too by the lack of a ground line or horizon line. The Nuttall and Borgia manuscripts come nearest to implying one, by the precision with which the feet are drawn, but the confusion of frame line and sandals in the Vatican manuscript is just that, a confusion, not a proper ground line. When one compares the Codex Borgia and its style to a Mixtec history manuscript such as Codex Nuttall, the similarities are thus striking.

The Codex Borgia and its somewhat less refined companion, Codex Vaticanus B, come from an undetermined place within what Vaillant called the Mixteca-Puebla culture area, although in a little-read footnote he classified the Borgia and Vatican codices as Mixtec within his larger Mixteca-Puebla culture, and contrasted them with the Aztec codices Telleriano-Remensis and Borbonicus.[23] Earlier classifications, made before his Mixteca-Puebla concept was published, are of less significance, and all classifications made since Caso's work establishing the history manuscripts as Mixtec are more important than those made before it.[24] Bernal calls attention to the fact that the culture of the Aztecs, and therefore their manuscripts, is in the main dependent upon the Mixtecs.[25] A recent synthetic study of Mexico by Frederick Peterson,

[23] Vaillant, *op.cit.*, ch. 9, n. 14, p. 291.
[24] For an early significant attempt at classification see Lehmann, *op.cit.*
[25] Bernal, *op.cit.*, pp. 8-9.

drawing upon Robert Barlow's knowledge in the area of manuscript studies, says, "The Mixtec (*sic*) codices were divided into
two groups: Borgia and Mixtec."[26] Franco in a recent article
agrees with the Peterson and Bernal allocation of a preponderant
role to the Mixtecs in Aztec civilization, but we think he goes
somewhat too far in identifying Codex Borbonicus and the Tonalamatl of Aubin as Mixtec, along with the Borgia Group.[27] He
points out that Covarrubias sought non-Mixtec traits in Aztec
culture and found few.[28] Covarrubias himself was a strong pro-
ponent of what can be called a pan-Mixtec interpretation of late
pre-Spanish Mexico, and attributed the ritual manuscripts to
the Mixtecs.[29]

The most important voice in any question concerning Mixtec
manuscripts is of course that of Caso, and his attribution is not
to the Mixtecs but rather to what he calls "*poblano-tlaxcalteca*."[30]
The basis of his attribution is threefold: the ritual manuscripts are
linked to the polychrome pottery of Cholula, near Tlaxcala; the
figure of Tezcatlipoca from the painted altar found at Tizatlán,
Tlaxcala (Pl. LI, 6) is similar to the same god in the ritual manuscripts (Pls. L, 3, 4; LI, 5); finally, this same god, so important
in the manuscripts with religious content, is almost entirely lacking in the Mixtec history manuscripts.[31]

Nicholson has recently proposed "cholultcca" to denominate
the Borgia style.[32] He did not give a detailed explanation or con-

[26] Peterson, *op.cit.*, p. 237.

[27] José Luís Franco C., "La Escritura y los códices," *Esplendor del México
antiguo*, Mexico, 1959, I, pp. 361-78.

[28] *Ibid.*, p. 377.

[29] Covarrubias, ch. 9, "The Mixtecs," pp. 293-311.

[30] Alfonso Caso, "Las Ruinas de Tizatlán, Tlaxcala," *Revista mexicana de
estudios históricos*, I, No. 4, Mexico, 1927, pp. 139-72, 4 plates showing frescos
restored. See also UNESCO, *Mexico: Pre-Hispanic Paintings* (Jacques Soustelle
preface; Ignacio Bernal introduction), New York, 1958, pls. x and xi for colored
photographs of the present state of the frescos.

[31] The bulk of Caso's demonstration is the iconographic study. His references
to Cholula pottery in connection with the manuscripts are more *en passant* than
Nicholson's (see next note). The pottery comparison is used more for understanding the iconography of the altars than in discussion of the manuscripts
themselves; however, the relationship is strongly implied by the article.

[32] Nicholson, "The Mixteca-Puebla Concept. . . ." For a contrary opinion to
the following explanation of the role of Cholula, see Henry B. Nicholson, "The

crete evidence but seems to rely upon the similarity of the manuscripts to Cholula polychrome wares (type not specified) and the fact that Cholula was a great emporium and religious center. We discuss the Cholula ceramics below. A possible definition of the Mesoamerican religious and political center as a concept is in order here. Cholula is like Rome during the Renaissance, a focus of pilgrimages from a widespread hinterland, yet Rome's main artists came from Florence, Perugia and other smaller towns in Italy. Rome itself produced few. Paris in the last century is an example of the political capital drawing upon a wide hinterland for artists, and acting as catalyst on artists from other parts of both France and Europe. We propose the parallels of Rome to Cholula and of Paris to Mexico-Tenochtitlán, as possible frameworks within which to place the problem of Mexican manuscript painting.

The ceramics of Cholula are among the richest of pre-Hispanic Mexico.[33] The polychrome wares have been studied extensively by Noguera, who treats them under several distinct rubrics, although they are sometimes carelessly lumped together as Cholula polychrome wares. His *"policroma firme,"* for instance, with its emphasis upon the linear patterns of the painter's brush and the use of parallel lines to condition areas of color in painterly fashion, is not so close to the manuscript style as what Noguera calls *"policroma laca,"* sometimes referred to as *"tipo códice."*[34] This codex-type pottery uses a style of painting almost identical to that of the manuscripts. Flat areas of color are applied with remarkable precision; none of the patterns due to brushwork found on most other Mexican pottery are to be seen.[35] The style uses a vocabulary of iconographic forms so close to the manuscripts that a

Use of the Term 'Mixtec' in Mesoamerican Archaelogy," *American Antiquity*, 26, No. 3, pt. 1, 1961, pp. 431-33.

[33] Eduardo Noguera is the main student of Cholula ceramics, and his investigations appear in the following publications: *La Cerámica arqueológica de Cholula*, Mexico, 1954; "Cerámica y estratigrafía," *Esplendor del México antiguo*, Mexico, 1959, 1, pp. 411-38; "Relaciones de Oaxaca con Puebla y Tlaxcala: culturas cholulteca, mixteca y zapoteca," *Revista mexicana de estudios antropológicos*, 16, Mexico, 1960, pp. 129-35.

[34] Noguera, *La Cerámica arqueológica de Cholula*; the polychrome wares are described on pages 120-42.

[35] *Ibid.*; see illustrations *passim*.

relationship is inescapable on both formal and iconographic grounds.

The reattribution of the manuscripts to the more northern area, and their removal from the Mixtec, runs counter to Vaillant and to other earlier writers. It results in breaking up a unity composed of Mixtec histories and Mixtec religious manuscripts which is in many ways a logical one, and it would associate them with parts of Mexico where less sophisticated and less refined styles dominate.

There are several possible explanations for the confusion that surrounds the study of ritual manuscripts. More recent work has been done on the history manuscripts on the basis of a firm knowledge of whence they came.[36] The ritual manuscripts, studied earlier in the century from the point of view of iconography and the religion of the area that Vaillant later called Mixteca-Puebla, have been treated in a somewhat indirect manner. The main pictorial information on native religion from the pre-Hispanic period is in these manuscripts. However, the main sources preserved to us from the sixteenth century, when knowledge of the religion was recorded either as a straight text or as glosses on a pictorial manuscript in European writing, are not from the Mixtec area but from the Náhuatl-speaking areas of Mexico. There is thus a tendency to interpret the Borgia Group from the point of view of early Colonial writers describing the religion of an area to the North of the Mixteca.[37]

Still another explanation lies in the fact that to understand the history manuscripts, the content of each by its very nature must be located in a more or less specific place as well as in a specific span of time; that is the stuff of which history is made. The religious manuscripts, on the other hand, describe something of a much less specific nature both in terms of time (religion notoriously changes slowly) and of geography. One can assume, as have Mexicanists since Seler, that there was a great unity of theology in the Mixteca-Puebla period. It is thus not so necessary for the understanding of the religious manuscripts to know where they came from nor when they were made. They do not record unique events taking place in time and space; rather they recount the

[36] See note 5 above.
[37] See especially the works of Seler cited above.

ever-recurring cycles of religious ritual, events that are repeated over and over again at various places but presumably at the same time in the ritual year.

One effect of this difference between history and ritual manuscripts is that the data of history, being a series of unique events, do not repeat themselves; thus they need to be specified in terms of persons, activity, place, and time. The history manuscripts record this kind of data for the history of the Mixtec area from the seventh to the late sixteenth century, or even into the seventeenth century when the history tradition dies out. Codex Bodley, for instance, records dated historical events from A.D. 692 to A.D. 1466, covering a span of 774 years on a strip of skin only slightly over twenty-one feet long, painted on both sides.[38] One of the characteristics of the history manuscripts is this concentration of information, and it dominates the dense, compressed layout of their pages. The religious manuscripts, on the other hand, order their materials in a more open and graphic format to help the reader follow their complexity, similar to the difference between a page from Toynbee and a page from the Roman Missal or Book of Common Prayer. This distinct organization of materials creates a difference in the gross appearance of the manuscripts sufficient, were only this aspect of pictorial style to be taken into account, to support another attribution of style for each type.

The fresco paintings of Tizatlán (Pl. LI, 6) are of more value in locating the Codex Borgia from the point of view of iconography than from that of artistic style, for the iconographic similarities are unquestionable. For example, Tezcatlipoca was a trickster god known from Toltec Tula by literary sources, and an important figure in the *tonalamatl* of both the Náhuatl and Borgia manuscripts. His name means "He of the Smoking Mirror," because his lost foot was replaced by a smoking mirror.[39] Tezcatlipoca in the Borgia manuscript and in the altar of Tizatlán exhibits significant style differences. The Borgia figures of the god (Pls. L, 3; LI, 5) show the more consistent and successful use of linear patterns to enrich areas of color applied within the outlines of the figures. This is apparent in such details as the feathers of

[38] Caso, *Interpretation of the Codex Bodley 2858*, pp. 79 and 81.
[39] Alfonso Caso, *La Religión de los Aztecas*, Mexico, 1936, p. 20.

the headdress, weapons, even feet and sandals. In details such as the ear plugs the superior readability of the Borgia forms is immediately clear. The Tizatlán artist, by drawing the mouth closed and omitting the teeth shown by the Borgia master, changes the whole expression of the face from one of determination to one approaching the "archaic smile." This difference is further reinforced by the rectangular shape of the eye and lowness of the headdress. By raising the knee bands too high he has created an area of confusion where the Borgia artist makes the articulation of the two parts of the leg quite clear. These differences indicate the Tizatlán figure as being derivative in comparison with the more completely understood and detailed Borgia figure. The Tizatlán painting might very well be copied from a manuscript model; the Borgia figure has the assurance of an original work.

The Cholula pottery implied as evidence for a Cholula or "cholulteca" attribution would be more convincing if we knew more about the source of the *policroma laca* wares of Cholula. The resemblance to manuscript painting is there and unmistakable. Noguera, the main authority on the Cholula pottery, however, admits that it is difficult to tell Cholula *laca* ware from Mixtec *laca* ware (Pl. XLIX, 2).[40] In this he is borne out by Paddock, currently working in the field.[41] Noguera, furthermore, seems to favor Cholula as the place of origin, but admits that it may have been introduced from the Mixtec area.[42] The Mixtec pottery which can usually be distinguished from Cholula pottery is also similar to the manuscripts in its designs. Association of the manuscripts with the pottery, then, can be used for either a Cholula or a Mixtec attribution. It is only by a study, not made as yet, of the details of the Mixtec and Cholula iconographic vocabularies, and a minute comparison with the studies by Seler of the iconography of the Codex Borgia, that results could be obtained which would be useful in this investigation. It is very possible that even such a detailed study would not give a conclusive answer. On the basis of information now available to us

[40] Noguera, *La Cerámica arqueológica de Cholula*, pp. 297 and 299; Noguera, "Relaciones de Oaxaca . . . ," pp. 129-30.
[41] Letter from Paddock to Robertson, July 24, 1961.
[42] Noguera, "Cerámica y estratigrafía," p. 419.

we can dismiss the pottery as a clue to provenience; it would work for both attributions and thus is not valid for either to the exclusion of the other.

Fresco paintings, unlike manuscripts, are not easily movable, although fresco artists like manuscript artists can migrate, taking their styles with them. The degree of sureness that we can apply to a fresco painting in this investigation, then, is greater than that to be had from those movable objects such as pottery, carved bones, cast gold, or mosaics. We have demonstrated that the Tizatlán fresco is of questionable value in locating the Borgia manuscript; we propose those of Mitla instead. There is agreement that the frescos of Mitla, on the opposite border of the Mixtec area, are Mixtec. Seler published versions of them which can still be checked against the remains to demonstrate the accuracy of his publication.[43] They differ from the manuscript painting in that they are red and white rather than using all the colors of the native palette, although this may be only underpainting, the overpainting having been of more fugitive colors.[44] They are similar in that they have a religious subject matter, which Seler has analyzed in detail, pointing out similarities between the murals and the Borgia manuscript itself. He finds in our illustration of the Mitla frescos (Pl. LII, 7), for instance, that Fragment 1 shows "the death god . . . whose face is painted like that of Tezcatlipoca, and who wears the stone knife as an ear plug and throws a lance with one hand."[45] In Fragments 6 to 9 he sees variants on the form of Quetzalcóatl as war and hunting deities. Fragment 10 is a similar series of variants upon the theme of the sun god. The content of the Mitla murals thus is like the Codex Borgia—religious. The forms are comparable to the Borgia manuscript as well.

[43] Eduard Seler, "Wall Paintings of Mitla: A Mexican Picture Writing in Fresco," *Bureau of American Ethnology, Bulletin 28: Mexican and Central American Antiquities, Calendar Systems, and History*, Washington, D.C., 1904, pp. 243-324, 3 plates of the frescos.

[44] Philip Dark with Joyce Plesters, "The Palimpsests of Codex Selden: Recent Attempts to Reveal the Covered Pictographs," *Actas del XXXIII Congreso Internacional de Americanistas, San José, 20-27 julio, 1958*, San José, 1959, 2, pp. 530-39. The authors show the history manuscripts use a red underpainting, are then colored, and the original red lines gone over with black.

[45] Seler, "Wall Paintings of Mitla . . . ," p. 318.

To look at what remains of the Mitla frescos is to see a manuscript design transferred to the wall and painted as though it were hung as a decorative frieze. The figures are finely drawn with the linear quality of Codex Borgia rather than the more painterly quality of the Tizatlán frescos. Large areas of the design are elaborated with linear patterns in details such as feathers, fur or costume, while double outlines are commonly used throughout. The world of forms is thus composed of the flat areas of the general Mixteca-Puebla conceptual style, with the added delicate and linear patterned enrichment of the Codex Borgia.

One feels that the absence from the history manuscripts of Tezcatlipoca, god of chance among the peoples of the Mixteca-Puebla culture, may very well be the result of one of his attributes—chance. An argument from an absence can always be answered by considering that the missing trait might very well have appeared in manuscripts not preserved to us. Another factor of importance is that the main bulk of material in the history manuscripts concerns people who once lived and acted; religious material is essentially extraneous or at most an addendum to the secular world of human beings. That one of the gods is not represented in such circumstances is not at all unlikely. In the list of names tabled by Caso in the recent edition of the Codex Bodley as few as five names of gods appear as the names of people.[46] The Mixtec pantheon of the people represented in Codex Bodley was certainly larger than this small listing would imply. Tezcatlipoca was one of the important gods of the *tonalamatl* as we know it from a wide variety of sources. The Mixtecs are assumed to use the *tonalamatl* also; therefore, Tezcatlipoca's absence from the history manuscripts is not an indication that the Mixtecs did not know him, but merely that he does not often appear in the history manuscripts.

The negative evidence from the absence of a trait, however, can be used in another context to throw light on the Borgia Group and its relation to the Náhuatl-speaking areas in the north. The extant religious pictorial manuscripts, the written sources of our knowledge of the *tonalamatl*, and the calendrics of native

[46] Caso, *Interpretation of the Codex Bodley 2858*, pp. 79-84.

America are rich in material from the north.[47] These sources, both pictorial and written, however, do not prepare us for the sophisticated elaboration and richness of the ritual content of the Borgia manuscript and its related Codex Vaticanus B. Seler had recourse to a "Venus Cycle" to interpret much of the content of our manuscripts, a Venus Cycle to which the Náhuatl sources make scant reference.[48] The difference between the religious content of Codex Borgia and of Codex Telleriano-Remensis is such that they can logically be related in terms of a major work from the seat of the religious cult and a simplified, almost adulterated version from a provincial center—the same sort of relationship we imply for the Tizatlán frescos and the Borgia manuscript.

Another point of similarity linking the Mixtec history manuscripts with the Borgia Group and also separating them from those coming from the area of Náhuatl speech is the fact that they are painted on animal skins. The tradition of manuscripts painted on skins seems, on the basis of the Mixtec histories, to have been a Mixtec tradition which continued even into the Colonial period. For examples, we have the map from the Relación of Amoltepec from the group of Relaciones Geográficas of 1579-81 and the Codex Gómez de Orozco, both from the Mixtec area and both continuing the Mixtec tradition into the sixteenth century.[49] It is of interest to note that all of the Borgia Group are painted on skins, while even the earliest of the Aztec manuscripts are on native paper including the Plano en Papel de Maguey, Codex Borbonicus and the Matrícula de Tributos.

There is a growing tendency in Mexican studies to divorce such things as art styles and archaeological divisions from linguistic associations. In many cases this clarifies issues; in some it tends to blur edges. For instance, a Náhuatl word for book is *amatl*, as in *tonalamatl* or Sun Book, and the Náhuatl word for paper

[47] See Caso, *La Religion* . . . ; and Vaillant, *Aztecs of Mexico*, chs. 10, "Religion," and 11, "Ritual."

[48] Seler Borgia Commentary, 1, pp. 238-80, 327-36; 2, pp. 1-75, 136-57. Seler Vaticanus B Commentary, pp. 87-121, 195-203.

[49] Donald Robertson, "The Relaciones Geográficas of Mexico," *Actas del XXXIII Congreso Internacional de Americanistas, San José, 20-27 julio, 1958*, San José, 1959, 2, p. 544, fig. 3; Alfonso Caso, *Interpretación del Códice Gómez de Orozco*, Mexico, 1954.

is also *amatl*. The usage of the Náhuatl speakers is thus conveyed to us by the language, and indicates that among them paper was the appropriate material for books. This is borne out by the fact that paper was used for the more natively-oriented books of the Colonial period. Colonial writers not only refer to paper, but the first books seen by the Spaniards at Cempoala on the Gulf Coast, according to Bernal Díaz, were of paper.[50] The use of skins seems to have been a more limited method of book production, and indications are that it was Mixtec.

The Náhuatl manuscript tradition in both Tlaxcala and Cholula has left no trace of being an important enough art in the pre-Conquest period to have produced the Codex Borgia. The main manuscript from this region, the Lienzo of Tlaxcala, indicates in the versions that have come down to us an art style very heavily acculturated and far removed from the tradition of the Codex Borgia, especially, considering that it is dated as early as ca. 1550.[51] In this respect we propose the Tlaxcala-Cholula area as bearing the same relation to the Mixtec area as did Mexico-Tenochtitlán to Texcoco: they were places where the manuscript tradition was newer and less important, and thus more susceptible to influence from Spanish art, than the cities with an older and more vital artistic tradition.[52] It is interesting to note in this connection that Ixtlilxóchitl says: ". . . there came from the provinces of the Mixtecs two nations [i.e. families] whom they called Tlailotlaques and Chimalpanecas . . . they were skilled in the art of painting and making histories. . . ."[53] Manuscript

---

[50] Bernal Díaz del Castillo, *Historia verdadera de la conquista de la Nueva España por Bernal Díaz del Castillo, uno de sus conquistadores, única edición hecha según el códice autógrafo*, Genaro García, ed., Mexico, 1904, 1, p. 126: "hallamos las casas de ydolos y sacrificaderos y sangre derramada, y Ensençios y de piedras, Con que sacrificavan, y plumas de papagayos, y muchos libros de su papel, cogidos a doblezes, Como a manera de paños de Cast.ᵃ"

[51] Charles Gibson, *Tlaxcala in the Sixteenth Century*, New Haven, 1952, p. 165.

[52] Robertson, *Mexican Manuscript Painting* . . . pp. 134, 143, and 196, discusses the Texcoco and Mexico-Tenochtitlán relationship.

[53] Fernando de Alva Ixtlilxóchitl, *Historia chichimeca*, Obras históricas, Mexico, 1892, 2, pp. 69-70. ". . . vinieron de las provincias de la Mixteca dos naciones que llamaban tlailotlaques y chimalpanecas . . . los cuales eran consumados en el arte de pintar y hacer historias. . . ."

painting came to Texcoco from the Mixteca; he does not mention Cholula or Tlaxcala.

Mixtec is the use of the interlocking "A" and "O" to indicate that one of the calendrical dates refers to the year, and not to a day in the calendar or the name of a person. This is found in Codex Borgia (Pl. LII, 8, page 71, top of main panel, left of center), the paintings of Mitla (Pl. LII, 7, Fragment 4, upper right), and the history manuscript Codex Nuttall (Pl. XLIX, 1, lower right corner). It also appears on pages 51 and 52 of Codex Borgia. This device for separating one of the important uses of the system of calendrical signs from the other usages is not known in the area of Náhuatl speakers during the Mixteca-Puebla period, although possible traces of it have been seen earlier at Teotihuacán and some Mayan sites. It is so common in the Mixtec manuscripts that it can be considered as one of the traits separating the Mixtec part of the Mixteca-Puebla culture from the other manifestations of this phase of pre-Columbian culture.

In summary we can say that this demonstration has placed the locus of origin of the Codex Borgia in the Mixtec area along with the Mixtec histories. It seems also probable, since Borgia and Vaticanus B are so close in content, that Vaticanus B also comes from the same area. This is another indication of the importance of the Mixtecs in the Mixteca-Puebla concept that Vaillant proposed, and gives support to the idea that, from the point of view of the art of late pre-Conquest Mexico, the Mixtecs were the source of the high art Cortés found in Mexico-Tenochtitlán when he visited that great metropolitan center. Mexico City drew upon its subject Mixtec city-states for artists and for artistic inspiration, rather than exporting artistic ideas and techniques to its southern provinces. Cholula was merely a station on the way.[54]

[54] Research support for this paper came from a grant of the American Council of Learned Societies which is gratefully acknowledged. I want also to thank John Glass for bibliographic help on the Borgia Group manuscripts and Professor R. M. Alford of the Newcomb College Art Department for making money available for complete kodachrome copies of several manuscripts from the Borgia Group.

THE GILT WOOD RETABLE IN PORTUGAL
AND BRAZIL

ROBERT C. SMITH

WOOD sculpture is as important to the churches of Portugal and of her former colony Brazil as marble is to those of Italy, or stone to those of France. Polychromed and gilded, wood was used for every aspect of the interior fitting—for the altars and their numerous accessories, for the pulpits and picture frames, for the railings of the chancel and for the columns of the choir loft at the entrance to the nave.[1] In many churches the very walls are sheathed in gilt oak and chestnut or tropical woods, in obedience to the Iberian ideal of a scintillating golden interior. Carried to extremes, the *talha dourada*, as gilt woodwork is called, impoverished the architecture of the Portuguese world in both a structural and a decorative sense. Where the woodcarving is badly executed or poorly composed, or where it has been lost, the interiors become lifeless or bare, for there is almost never any other element to compensate and take its place. In the case, however, of the relatively few great woodcarved interiors that have been preserved intact in both Portugal and Brazil, their effect is overwhelming and the beauty of the ensemble is unlike that of any other nation's art.

The history of the Portuguese wooden retable begins effectively in the reign of Manuel I (1495-1521), when Flemish woodcarvers built gigantic screens of Late Gothic decorative architecture behind the altar tables in most of the cathedrals and major churches. One great example survives in the Old Cathedral of Coimbra, executed by Olivier de Gand for the bishop D.

[1] For further accounts of the subject see: Lucio Costa, "A arquitectura Jesuitica no Brasil," *Revista do Serviço do Património histórico e artístico nacional*, v, pp. 9-104; Robert C. Smith, "The Portuguese Woodcarved Retable, 1600-1750," *Belas Artes,* II, 1950, pp. 16-57; Reynaldo dos Santos, *A escultura em Portugal*, Lisbon, 1950, II, pp. 48-73; Germain Bazin, "Morphologie du rétable portugais," Belas Artes, v, 1953, pp. 3-28 and *L'architecture religieuse baroque au Brésil*, Paris, 1956, I, pp. 227-329; George Kubler and Martin Soria, *Art and Architecture in Spain and Portugal and Their American Dominions, 1500-1800*, Baltimore, 1959, pp. 188-96.

Jorge de Almeida between 1498 and 1508. Stylistically the retable resembles that of the cathedral of Toledo, begun in 1498. It represents the closest approach to a common Hispanic style that the woodcarving of the Peninsula was to know during the period of three centuries from 1500 to 1800, for the Portuguese altarpieces soon developed marked characteristics that distinguish them from those of Spain.

In Portugal academic Renaissance retables of wood appear only at the close of the sixteenth century, for following the period of the Late Gothic examples there seems to have been an hiatus of several decades caused by a vogue for altarpieces of stone. These were the first retables with Renaissance ornament. It is not surprising that the character of this ornament is distinctly French, since Portuguese sculpture was dominated for a long period by a group of brilliant artists from Rouen headed by Nicolas Chanterène, who more than anyone else seems to have popularized in Portugal the use of classicizing decoration.

Some of the earliest wooden retables of Renaissance style are in the church of Sta. Maria do Castelo at Estremoz. They are extremely simple in design, based upon the edicule frame of Italian marble altarpieces, like those of the aisles of S. Giorgio Maggiore in Venice. In one transept retable the motif is twice repeated to produce a thin tall composition like those found in Mannerist architecture all over Europe at the close of the sixteenth century. Even more striking is the resemblance afforded by the more conventional three-bay retable of the high altar of the Augustinian church of N. S. da Graça in Coimbra, because of the Serlian doubling of the columns framing the panels occupied by paintings and free-standing statues. The Augustinian altarpiece seems to date from the early seventeenth century, for it contains decoration typical of that period, including sheaths of ornament on the first third of the shafts of the columns, friezes of angel heads in trailing foliage and swags of fruit framing the third story and pediment areas.

All of these elements can be seen in the two great retables which the wood sculptor Gaspar Coelho prepared about 1590-1600, by order of Frei Dom Amador Arrais, third bishop of Portalegre, for the high altars of the cathedral of Portalegre and the church of the Carmelite college in Coimbra (Pl. LIII, 1). Both, however, show a new composition in which a series of rectangular compartments is dominated by a heavy arch that completely locks the retable into the wall of the building. This produces a closed outline, and a feeling of interior outline movement, which were to characterize Portuguese retables for over a century and provide them with a compositional unity found nowhere else in Europe. In most of these examples of the early seventeenth century sculpture and painting are given almost equal importance in the panels of the columned compartments and in the predellas at the base of the first tier of the retable.

It was from such elements as these that the first great retables of the Jesuit churches of Portugal were fashioned. Beyond doubt the finest and best preserved is that of the high altar of S. Roque, the former church of the Company of Jesus in Lisbon. Dating from about 1625, it shows two new characteristics of the period, the use of a tondo or oculus in the top story, derived from Serlio, and the greater importance now given to sculpture than to painting.

Corresponding to this phase in the development of the metropolitan altarpieces are those of the destroyed Jesuit church of Rio de Janeiro, now at the church of the Santa Casa da Misericórdia of that city. Among the oldest surviving retables in Brazil, they are thought to have been exported from Portugal and are to a certain degree miniature versions of that of the high altar of S. Roque, the design of which also served as model for the principal retable of the church of the Jesuits in Évora.

The last altarpieces of the Renaissance style in the mother country, which date from approximately 1640 to 1675, are distinguished by the use of relief sculpture in the panels formerly occupied by paintings, and by the extension of the sheaths of ornament to the entire shaft of the column. The design of the frames of these new retables remains essentially the same as in the earlier seventeenth-century examples—a Serlian composition like that of the original section of the courtyard of the Louvre.

This can be well seen in an altarpiece of St. Anthony of ca. 1650-60 in the former Jesuit church, now New Cathedral, of Coimbra, which also shows the real innovation of this last phase of Renaissance style (Pl. LIII, 2). That is the freer and more naturalistic use of ornament on the shafts of the lower columns, where voluted leaf forms are set in vertical compositions of swinging movement that reveal the slow progress being made toward the Baroque. At the same time the style itself was moving slowly westward, under the auspices of the Company of Jesus. The retable of the high altar of the former Jesuit church at Funchal in Madeira, decorated in this style, is dated 1660; that of the former church of the order in Salvador, the old capital of Brazil (Pl. LIII, 3), appears to have been installed shortly before the inauguration of the building in 1672, at a time when the style reached the height of its development in Portugal in the decoration of the circular reliquary chapel of the Cistercian abbey of Alcobaça.

In the last quarter of the seventeenth century Portuguese woodcarving underwent a profound change. The old Renaissance patterns were abandoned in favor of a new style based on the use of a pseudo-Solomonic column decorated with grapes and acanthus leaves, cherubs and phoenix birds, symbolic of the Resurrection and the Eucharist. This was a free interpretation, which had already been evolved in Spain, of the columns of Bernini's baldachin of St. Peter's. During the 1680's in Portugal, and continuing until the second quarter of the eighteenth century, this type of column was effectively combined with concentric arches and huge supporting brackets to produce an impression of continuing vigorous movement throughout the frame of the typical Portuguese closed composition. Such grandiose altarpieces as those of S. Bento da Vitória in Oporto, which dates from the last years of the seventeenth century, and that of the Carthusian monastery of Évora, which was gilded by the brothers Abreu do Ó in 1729 (Pl. LIII, 4), offer convincing evidence that the new model is in many respects a Baroque version of the basic Renaissance form.

For a number of reasons the style can be called a National style. One reason is this very resemblance to the Renaissance retable formula as established by Gaspar Coelho at Portalegre. Another is the relation of the concentric arches to Romanesque and Manueline prototypes in Portugal (Alcobaça and Tomar,

1515). Furthermore, the new decoration of grapes, acanthus leaves, boys and birds, has strong antecedents in Manueline sculpture (Tomar, 1510) in stone, which had imitated similar ornament in Luso-Flemish woodcarving (Coimbra, retable of the Old Cathedral). Still another reason why the style can be called National is the great number of retables built in this manner, for there is scarcely an old parish church throughout the country which does not retain at least one example. A last compelling reason why the style should be called National is the fact that it coincided with the introduction in all major altarpieces of a niche containing a pyramid of pedestals for the exposition of the Sacrament; called a "throne," it is unknown outside Portuguese-speaking lands, but a constant of the religious art of those countries.

With the National or Early Baroque style is associated the new concept of a church covered entirely in gilt woodwork, an *igreja toda de ouro*, with a dado of blue and white pictorial tiles and a zone of paintings above to provide the essential contrast of polychromy. One of the finest examples is the small church of Sto. António in Lagos, decorated about 1700-20 (though with a painted ceiling of ca. 1769), where angelic figures link the concentric arches of the retable and provide three-dimensional counterparts of the painted angels of the vault, thus emphasizing the Baroque tenet of the unity of visual arts (Pl. LIV, 5).

In Brazil, where the new style was introduced at the moment of the local discovery of gold and at a time of increasing colonial prosperity, the golden interior became a feature of at least one wealthy church in each of the major coastal communities. At Recife in Pernambuco, the brothers of the Venerable Third Order of St. Francis employed in 1698 the sculptor António Santiago to carve part of the interior of their Capela Dourada, the pictorial tiles for which were imported from Lisbon in 1704 (Pl. LIV, 6). In all important aspects the chapel repeats the characteristics of Sto. António of Lagos.

From this time onward more specific relations between Portuguese and Brazilian *talha* can be cited. A good example is the gilt interior of the Benedictine church of Rio de Janeiro, carved by Alexandre Pereira and his assistants beween 1717 and 1733 on designs of Frei Domingos da Conceição (Pl. LV, 7). The latter appears to have taken as his model the magnificent decoration of the choir loft of the Benedictine church of Oporto, which Domingos Nunes and António de Azevedo Fernandes contracted to carve in 1704, and for which wood was imported from Brazil (Pl. LV, 8). It is easy to see the close relationship of the grouping of panels and the plume-like handling of the acanthus fronds in the two Benedictine interiors. The statues of illustrious members of the order which decorate the nave in Rio de Janeiro could well have been inspired by those, in the flatter style of the Renaissance, which were carved for the choir stalls of the Benedictine abbey of Tibães near Braga in northern Portugal in 1667 and gilded in 1706.

The largest and richest monument of the National style in the Portuguese-speaking world is the interior of the Franciscan church at Salvador in Brazil (Pl. LV, 9). This was begun about 1720 by local woodcarvers, at least one of whom, Frei Luiz de Jesus, was a member of the order. Since the work was prolonged for at least two decades, it is not surprising that parts of the *talha* incorporate elements not found in the National style woodcarving so far surveyed, elements which reveal the increasing influence of Italian baroque architecture and sculpture.

The change seems to have begun in Portugal about 1717, when the immensely rich King John V began to build the royal library at the University of Coimbra and the palace-convent of Mafra. From this time onward there was a large importation of statues, religious silver, and carved coaches from Rome, which influenced the woodcarved retables of the great churches of Lisbon. Volutes and other pedimental fragments were now added to the otherwise rigid profiles of their bonnets, as well as angels in dramatic attitudes. This produced an approximation to Roman marble altarpieces (retable of the convent of N. S. da Encarnaçao, Lisbon, and retable of Sta. Maria in Vallicella, Rome, 1608). The same resemblance can be seen between the gilt wood reliquary of the choir loft of the convent of Madre de Deus in Lisbon and the gilt bronze "Gloria" of the high altar of Sta. Maria in Campitelli in Rome of 1667. It should be noted, however, that the Portuguese piece employs the pseudo-Solomonic columns of the National style, while the Roman example displays the correct Berninian version.

The use of true Solomonic columns, in which the first third of the shaft is striated and garlands of flowers decorate the upper depressions, characterizes the great altarpieces with allegorical figures that constitute a Joanine style in the second quarter of the eighteenth century. Towering in their apses and dramatically crowned with statues, these impressive compositions are framed by tiers of richly gilded woodcarving on the lateral walls. Among the finest examples are the retable of the high altar of the Lisbon church of Paulistas, possibly the work of Bento de Fonseca Azevedo, and that of the chapel of the Third Order in S. Francisco at Évora. Characteristic of the heroic qualities of this new phase of woodcarving are the supporter figures of the brackets. From them rise the Solomonic columns and the High Baroque compositions of architectural forms and angelic figures that fill the side walls of the apse at the Paulistas, and cover the lower surface of the immense retable of the high altar of the cathedral of Oporto, designed in 1726 by the Lisbon sculptor Santos Pacheco (Pl. LV, 10). Smaller altarpieces by the Medallion Master at S. Miguel de Alfama in Lisbon (Pl. LVI, 11) show motifs closely resembling those used by the woodcarvers Manuel and Francisco Xavier de Brito, who decorated the church of S. Francisco da Penitência in Rio de Janeiro between 1726 and 1739 (Pl. LVI, 12), the first great example of the Joanine style in Brazil.[2]

In the colony the Italianate style flourished for half a century. At Salvador it produced a brilliant local school represented by João Moreira, who built the retable of the high altar of N. S. da Conceição da Praia in 1765 (Pl. LVI, 13). By this time, however, in Brazil as well as in Portugal, rococo motifs derived from both French and German models were being freely intermingled with Italianate Baroque elements.

The chief source of this new strain, which was to play a great part in the colonial art of Minas Gerais in Brazil, was the woodcarving of the area north of Oporto, the Alto Minho. Here, as early as 1746, the architect Manuel Pinto Vilalobos had de-

---

[2] Bazin ("L'architecture . . . ," p. 298) would identify this woodcarving with Manuel de Brito.

signed the key Rosary altarpiece which Domingos Magalhães carved for the church of S. Domingos in Viana do Castelo. The almost aquatic plasticity of shifting forms enriched with asymmetrical passages of shells and volutes, of this retable, as well as its columns with straight shafts entwined with frilled ribbons, are all repeated in a fuller scale in the grand anonymous interior of the Benedictine church of Tibães (Pl. LVI, 14). From this *talha gorda* the gifted Mineiro sculptor António Francisco Lisboa, called Aleijadinho, derived elements which, rendered more delicate, he combined in a highly original way, in his two major retables, with decorative schemes still Joanine in flavor. In the first of these, for the high altar of the church of the Venerable Third Order of St. Francis in S. João d'El-Rei (1781), he created a new unity between the retable and the vault of the apse, which a decade later he greatly dramatized in the chancel of the Third Order of St. Francis at Ouro Preto (Pl. LVI, 15).

Meanwhile, in Lisbon, the woodcarved retable was gradually losing the impulse of creativity under the impact of Luigi Vanvitelli's chapel of St. John the Baptist, imported from Rome and set up in the Jesuit church of S. Roque in 1749. In their efforts to imitate in polychromed gilt wood the columns of lapis lazuli, the marble revetments and porphyry plaques of this taste-changing monument of the new Italian classicism, the court woodcarver Silvestre de Faria Lobo and his followers developed a prodigious technique and effects of extreme elegance. These scarcely compensate, however, for the increasing dryness of their imitative effects, which paved the way toward Neoclassicism, both at home and in Brazil.

In summary, the history of the flowering of the gilt wood retable in Portugal and Brazil can be subdivided in this fashion: 1) a Renaissance phase extending from ca. 1520-1680; 2) an Early Baroque phase, here called the National style, from ca. 1680-1725; 3) a Full Baroque period, called the Joanine style, from ca. 1720-50; 4) a Rococo phase from ca. 1740-1800.

LA ARQUITECTURA EN MADERA DE LAS MISIONES DEL PARAGUAY, CHIQUITOS, MOJOS Y MAYNAS

MARIO J. BUSCHIAZZO

CUANDO en 1540 se fundó la Compañia de Jesús, ya habia comenzado la obra evangelizadora de los indios americanos gracias a los frailes franciscanos, domínicos y agustinos, especialmente en México y Perú. Pero acaso como consecuencia del espíritu más combativo que desde su fundación caracterizó a los jesuitas y al entusiasmo que la nueva organización despertó, ese atraso cronológico fué compensado con un empuje que se tradujo rapidamente en una obra misional amplísima. A fines del siglo XVI ya estaban practicamente fundados los principales Colegios jesuiticos de Hispanoamérica, muchos de los cuales fueron el origen de Universidades que aun hoy subsisten, como las de San Marcos de Lima, Chuquisaca en Bolivia o Córdoba en la Argentina. Tomando como base de operaciones estas fundaciones urbanas, rapidamente se lanzaron a la obra de catequización de los indígenas, fundando misiones que fueron verdaderas avanzadas civilizadoras en zonas totalmente salvajes y desconocidas.

La cantidad de establecimientos asi fundados fué enorme y su estudio escapa a los límites y objetivos de este trabajo, pero aunque sea brevemente debo mencionar ciertos grupos misionales que constituyeron un verdadero sistema o cadena de establecimientos, no siempre ligados entre si pero de todos modos vertebrados por una idéntica organización. Esos grupos eran, de norte a sur, los del Orinoco en el límite actual de Colombia y Venezuela, Meta (Colombia), Maynas (Perú), Mojos (Bolivia), Chiquitos (Bolivia), y Paraguay (Paraguay, Argentina y Brasil). Aun cabría agregar a estos grupos otros más, como los de Darien, México y Sonora, integrando así el sistema que llegó a abarcar practicamente toda la América española. Pero como solo poseo documentación relativa a los grupos meridionales me concreto a mencionarlos.

Si se observa la ubicación de estas misiones sobre un mapa de América del Sur (Pl. LVII, 1) es fácil notar que todas ellas estuvieron situadas en las fuentes de los grandes rios—Meta, Orinoco, Marañon, Beni, Paraguay, Paraná y Uruguay—en tierras cuya altitud no pasa de los 500 metros y a veces mucho menos, como por ejemplo en Mojos y Chiquitos, donde ocuparon zonas bajas y anegadizas que hicieron y aun hoy hacen muy dificil la comunicación. Logicamente, se trata de tierras muy fértiles en las que los grandes bosques dominan, o por lo menos se encuentran lo relativamente cerca como para proporcionar facilmente abundante madera de construcción.

Prescindiendo de las misiones del Meta y Orinoco—que dejo de lado por falta de documentación y conocimiento directo— observamos que tres de los cuatro grandes grupos de misiones se recuestan sobre las ultimas estribaciones orientales de los Andes, formando una especie de arco o media luna, exactamente donde la topografia señala el fin de la gran zona rocosa andina y el comienzo de la llanura o meseta brasílida. El cuarto grupo, o sea el paraguayo, está ubicado estrategicamente en otra zona de deslinde, donde terminan las tierras rojas paulistanas y comienzan las tierras negras, de riquísimo "humus," frontera o borde señalado por las cataratas del Iguazú.

Conocido es el sentido centrífugo y expansivo de la colonización portuguesa, que les llevó rapidamente a pasar por alto el Tratado de Tordesillas y adentrarse en pleno corazón de América, tratando de llevar sus fronteras hasta las fuentes mismas de los grandes rios que surcan el territorio que hoy constituye el Brasil. Continuamente en la documentación que he consultado sobre las misiones jesuiticas[1] se habla de choques entre indios misioneros y portugueses, ya sea por que estos trataban de apoderarse de ellos para venderlos como esclavos, o simplemente porque pretendían llevar mas adelante sus fronteras. Puede afirmarse que toda las misiones que estuvieron situadas al borde de un gran rio tenían en la margen opuesta una población portuguesa, las mas de las veces un fortin o guarnición militar. De no haber existido esas misiones, los portugueses hubiesen llevado su avance

[1] Archivo General de la Nacion, Buenos Aires, y Archivo Jesuitico de San Miguel.

hasta plena zona andina. En este sentido aun no se ha estudiado bien ni se ha hecho debida justicia a la obra defensiva de las fronteras que desarrollaron los jesuitas españoles.[2]

Las misiones de Mojos y Chiquitos ocupaban las zonas mas bajas y anegadizas, a tal punto que desde septiembre hasta abril toda comunicación quedaba interrumpida, y aun en los meses restantes la vinculación de Mojos con el resto del mundo se hacia siempre a través de Chiquitos, y de aqui por Santa Cruz de la Sierra, a Juli, donde los jesuitas tenian un centro importantísimo, con tres iglesias, colegio, seminario, imprenta, etc. La comunicación entre las misiones de Chiquitos y las del Paraguay era tambien dificil, pues atravesar en diagonal el Chaco era empresa titánica. Habitualmente se hacía en forma de angulo recto, yendo de Chiquitos a la altura del paralelo 18 hasta el rio Paraguay, y luego por éste aguas abajo hasta Asuncion o viceversa. Tan solo al final del periodo jesuitico, es decir poco antes de la expulsión de éstos, el Padre Juan Bautista Neumann descubrió un camino en linea directa, pasando por esa razon a depender las misiones de Chiquitos de la Provincia del Paraguay, habiendolo sido siempre de la del Perú.

Las tribus indígenas de los cuatro grupos que estudiamos pertenecian a razas diversas, principalmente guaraníes, chiquitos, baures, mojos, pebes y gíbaros o jeberos. En realidad eran una mezcla de muchas tribus, y tan solo las misiones del Paraguay agrupaban a una raza única: la guaraní, más dócil e inteligente que el resto de las tribus sudamericanas. Pero no solo hubo guaraníes en las misiones del Paraguay, pues se extendieron por el Chaco llegando hasta las regiones ocupadas por las misiones del Beni. Así lo afirma D'Orbigny, quien en varios pasajes de su famoso diario de viaje relata su sorpresa al ver que pudo hablar guaraní con muchos de los indios de Chiquitos y Mojos. Textualmente dice "me habia llamado la atencion el lenguaje del escaso número de cruceños que habia visto, encontrandoles el acento, los modales y hasta los rasgos de los habitantes de Corrientes. . . . creí reconocer a los guaraníes. Sin embargo, ? Cómo suponer que esa nacion habitaba al pié de los Andes, tan lejos de su cuna?

[2] Constantino Bayle, S. J., *Las Misiones, defensa de las fronteras. Mainas*, Madrid, 1951.

Impaciente por fijar mis ideas acerca de esa curiosa analogía, me arriesgué a decirles algunas palabras en guaraní. Me contemplaron estupefactos, no concibiendo sin duda, que un extrangero conociera su lengua; me respondieron y tuve la certeza de que son verdaderos guaraníes, así como todos los chiriguanos de la provincia de Cordillera."[3] Mas adelante afirma que todos los indios de la misión franciscana de Bibosi "hablan el guaraní puro,"[4] comentando luego que "ese descubrimiento era para mi muy importante, puesto que me demostraba que los guaraníes llevaron sus migraciones hasta esas comarcas, mucho antes de la llegada de los chiriguanos, cuya época es conocida (1541)."[5] Tambien en Mojos halló D'Orbigny influencias guaraníes, pues dice que al llegar a Trinidad de Guarayos "los habitantes huyeron, pero como les hablé en su lengua (en guaraní), se tranquilizaron y me ofrecieron cuanto poseían."[6]

Lo evidente es que los indios de las misiones de Chiquitos, Mojos y Maynas no fueron tan dóciles y despiertos como los del Paraguay, ya que solamente en estas misiones púdieron desarrollar ese sistema de pseudo-gobierno democrático, basado en Platon,[7] con el cual lograron dar a los indígenas una relativa libertad.

En cuanto al número y advocación de las misiones que estudiamos, varió segun las épocas debido a que muchas fueron trasladadas, otras abandonadas, o en otros casos se fundaron nuevas. Pero tomando como base las que existían cuando sucedió la expulsión (1767), hallamos las siguientes misiones de acuerdo al estudio del Carrez:[8] En Chiquitos: San Ignacio (capital), San Francisco Javier, San Rafael, San José, San Juan Bautista, La Concepción, San Miguel, Santiago, Santa Ana, Santo Corazon de Jesús; En Mojos: San Pedro (capital), Loreto, Trinidad, San Javier, Santa Ana, Exaltacion, San Ignacio, San Borja, Reyes, Magdalena, Con-

---

[3] Alcide D'Orbigny, *Voyage dans l'Amerique Meridionale*, Paris, 1844, III, pp. 1088-89. (Hay edicion en castellano, Buenos Aires, 1945.)

[4] *Ibid.*, III, p. 1105.

[5] *Ibid.*, III, p. 1106.

[6] *Ibid.*, IV, p. 1302.

[7] Jose Manuel Peramas, S. J., *La República de Platon y los guaraníes*, Buenos Aires, 1946.

[8] P. Lud. Carrez, *Atlas Geographicus Societatis Jesu*, Paris, 1900.

cepción, San Simon, San Martin, San Joaquin, San Nicolás; En Maynas: San Borja (capital), San Luis, Santa Teresa, Santiago, Jaen de Bracamoros, Cumba, Lemeibamba, Chachapoyas, Concepción de Geberos, Laguna, Santa Bárbara, Santa Cruz, San Miguel, San Ignacio de Pebas, San Joaquin, Quematé, Guacuraté, San Pablo, Nuestra Señora de las Nieves de Yurimaras. Las del Paraguay sumaban treinta, distribuidas entre la Argentina, el Paraguay y el Brasil actuales. Omito su nómina por ser muy conocida. La capital era Candelaria, y a los efectos eclesiásticos las misiones situadas sobre el rio Paraná dependían de Asuncion y las del rio Uruguay de Buenos Aires, si bien en la realidad todas estaban supeditadas a la capital del virreinato por que el puerto de Buenos Aires era la salida natural y única de sus productos agropecuarios.

No voy a entrar en mayores detalles sobre la forma y traza de todas estas misiones por que nada nuevo podría agregar a lo mucho que se ha publicado sobre el tema.[9] Pero sí quiero referirme a dos anomalías que aparecen en las misiones de Concepción de Mojos y San José de Chiquitos (Pl. LVIII, 2, 3). En la primera de ellas la plaza forma un octógono en lugar del habitual cuadrado, formado por el templo y colegio, mas dos largos edificios de destino desconocido y cuatro pequeñas capillas que constituyen los lados menores del octógono. Aqui es donde radica la diferencia con las misiones guaraníes, que no tenían dichas capillas. Al estar tan cerca de la iglesia y precisamente en la plaza, todo hace suponer que se trataba de algo asi como las capillas-posas tan utilizadas en México durante el siglo XVI.[10] Tambien aparecen estas pequeñas capillas en la plaza de San José de Chiquitos, aunque en ubicación menos simétrica. Asimismo la Purísima Concepción de Baures tenía esas capillas, pues D'Orbigny decia que "la plaza, bastante grande, está dotada de capillas en sus cuatro esquinas."[11] En otro párrafo aclara mas explicitamente el viajero

[9] Entre muchas otras obras con abundante bibliografia sobre las misiones del Paraguay, citamos especialmente P. Pablo Hernandez, S. J., *Organizacion social de las doctrinas guaraníes de la Compañia de Jesús*, Barcelona, 1913, y Diego Angulo Iñiguez, *Historia del Arte Hispano-Americano*, Barcelona, 1945-56.

[10] George Kubler, *Mexican Architecture of the Sixteenth Century*, New Haven, 1948.

[11] D'Orbigny, *op.cit.*, IV, p. 1313.

francés que en San José de Chiquitos había "en los cuatro angulos de la plaza capillas destinadas a las procesiones."[12] Si a estos casos agregamos los ya conocidos de Santiago del Paredon, Copacabana,[13] Tomave y Tahua,[14] será preciso reconocer que las capillas-posas tambien se usaron en America del Sur, a modo y semejanza de las utilizadas en México. Precisamente en Concepción de Mojos el sistema aparece completo, pues además de las cuatro posas situadas en los angulos de la plaza, existe otra, llamada de la Misericordia, destinada a velar los cadáveres.

En el plano de San José de Chiquitos levantado por D'Orbigny aparece la torre situada en el eje del patio, a mitad de distancia entre la iglesia y la residencia. Esta ubicación, insólita, asi como el uso de bóveda de ladrillo en los edificios principales de la misión, hace sospechar que se trata de obras posteriores al extrañamiento de los jesuitas, puesto que en el inventario levantado cuando la expulsión solo se menciona "una iglesia con sus paredes de adobe y el techo de teja."[15] Sin embargo, ya a mediados del siglo XVIII trataron los propios indios de hacer nuevo templo abovedado, en parte por sentirse capaces y en parte porque ya era dificil lograr maderas de las dimensiones requeridas para hacer un esqueleto portante. En efecto, un Memorial del Padre Lizoain, del 28 de agosto de 1752 dice que "los Indios principales de el Pueblo [de San José de Chiquitos] instan que se les permita trabajar la casa de el Padre con cal y piedra. . . que no se hallan ya palos proporcionados para fabricar con madera sino con mucha dificultad y distancia."[16]

Veamos ahora el aspecto a mi juicio mas interesante en la arquitectura de estas misiones, a saber, la utilizacion de un sistema de esqueleto de madera que posibilitó la erección de templos

[12] *Ibid.*, IV, p. 1180.

[13] Diego Angulo Iñiguez, *op. cit.*, III, p. 489.

[14] Martin S. Noel, *Rutas historicas de la arquitectura virreinal altoperuana,* Documentos de Arte Colonial Sudamericano publicados por la Academia Nacional de Bellas Artes, Cuaderno V, Buenos Aires, 1948.

[15] Francisco Javier Brabo, *Inventarios de los bienes hallados a la expulsión de los Jesuitas y ocupación de sus temporalidades por Decreto de Carlos III*, Madrid, 1872, p. 529.

[16] Memorial del Padre Lizoain, Archivo General de la Nacion, Misiones de Chiquitos, legajo 54, Buenos Aires.

enormes, fáciles de construir, funcionales y perfectamente adaptados a las necesidades de las misiones y al clima torrido.

El Padre Cardiel nos ha dejado una minuciosa descripción del sistema empleado, que no obstante ser un documento relativamente conocido, voy a transcribir in extenso por su importancia. Dice asi: "Todos estos edificios se hacen de diverso modo que en Europa, por que primero se hace el tejado, y después las paredes. Clávanse en tierra grandes troncos de madera, labrados a azuela. Encima de ellos se ponen los tirantes y soleras; y encima de estas las tijeras, llaves, latas y tejado; y después se ponen los cimientos de piedra, y 2 o 3 palmos hasta encima de la tierra, y de ahi arriba es la pared de adobes, quedando los troncos o pilares, que aqui llaman horcones, en el centro de la pared, cargando todo el tejado sobre ellos y nada sobre la pared. Esto se hace por no haberse hallado cal en todo este territorio, pues aunque hay piedra en todas partes, toda es arenisca o de fierro, inútil para cal. . . . Las iglesias, como casas de Dios, son la fabrica principal en todos los pueblos. Son todas muy capaces, como catedrales de Europa, porque como no hay más que una en cada pueblo, es preciso que sea capaz de tantos millares de personas que los dias de fiesta entran por lista a sermon y misa. Son de tres naves y dos hay de cinco. El modo de fabricarlas es éste. Córtanse en las menguantes de invierno unos arboles muy altos y gruesos llamados Tajivos, u otros llamados Urundey, mas fuertes que el roble de Europa, para pilares u horcones; y otros de cedro y sus especies y de laurel, para tijeras y latas y tablas. Secos ya, se traen al pueblo cada horcon con 25 o 30 pares de bueyes. Hácense en las naves de enmedio y en donde ha de ser la pared, unos hoyos de 9 pies de profundo y 12 o 14 de circulo. Enlósanse bien, y con máquinas de arquitectura meten dentro los horcones labrados ya en forma de columna, o cuadrados para después aforrarlos con tablas de cedro pintadas y doradas. Los 9 piés que quedan dentro están sin labrar, y aun con parte de las raices del arbol para mayor fortaleza, y se quema esta parte paraque mas resista a la humedad."[17]

[17] P. Guillermo Furlong, *José Cardiel S. J., y su Carta-Relación de 1747*, Buenos Aires, 1953, pp. 154-55. Otra variante de la descripción del sistema constructivo misionero la hace el propio P. Cardiel en P. Pablo Hernandez, *op.cit.*, ii, p. 522.

En la mayoria de las misiones de indios guaraníes, sin perjuicio de seguir utilizando el esqueleto de madera, los muros se hicieron de piedra en lugar de adobe. Asi, en San Ignacio Miní, Argentina (Pl. LIX, 4), aun pueden verse las paredes del templo, de asperón rojo, con las canaletas donde estuvieron empotrados los troncos, desaparecidos a raiz del incendio de la misión. Cuando se construyó el templo aun no se habia descubierto la cal en esas zonas, por lo cual el uso de un esqueleto portante era de rigor.

Desde luego, no hay dudas de que este fué el sistema utilizado en las misiones del Paraguay, Chiquitos y Mojos, hasta que en las primeras se acometió la obra de nuevos templos, totalmente abovedados y de piedra (Pl. LIX, 5). Como no he visitado personalmente las misiones de Maynas, suponía que tambien en ellas se habia seguido idéntica técnica, hasta que el hallazgo del Diario del Padre Manuel Ugarte, S. J., vino a corroborar mi sospecha. En efecto, refiriéndose a la misión de San Joaquin de Omaguas, escribía el Padre Ugarte: "Habia caido un par de años antes, el 5 de septiembre de 1752, la iglesia con un vendaval, pero con la providencia de Dios pudo el P. Martin Iriarte sacar el Sagrario con el Sacramento (obra del P. Samuel Fritz) y desencajar el hermoso retablo grande con columnas, todo de cedro y plateadas y pintadas (trabajo del Hermano Jorge Vinterer, que a su modelo hizo mayor el célebre del Colegio Máximo de Quito, que llevó La Condamine dibujado a Paris). Por esto, se suplía con una casa para la misa y rezo, y estaba el Padre haciendo una nueva iglesia capaz, de tapiales de vara de grueso, y cuando yo llegué, trabajaba ya hacia el remate del altar y sacristía (a causa de dar la fachada al Oriente y el frente al Marañon) se aseguraba con estantes de palo fuerte en medio, y en todas partes se cavaron cimientos de dos varas con tierra y cascajo bien golpeados. Tenía por todo su cuerpo la iglesia estantes [columnas o pilares] gruesos, derechos, y altos de 15 varas, que hacian como tres naves y afirmaban la techumbre con traviesas de cedro. Habia seis ventanas vistosas con barandillas torneadas, una puerta principal y dos laterales, todas de a dos postigos y de cedro labrado y por decirlo

---

Una tercera descripción, concordante con las dos anteriores, es la del P. Antonio Sepp, S. J., *Viagem as Missões Jesuiticas e Trabalhos Apostólicos*, Sao Paulo, 1943, p. 211.

de una vez, con lo que después se añadió, vistosísima, pues se puso un retablo lucido en el presbiterio. A este se hizo su tumbado de tablas de manapanba, blancas y fuertes, que se blanquearon mas con yeso. . . . Tenia delante [de la fachada] su alpendio o pórtico que recorría el ámbito de la iglesia a lo largo como 16 varas y de ocho de ancho, cerrado con tapia francesa (bahareque doble) ancha de dos cuartas (Pl. LIX, 6)."[18]

Y llegamos con esto a uno de los puntos capitales de nuestro trabajo: ? debe considerarse este sistema constructivo como una reedición de prácticas tectónicas de uso corriente en otras partes del mundo, o es una creación americana? Si nos atenemos escuetamente al uso de un esqueleto de madera, es obvio decir que su uso es muy anterior y común. Sin remontarnos a épocas muy remotas, cabe recordar que el uso de entramados de madera fué frecuentísimo en la arquitectura civil medieval. Pero si nos detenemos a analizar ciertos detalles, parecería que nos encontramos frente a una solución local, orginada por la abundancia de grandes arboles y la carencia de cal, como bien lo aclara el P. Cardiel. Al no poder levantar muros suficientemente consistentes como para soportar la techumbre, la armazón de madera debió transformarse en un verdadero esqueleto portante, reduciendose el muro a un simple elemento de cerramiento. Por otra parte, no olvidemos que las columnas eran en realidad árboles íntegros con sus raices calcinadas, cosa que creo que no se usó en Europa. La minucia con que describen el sistema los Padres Cardiel, Ugarte y Sepp, y el Obispo Martí de Venezuela, parecería confirmar que se trata de algo novedoso. Aun más, en 1732 el Padre Antonio Sepp, S. J., escribió un Tratado-Reglamento con advertencias referentes al gobierno temporal de los pueblos, y en él se refiere nuevamente al sistema de estructura de madera y da consejos sobre la calidad y tipos a usar: "para los postes, Yrundaly [Urunday], llamado quiebrahachas y Tuxifo. Los cedros se usan para todas las cosas que han de tener oro y plata."[19]

[18] P. José Jouanen, S. J., *Historia de la Compañía de Jesús en la antigua provincia de Quito*, Quito, 1941-43, pp. 511-12.
[19] El Padre Antonio Sepp, S. J., escribió en 1732 un Reglamento para las obras temporales de las misiones, que no ha sido editado, y cuyo original está en poder del historiador brasilero D. Alberto Lamego, segun informa Wolfgang Hoffmann Harnisch en Padre Antonio Sepp, *op.cit.*, p. 40.

Ignoro si el esqueleto de madera se usó en las misiones del Meta y Orinoco, aunque la similitud de condiciones del medio físico hacen sospechar que sí, en cuyo caso estaríamos en presencia de un verdadero sistema americano. No debemos olvidar que en casi toda América (con excepción de la zona andina) los indios construian sus viviendas haciendo descansar el techo sobre "horcones" de madera, cerrando luego el rancho o bohio con muros de tapia, morrillos, "chorizo" de barro, encañado, "bahareque," etc.

En las misiones paraguayas, a juzgar por los escasos restos y la única foto antigua que nos ha llegado, esos enormes troncos burdamente desvastados se revestían con tablas en toda su altura, dándoles aspecto de pilar de sección cuadrada. En cambio en las de Mojos y Chiquitos se prefirió tallar directamente los troncos con estrias helicoidales, que desde luego no respetaban los cánones viñolescos. Por el contrario, había una absoluta libertad formal, de tal modo que en un mismo templo unas columnas tenian gran cantidad de espiras, otras muy pocas, e incluso no faltó alguna con estrias verticales. D'Orbigny dice que se dió amplia libertad a cada jesuita "para variar la arquitectura de su iglesia o de su colegio. Templos dignos de nuestras ciudades [de Europa] fueron levantados por las manos de los indios. Transformados en columnas, unas retorcidas y cargadas de ornamentos esculpidos con gusto, otras mas sencillas, los mas bellos arboles de las selvas sostuvieron magníficos frontispicios o la amplia armazon del cuerpo de las fábricas."[20]

Hace ya muchos años observé la similitud existente entre el sistema jesuitico misionero y algunas iglesias de Panamá (San Francisco de Veragüas, Penonomé, Las Toblas, Parita) aunque solo se trataba de un tímido avance de opinión por falta de informacion directa. Estudios recientes—especialmente por parte del Arquitecto Graziano Gasparini—han venido a corroborar esta presunción. El citado investigador menciona varias iglesias venezolanas construidas con la misma técnica (Caigüa, Santa Cruz, Pecaya, Rio Tocuyo, El Carmen de Maracaibo, Cariaco), haciendo notar que todas ellas se levantaron en zonas donde

[20] D'Orbigny, *op.cit.*, IV, pp. 1256-57.

abunda la madera y se carece de piedra, y a veces hasta de tierra apta para fabricar buenos ladrillos. . . .[21]

Sea por herencia indígena, por creacion jesuitica, o una simple solucion determinada por el medio físico y la necesidad, lo cierto es que esa arquitectura de estructura maderera dominó en todas las zonas cercanas a las misiones, llegando en mi patria hasta Santa Fé.[22] En esta ciudad se levantó el templo de San Francisco, construido por indios abipones, cuyo magnífico techo de artesonado y boveda baida en el crucero descarga sobre gruesos pilares de madera empotrados en muros de tapiería (Pl. LX, 7, 8). Es verdad que en este caso se trata de una obra mucho mas rica que la de las misiones, en la que se confunden aportes indígenas con técnicas mudéjares, pero en cuanto al esqueleto portante vemos que se repite la técnica jesuitica. Otro tanto cabe decir de la "Estanzuela de los Echagüe" (Pl. LX, 9), simpática casona de campo con techo a cuatro aguas y amplia galeria perimetral, que se encuentra en Guadalupe, muy cerca de la cuidad de Santa Fé.

Si remontamos el rio Paraná veremos que en la ciudad de Corrientes hubo hasta no hace muchos años una arquitectura popular en la que el uso de los pilares, dinteles y zapatas e incluso tejas de madera de palma le dió notable color regional. Hoy en dia han desaparecido todas esas casas, pero aun se conserva el claustro del convento de San Francisco, con idéntica arquitectura maderera. Y si seguimos hacia el norte, internandonos en el Paraguay, observaremos que muchas de las iglesias parroquiales esparcidas por la campiña son verdaderas réplicas de las iglesias misioneras. Tales son las de Yagüaron (Pl. LXI, 10), Caacupé, Piribebuy, Valenzuela, etc. Todas ellas fueron construidas bajo la direccion de franciscanos con posterioridad a la expulsion de los jesuitas, pero evidentemente los indios recordaban los procedimientos jesuiticos y tenían a la vista los templos misioneros, aun no destruidos en esa época, lo que explica esa reedición tan fiel. Algunas de esas iglesias, como la de Capiatá (Pl. LXI, 11), son tan parecidas a las que describen los inventarios de Francisco Javier Brabo que cuesta

[21] Graziano Gasparini, *Templos colonials de Venezuela*, Caracas, 1959.
[22] Mario J. Buschiazzo, *La arquitectura colonial en Hispano-America*, edicion cuatrilingüe de la Sociedad Central de Arquitectos, Buenos Aires, 1940.

creer que se está en presencia de obras franciscanas y posteriores a la pragmática de Carlos III.

No se detiene en el Paraguay esa influencia misionera. La ciudad de Santa Cruz de la Sierra, en Bolivia, ofrece las mismas características tanto en su arquitectura religiosa como en la civil. La relación que en 1793 hacía Francisco de Viedma y que podría servir para una descripción actual, era como si se estuviese refiriendo a cualquier población paraguaya o correntina: "las casas principales se hallan en el centro de la ciudad; sus paredes son de adobe, unas cubiertas con teja, otras con una especie de canal de tres varas de largo y una cuarta de ancho, que labran de la madera de palma, y estando en sazon dura hasta doce y más años."[23] Las desaparecidas iglesias de La Compañia, La Merced, San Andrés (Pl. LXII, 12, 13), La Misericordia, Buenavista, Ayacucho, y Santa Rosa del Sara (ésta última a 22 leguas de Santa Cruz de la Sierra) tenian todas ellas estructuras de madera como las descriptas, techo a dos vertientes, muros de adobe, etc. Solo se conserva, por milagro, la iglesia de San Roque, que repite el tipo misionero paraguayo. Para mayor similitud, todas las casas de Santa Cruz de la Sierra tienen en su frente una amplia galeria o corredor soportado por pilares de madera, de tal modo que se puede recorrer el perimetro de cada manzana a cubierto del sol o de las lluvias tropicales, tal como dijimos que era la ciudad de Corrientes hasta no hace muchos años. Ya lo habia observado D'Orbigny cuando al describir la ciudad de Santa Cruz de la Sierra decía que "las viviendas solo tienen una planta baja; todas cuentan con galerias exteriores destinadas a protegerlas de la lluvia. . . . asi como en Corrientes, suelen estar cubiertas de troncos o de palmera corondai, aunque ya se empieza a construir de tejas cocidas."[24]

Dejemos ahora el estudio de la parte estrictamente arquitectónica para referirnos a algunso aspectos de las otras artes que se practicaban en las misiones. Es una notable y feliz coincidencia que precisamente hoy—10 de septiembre de 1961—se inaugure la VI

[23] Francisco Viedma, "Descripción de la provincia de Santa Cruz de la Sierra," en Pedro de Angelis, *Colección de obras y documentos relativos a la historia antigua y moderna de la provincia del Río de la Plata*, Buenos Aires, 2a edicion, 1910, III, p. 463.

[24] D'Orbigny, *op.cit.*, III, p. 1135.

Bienal de San Pablo, Brasil, con la concurrencia de 50 paises, y que la sala principal de la exposición esté destinada a exhibir 60 piezas de arte barroco misionero-guaraní. El gobierno del Paraguay las ha facilitado a requerimiento del Sr Livio Arbamo, delegado del Museo de Arte Moderno de San Pablo, y asi por primera vez se realiza una exhibición del arte misionero jesuitico con carácter internacional. Destaco el hecho, no solo por simples razones de coincidencia sinó porque ello significa que estamos asistiendo al descubrimiento y valoracion de un capítulo del arte barroco popular hasta hoy semiignorado.

No voy a analizar la pintura y escultura misioneras por que el tema estricto y el tiempo no lo permiten, aunque la verdad es que hace falta un estudio a fondo, aun no realizado. Quiero referirme a cierto aspecto de la artesania y artes menores porque acaso alli se encuentre la clave de cierto problema estético, segun veremos de inmediato.

Gabriel René-Moreno, en el estudio que precede a su publicación del archivo de las misiones jesuiticas en Bolivia, escribe que "los consumidores se disputaban ciertos artefactos de agrado, como totumas coloridas, pelotas elásticas, mates tallados [Pl. LXIII, 14], tableros de damas y de chaquete, cigarreras, cañuteros y rosarios de hueso, bastones, medias labradas, redecillas, sortijas de coco, escritorios y cofres con incrustaciones de concha fluvial, taburetes, poltronas, y hasta cunas y cujas de jacarandá."[25] De idéntico modo se expresa D'Orbigny a propósito de los artistas indígenas de la Purísima Concepcion de Baures, quienes en la época que la visitó (1832) aun mantenian vivos los procedimientos de la artesanía que les fuera enseñada por los jesuitas: "visité a menudo los talleres de tejido, de pintura o de ebanisteria, en donde admiraba sus cofrecillos y sus cajitas, encantadoras obras en madera de palisandro (jacarandá) con incrustaciones del brillante nácar de las conchillas de agua dulce. Tambien fabrican allí camas de viaje, valijas, etc. Otros obreros hacen cosas muy lindas con trenzas de paja, como sombreros y costureritos; sobre un barniz tan bello como el de China pintan calabazas; tornean cocos para convertirlos en cajitas elegantes y fabrican muchos pequeños

[25] Gabriel René-Moreno, *Biblioteca Boliviana; Catálogo del Archivo de Mojos y Chiquitos*, Santiago de Chile, 1888, pp. 42-43.

objetos con cuernos y huesos o los dientes de los caimanes. Son los hombres más habiles de la provincia, y uno se asombra de la perfección de sus trabajos al pensar que por toda herramienta tienen sus cuchillos."[26]

Estos testimonios, sumados a la gran cantidad de piezas artisticas existentes en los museos y colecciones argentinas y peruanas, prueban que las misiones jesuiticas no solo exportaban productos agropecuarios (especialmente yerba-mate y cueros) sinó que había una abundante producción de objetos de artesania, que se vendían por toda la América meridional. Y es precisamente en esta produccion y difusión donde acaso se encuentre la clave de un problema artistico al cual me referiré de inmediato.

Una de las zonas mas densas en arquitectura religiosa del periodo colonial es la meseta del Collao o altiplano que rodea al lago Titikaka, donde desde mucho antes de la llegada de los españoles vivían gran cantidad de indigenas, especialmente collas y aymaras. Es una region inhóspita, de vida dura como consecuencia de la altura, cuyo promedio puede estimarse en unos 3.500 metros sobre el nivel del mar (10.500 piés). No obstante estas condiciones adversas, tuvo activo comercio por la abundancia de llamas, guanacos, ovejas y cabras, y sobre todo por la minería. Domínicos y jesuitas se disputaron el derecho a misionar y catequizar en esa zona, levantando gran cantidad de templos magníficos, como los de Santiago de Pomata, San Pedro de Zepita, Santiago de Pupuja, Santa Barbara de Ylave, la catedral de Puno, y los tres templos de Juli: San Pedro Mártir, Santa Cruz y San Juan. En Juli, llamada "la Roma indígena," tuvieron los jesuitas un centro doctrinal importantísimo, una verdadera base de operaciones. El Colegio de Juli alcanzó gran predicamento y en su imprenta—una de las mas antiguas de Sudamerica—se imprimió el primer diccionario de la lengua aymara.

La importancia artistica de esta zona no radica tanto en la cantidad o magnitud de dichos edificios sinó en su decoración, típica e inconfundible labor de canteros indígenas que trabajaban la dura piedra andesita con acentuados claroscuros, en cortes a bisel e incisiones profundas, dentro de un planismo o achata-

---

[26] D'Orbigny, *op.cit.*, IV, p. 1314.

miento caracteristicamente regional. Tan típica es esta decoración que todos los historiadores del arte que se han ocupado de este tema definen la arquitectura del Collao como una variedad americana del barroco, denominándola indo-hispana, criolla, mestiza o de fusión.

Mas lo verdaderamente interesante estriba en los motivos utilizados para esa decoración plana y angulosa. En su gran mayoria son elementos zoomorfos o fitomorfos extraños a la region, de evidente procedencia tropical (Pl. LXIII, 15, 16). Exceptuando desde luego los temas antropomorfos inspirados en los propios indios, y algunos motivos animales como el del "alcamari," y el zorrino, o vegetales como la "ccantucta" y el "sanccaio," los restantes son de evidente procedencia de zonas bajas, fértiles y calientes, como eran los de las misiones de Mojos y Chiquitos. Un rápido inventario de los temas utilizados nos muestra monos, tucanes, loros, iguanas, colibríes, pumas, o sinó papayas, cacao, uvas, plátanos, zapallos, etc. Volvamos ahora al tantas veces citado D'Orbigny, y leyendo su descripción de la region del Beni nos parece encontrarnos ante el inventario de la decoración de los templos del Collao: "monos ligeros, de variadas especies, recorren incesantemente los bosques más cálidos, mientras que manadas de pecarís devastan las plantaciones. . . . una multitud de especias de tangaras, de manaquines y cotingas disputan las copas de los árboles a las cotorras y a los papagayos, cuyo plumaje se confunde con el follaje. Esas bandadas en movimiento, mezcladas a los caciques, tucanos y a multitud de otras especies. . . . Entre las plantas cultivadas se distinguen el cacao, el tabaco, el índigo, el algodon, el maiz, la coca, la batata, la yuca o mandioca, la gualusa, la ajipa, la suculenta sandía, la chirimoya, la papaya o aguacate, las guayabas, las naranjas, tal vez las mejores del mundo, la toronja, el limon, la granada, muchas especies de bananas, ananâs, caña de azucar y gran número de otras frutas cuyo nombre he olvidado."[27]

El problema es desde luego intrigante y merece su análisis. Se ha sugerido algunas hipótesis, sin que cualquiera de ellas zanje la cuestión de modo definitivo y satisfactorio. Enrique Marco Dorta, al hablar de los movimientos o traslaciones de indios "mi-

[27] *Ibid.*, III, p. 1013.

tayos" . . .[28] deja entrever la posibilidad de que esos indios de las misiones tropicales, tan hábiles artistas y artesanos, hubiesen podido ser trasladados para trabajar en los templos del altiplano. Pero esto debe descartarse por que está probado que el indio de las tierras bajas y calientes no soporta el clima terriblemente duro de las alturas. La muerte de indígenas por esa razón está abundantemente documentada en los frecuentes conflictos entre las autoridades españolas y los encomenderos que abusaban de su poder sacando a los naturales de sus sitios de origen. Además, en la guerra del Chaco que sostuvieron Paraguay y Bolivia hace treinta años se repitió el caso de traslados masivos con gran índice de mortandad.

Harold Wethey refiriendose a la decoración de la iglesia de Santa Cruz en Juli dice que "los monos juegan aqui un papel excepcionalmente prominente. Aunque pertenecen al repertorio mestizo de la region del lago, en ninguna otra parte son tan abundantes y divertidos. Deben ser vistos como una herencia del arte precolombino. Son ubicuos en los tejidos y alfareria de las culturas indígenas tardias."[29] Sin cescartar la posibilidad de que este fuese el origen, el problema no queda resuelto sinó trasladado en el tiempo, pues en todo caso habria que ver cómo se explica que aparezcan monos y papayas en obras indígenas del altiplano, sean tejidos o alfareria. Wethey no aclara si se refiere a culturas indigenas del altiplano o de la costa. Pero aun tratándose de obras de las culturas nazca o chimú el problema subsistiría, pues tampoco hubo esos animales (monos, tucanes, colibríes, iguanas) en la zona de la costa. Acaso Wethey se ha referido a obras hechas por los indígenas de la zona del Beni, es decir, Mojos y Chiquitos, en cuyo caso estaríamos dentro de la explicación que considero como más lógica y racional.

En efecto, Pedro Juan Vignale adelantó hace años la opinión de que probablemente el autor de la extraordinaria portada de

---

[28] Se llama "mita" al servicio personal que debían prestar los indígenas en las zonas mineras, especialmente en Potosí. Los "mitayos" podían ser trasladados de lugar, y debían trabajar una semana y descansar dos, hasta sumar cuatro meses de labor, pero en la realidad esto no se cumplía por los abusos de los "encomenderos."

[29] Harold E. Wethey, *Colonial Architecture and Sculpture in Peru*, Cambridge, Massachusetts, 1949, p. 165.

San Lorenzo de Potosí fué algun artista misionero trasladado a la famosa ciudad minera, acostumbrado a trabajar la dura madera de coco. "Salta a la vista—y casi diriamos al tacto—que el maestro anónimo de San Lorenzo hubo bajado de Mojos para ejecutarla. . . ."[30] Pero Vignale expuso su teoria concretándola al caso potosino, que si bien es bellísimo, no es el mas representativo de la escultura mestiza con motivos tropicales. Aun mas, afirma rotundamente "que la escuela limeña que diera nacimiento a la de Juli y Pomata, puntos extremos al sur, de su avance sobre el Cuzco, no llegó a Potosí."[31] Es decir, que terminantemente se desentiende de toda la arquitectura del Collao—que es precisamente la que nos interesa en nuestro estudio de hoy—y además la vincula con Lima en lugar de Arequipa, como es hoy sabido y aceptado.

Hace años sugerí una explicación ligada en cierto modo a la de Vignale, relacionando esos temas de la decoración mestiza del altiplano con la gran variedad y cantidad de objetos que producía la industria de Chiquitos y Mojos, que se llevaba a Juli y demás ciudades del Alto Perú e incluso llegaban a Buenos Aires. Ya hemos citado lo que decían D'Orbigny y René-Moreno sobre los los productos de dicha artesania, y si a ello agregamos la comparacion de las tallas mestizas con las piezas misioneras que se conservan en los museos y colecciones argentinas, el parecido salta a la vista. No solo la identidad de motivos sinó la técnica y factura de la talla son similares, pues si bien en un caso se trata de piedra y en el otro de madera, en ambas escuelas domina la dureza, el biselado, la incisión profunda, el claroscuro.

Resumiendo todo lo expuesto llegamos a una serie de conclusiones, unas de carácter afirmativo, otras menos precisas y por lo tanto discutibles, que someto al juicio de esta asamblea de expertos:

1. Los jesuitas crearon una serie de misiones en la vertiente oriental de los Andes y Chaco, que aun cuando no estaban siempre ligadas entressi, formaron todo un sistema, idéntico en su organizacion y arquitectura.

[30] Pedro Juan Vignale, "El maestro anónimo de la portada de San Lorenzo de Potosí," *Revista de Arquitectura*, No. 280, 1944, p. 161.
[31] *Ibid.*, p. 162.

2. Salvo contadas excepciones, utilizaron para los templos y demás edificios de estas misiones una técnica de esqueleto de troncos, sin que las paredes soporten el peso del tejado, lo que puede considerarse como una creación americana.

3. Dicha técnica está ligada a las caracteristicas boscosas de las zonas donde se levantaron las misiones, y su influjo se extendió a las regiones vecinas donde abundaba la madera, como por ejemplo Santa Cruz de la Sierra en Bolivia y la zona mesopotámica argentina.

4. Los motivos decorativos utilizados en la arquitectura misionera, como asimismo en las artes menores, se inspiraron en ejemplos tomados de la fauna y flora de las zonas bajas y tropicales.

5. Esos motivos, ajenos a la region del altiplano perú-boliviano, son los mismos que aparecen en la arquitectura mestiza del Collao, por lo que cabe suponer que fueron llevados desde las misiones de Mojos y Chiquitos, probablemente por la via comercial de objetos relativamente pequeños y transportables. Se estaría asi en presencia de una decoración de origen lignario, traspuesta a la piedra.

6. Con excepcion de las misiones del Paraguay, que han sido bien estudiadas e incluso restauradas algunas de ellas por los gobiernos de Brasil y Argentina, las restantes están desapareciendo rapidamente por el abandono y la incomprensión. Varias han sido demolidas y sus tallas y pinturas vendidas a anticuarios y coleccionistas. Tengo noticia de que en las misiones de Maynas—que nadie ha estudiado todavia—quedan verdaderos artisticos cuya salvación urge, antes de que el tiempo, la incuria o intereses mercenarios los hagan desaparecer.

MEXICAN ARCHITECTURE AND THE
BAROQUE

JOSEPH ARMSTRONG BAIRD, JR.

ALMOST no era in the history of architecture has been so misunderstood as that in Mexico from the effective revival of building following the Conquest to the end of the viceregal period. In this span of almost three centuries, Mexico produced building of unusual quantitative magnitude, combining structural, stylistic and ideational considerations with special vigor in both metropolitan and regional variations. The church was the particular focus of architecture: first, as the center of the friars' communities, and then in the development of the cathedral in the metropolitan center and the parish church in the town. The town palace, also, was built with distinction; and away from city and town, great haciendas provided another focus for architecture of high economic potential. From these arose a fascinating multiplicity of humbler variants, with particular creativity in architecture, as in all the arts, at the folk level. Despite the considerable interest that scholars of Spain, Latin America and the United States have shown in this richly endowed period (serious, critical studies by scholars of other European countries have, as yet, been rare), one aspect of almost two-thirds of the viceregal era has been insufficiently remarked. That is the curious relationship of Mexican architecture to the Baroque.

The relationship of Spain and the viceroyalty[1] is of particular importance in this respect; few have been able to read this economic-political and architectural equation accurately. In Spain, partly because of its more continuous architectural history, and partly because of the continuing interrelation of Spain with the artistic currents of Italy and the North, there was a richer variety of formal sources available to architecture than in Mexico. But one must guard against a too easy leveling of the relations of

[1] A conference at The Museum of Modern Art, New York City (May 28-31, 1945) explored many of the basic problems of the relationships of Mexico and Spain and special facets of Mexican viceregal architecture; see *Studies in Latin American Art*, edited by Elizabeth Wilder, Washington, 1949.

Spain and Mexico. The cliché image of mother-child, or great nation and its colonial dependency, is misleading for this relationship. It is easy and fallacious to think of Spain as the center of infinitely various approaches to architecture, and of Mexico as a stereotyped by-product of the least sophisticated of those approaches. Formal and ornamental developments there were in Spain; still Mexico constantly surprises with its irregular display of a high level of conception and execution, often paralleling rather than imitating the background from which it came. The special character of Mexican architectural history goes far to explain its apparent naïveté in some periods and areas.[2] There were examples of planning and formal architectural conception in Mexico, but Mexico's special genius was not concentrated on the dramatic plan and space effects of Baroque Europe, which were occasionally seen in Spain.[3]

Certainly one of the factors to be noted was a more progressive architectural training in Spain. Young architects had the advantage of contact with fashion-conscious and highly competitive metropolitan centers of influence within the country, and also of the opportunity to travel to such centers elsewhere in Europe. Mexico's distance from Europe and its viceregal status denied it certain contacts that enriched Spanish architecture over many centuries. Apprentice craftsmen in Mexico might develop into important architects, but itinerant Spanish designer-architects often received the major commissions.[4] The patronage sys-

[2] For example, there is the complete absence in the pre-Conquest period of the developed structural experimentation of Europe before A.D. 1500. This can also partly be explained in terms of the ruinous colonial economic policy of Spain; cf. H. G. Ward, *Mexico in 1827*, London, 1828, I, p. 112: "If a system of absolute prohibition could ever prove a good one in the end . . . the policy of Spain might be held out. . . . From the first she reserved to herself the exclusive right of supplying all the wants of her colonies. . . . No foreigner was permitted to trade with them, or foreign vessel to enter their ports."

[3] As in Narciso Tomé's *Transparente* for Toledo Cathedral (1732), an adaptation of an older structure to late Baroque spatial extension and illusionism; in the extraordinary proscenium-retable of the Capilla de la Pasión (ca. 1765-70) in El Salvador at Sevilla—combining the actual space of a *camarín* with illusionistic space above in the great retable frame; or in the apse of San Martín Pinario at Santiago de Compostela with its approximations of German and Bavarian sculpture-architecture in a dazzling sequence of screens, figures, etc.

[4] The older sources for Spanish architectural biographical information are E.

tem of the viceroyalty made much of this natural and inevitable. This field is still incompletely studied, but future research will undoubtedly clarify architectural status and training in Spain and Mexico, and may create important modifications of the nature of the relationship between the two countries.

Much of the question of training and status was influenced by fashion and by the nature of the Spanish empire. Competent architect-designers in the New World were usually not as up-to-date as those in Spain, despite the rapid transfer of prints (engravings, etc.), and the waves of itinerant, progressive designers who set new fashions and developed them. Spanish-trained architect-designers executed commissions and influenced the character of architecture over a vast area of the world's surface, and Mexico received these waves of influence and translated them into distinctly regional idioms. The surprising fact is that there was almost no reciprocal transfer of formal ideas. Despite efforts to prove the importation of colonial architectural forms and ideas from Mexico to Spain, careful study of the facts reveals virtually none.[5]

Llaguno y Amírola, *Noticias de los arquitectos y arquitectura de España* (with notes, additions and documents by J. A. Ceán Bermúdez), Madrid, 1829; J. A. Céan Bermúdez, *Diccionario historico de los mas ilustres profesores de las bellas artes en España*, Madrid, 1800 (with addition by the Conde de Viñaza, 1889); Sir W. Stirling Maxwell, *Annals of Artists in Spain*, London, 1891. For more contemporary references see G. Kubler, *Arquitectura de los siglos XVII y XVIII*, Madrid, 1957 (*Ars Hispaniae*, XIV), pp. 361-67. Kubler's studies of architectural practice in Spain and Mexico are being supplemented and enlarged by scholars like Margaret Collier (Ph.D. Diss. on Lorenzo Rodríguez and the Sagrario Metropolitano, Yale University), and by continuing archival work in Mexico City. Heinrich Berlin has also provided valuable material on time schedules and division of work for the architecturally inspired retable designers and craftsmen.

[5] Almost nothing has been written to support this contention, particularly advanced by a few Latin American art historians. The slight volume by Genaro Estrada, *El arte mexicano en España* (*Enciclopedia ilustrada mexicana*, V, Mexico, 1937), is concerned with minor decorative works that happen to have found their way into Spanish collections, and not with attempting to prove the West-East stream of influence. Taylor has given the most convincing printed proof of the indefensibility of the idea (see R. C. Taylor, "Francisco Hurtado and His School," *Art Bulletin*, XXXII, 1, 1950, pp. 45-48). A particular degree of absurdity is reached in the allegation that there are New World corn (maize) motifs in the Cartuja Sacristy at Granada.

Though the influence of Spain was consistent throughout the viceregal period, there was something essentially different about individual monuments and their parts in Mexico, and also in the total character of architecture in this viceroyalty. Something has already been said in various publications about a so-called "indigenous character," as well as the nature of "Indian sources."[6] It is well to emphasize at this point that wishful thinking has interpreted in an exaggerated manner certain sources and their influence in Mexico. After the Conquest, there were only a few Indian formal conventions that continued into the mid-sixteenth century—notably in sculpture, painting and in certain ornamental details of architecture.[7]

In the pre-Conquest Indian world there was a well-established tradition of construction in stone which was of inestimable value to the builders of the post-Conquest period. A good Indian craftsman would naturally respond to the challenges of post-Conquest building with more knowledge and skill than someone completely unacquainted with monumental building and sculptural techniques. Still, the direct influence of Indian ideas on the post-Conquest period was exceedingly small. The types of building and sculptural commissions were completely different, and the techniques of post-Conquest architecture demanded a knowledge of traditional medieval and Renaissance forms which were alien to the Indian world. The special character of viceregal architecture in Mexico was based on something more complex than direct utilization of "Indian sources." This special character was founded on an aesthetic preoccupation with ornamental and ornamental-sculptural, rather than architectural, developments, and on a general rejection of the over-all planning and spatial conceptions of the Baroque period in western Europe.

Mexican architecture from 1550 to 1810, in a very large sense, was thus devoid of the complex planning of building and site

[6] The best modern study of the problem is in George Kubler and Martin Soria, *Art and Architecture in Spain and Portugal and Their American Dominions*, Baltimore, 1959, pp. 73, 78.

[7] Cf. R. García Granados, "Reminiscencias idolátricas en monumentos coloniales," *Anales del Instituto de Investigaciones Estéticas*, III, 1940, pp. 54-56, and Alfred Neumeyer, "The Indian Contribution to Architectural Decoration in Spanish Colonial America," *Art Bulletin*, xxx, 1948, pp. 104-21.

which was the basis of most Baroque Italian, French, and Spanish architecture. It is significant that there was no Versailles in Mexico, no St. Peter's. There were no villas in the Italian manner, no country estates in the English manner—although the hacienda provided a special variant of seignorial country living, medieval rather than post-Renaissance in pattern. This does not imply that there were no town plans and no instances of topographical sensibility. There were certainly many of these.

Towns in Mexico were early and consistently laid out in a regular checkerboard, showing responsiveness to ideal Renaissance-Roman sources (Pl. LXIV, 1). However, ideal Baroque sources were less important. The presence of a few great radiating streets in Mexico City is due to late nineteenth- and twentieth-century additions to the old city, in the manner of Baroque Paris. Perhaps the most thoughtfully planned ensembles of the vice-regal period were the sixteenth-century friars' complexes, which were laid out with a fine regard for site and with local modifications of the building plans of medieval Europe.[8] In Mexico after 1600, however, there was comparatively little of the carefully conceived spaces before individual buildings, or of the elaborate interrelation of scale and mass, in terms of streets and the *piazze* or *places* of a metropolis, which were developing in Baroque Rome and Paris. (Morelia's Cathedral area is a special case of Baroque scale with double Renaissance spaces, partially planned in the nineteenth century: Pl. LXIV, 2.)

The result is that Mexican architecture often consisted, after the sixteenth century, of isolated buildings related in a physical, but rarely in a cohesively planned, manner to their metropolitan, town, or country sites. Such simple devices of protection and emphasis as enclosing walls or staircases, or a simple forecourt, followed Early Christian and medieval precedents. The history of the Basilica of Guadalupe and its surroundings is symptomatic (Pls. LXIV, 3; LXV, 4, 5). Before the recent paving of the forecourt and surrounding area of the Basilica proper, this important site was a haphazard mingling of handsome individual buildings and special areas of veneration. There was no integrated attempt to

[8] G. Kubler, *Mexican Architecture of the 16th Century*, New Haven, 1948, chs. VI and VII.

relate the Basilica proper to the Chapel of the Holy Well, nor to relate the Basilica to the functionally important Hill of Tepeyac, where the miraculous vision took place. Another instance can be seen in the relationship of the Cathedral of Mexico City and the Zócalo. Here, a pre-Conquest plan established the pattern of a large traffic area, girdled by buildings significant to the secular life of the metropolis. Various modifications to both the Zócalo and the space in front of the Cathedral were made,[9] especially in the nineteenth and early twentieth century (Pl. LXVI, 6), but there was no rethinking of this space as Bernini had rethought the area before St. Peter's. Mexico continued to depend (often with an indefinable magic of combination) on the Renaissance grid, with additions of regional materials, planting, the color of crowds, and that extraordinary Mexican genius for using accidental qualities for a total visual effect.

Mexican viceregal building and site planning received its strongest direction in the sixteenth century. The character of that period echoed down to the end of the eighteenth century, and generally precluded any major changes to a town plan already laid out in a grid. Furthermore, there was apparently no real desire to modify those plans. Personal aggrandizement, of cleric or civilian, lay in some striking individual monument—not in the rethinking of a whole town. It is indicative that the wealthy mining magnates of the eighteenth century were content to construct a new parish church (José de la Borda) or a rather modest palace (Conde de Rul). One can see parallels in any smaller European town of the eighteenth century, where similar churches and palaces were built. It is interesting, however, that the charming and complete replanning of Nancy's center, the crescents of Bath, or the rebuilding of Noto, Sicily, by Jesuit planners in the eighteenth century, had no direct parallels in Mexico.

Building types in Mexico were generally simple. There were examples of spatial thinking in the colonial period (the open chapels of the sixteenth century, the space effects of the *camarines* of the eighteenth century), but most buildings were conceived as backgrounds for ornamental enrichment of certain sections. The

[9] See M. Romero de Terreros, *La plaza mayor de México en el siglo XVIII*, Mexico, 1946, and J. Olvera, "La Catedral Metropolitana de México," *Artes de México*, no. 32, 1960.

façade and parts of the interiors of churches, especially the retable, the fronts and courtyards of palaces and public buildings, were the aesthetic foci of viceregal Mexico.

Pattern and ornament thus assumed a major role in Mexico—indeed, many of the architects were ornamental designers.[10] And it is here that the notable character of Mexican architecture can be seen. The strong preference in the viceregal period was for bilateral symmetry of design, with an enrichment of certain parts.[11] Underlying this bilateral symmetry was a complex aesthetic history—partly European, partly American. It is in this area that so much misunderstanding of "indigenous or Indian sources" develops.

What one might call the sense of organized pattern in viceregal Mexico was reinforced by Islamic backgrounds in Spain, by the classical backgrounds of Renaissance Italy, and to a lesser degree by the conventions of the pre-Conquest Indian cultures, which sometimes emphasized non-figurative and sometimes figurative forms. The Mudéjar or Islamic influence was in terms of geometric, non-figurative ornament of rigidly controlled patterns.[12] This influence can be exaggerated, although there were a considerable number of Mudéjar-inspired ornamental motifs in viceregal Mexico as late as the eighteenth century. The classical-Renaissance and Mannerist ornamental language of the sixteenth century in Italy, and especially in Spain and her northern dominions in Europe, was the most immediately important for motifs.[13]

[10] The use of internationally circulated ornamental source books was apparently common. For studies of such sources see J. Weingartner, *Das kirchliche Kunstgewerbe der Neuzeit*, Innsbruck, 1927. Fundamental also are D. Guilmard, *Les maîtres ornemanistes*, Paris, 1888; P. Jessen, *Der Ornamentstich*, Berlin, 1920; R. Berliner, *Ornamentale Vorlage-blätter*, Leipzig, 1925-26; J. Evans, *Pattern*, Oxford, 1931; *Katalog der Ornamentstichsammlung der Staatlichen Kunstbibliothek Berlin*, Berlin, 1936.

[11] The fundamental Hispanic preoccupation was also with animated surfaces, symmetrically planned; cf. Oskar Hagen, *Patterns and Principles of Spanish Art*, Madison, 1948, and J. A. Baird Jr., "The Ornamental Tradition in Spanish Architecture," *Country Life Annual*, 1961, pp. 82-87.

[12] The treatise by Diego López de Arenas, *Carpintería de lo blanco* (1633, reprinted 1727 and 1867), preserves the technical details of Mudéjar work. See also Georgiana G. King, *Mudéjar*, New York, 1927, and M. Toussaint, *Arte Mudéjar en América*, Mexico, 1946.

[13] The importance of northern Mannerism has never been fully evaluated

That this was usually bilaterally symmetric reinforced the other aesthetic backgrounds, although its language was very different from theirs. The classical and Mannerist-based figurative and ornamental styles of Italy, blending with those of Mudéjar-medieval Spain and Mannerist Germany and Flanders, replaced the ferocious vigor and naturalistic power of Aztec ornamental ideas.

After the Conquest, the principal exterior focus of this determined sense of organized pattern was on the façades of churches and civil buildings. An important interior focus of design enthusiasm was the retable,[14] or decorated screen behind the high altar of the church (and later, the screens behind the side altars of the transept and nave). In both instances there was a consistent enthusiasm for wall surfaces embellished with a variety of carefully controlled and richly patterned ornament. It is in the stone façades and the great gilded, wooden retables that one sees the major changes of fashion—the inevitable response to new ornamental persuasions. Painting was, to a certain extent, peripheral in decorative thinking; sculpture and the related crafts were fundamental. Mexican architecture of both pre- and post-Conquest eras was profoundly sculptural. A great deal of building was done

---

in connection with Hispanic and Mexican work of the 18th century. O. Schubert, *Geschichte des Barocks in Spanien*, Esslingen, 1908, pp. 224-39, discusses the Mannerist qualities of the 18th century *Plattenstil* in Galicia. Studies of Wendel Dietterlin (born 1550 or 1551 at Pullendorf; died 1599 at Strasbourg), Jan Vredeman de Vries (born 1527 at Leeuwarden, Friesland; died ca. 1604 or as late as 1623), and the other late 16th century northern Mannerist ornamental masters, have still to be written in terms of their role in the creation of a decorative language and complex of attitudes which led to the so-called "Mexican Churrigueresque" or "Ultra-Baroque." See Kubler and Soria, *op.cit.*, p. 371, n. 20, for discussion of Vredeman de Vries.

[14] The word comes from the low Latin, *retaulus* (Latin: *retro-tabula*). The Spanish word *retablo* is used in two senses; for works before 1800, it refers to the great screens behind altars, and after 1800, it may also refer to small, votive paintings created by "popular" artists as thank-offerings for miraculous recoveries. The colonial period seems to have used *altar* as synonymous with *retablo* as a screen. Distinction between the screen behind the main altar and side altars is usually in terms of *retablo mayor* and *retablo colateral* (or *colateral*, alone). The Anglican church has yet another specialized meaning for the English word, retable, as the shelf behind the altar. Attributions, based on archival information and secondary sources (particularly the *Gaceta* of 18th century Mexico), are still in progress for many important works.

(indeed, in the seventeenth and eighteenth centuries it is stupefy-
ing in quantity). Yet, there was generally more interest in an
animated surface—what one might call the "ornamented wall"—
than in the structural problems of architecture proper.

More scholarly attention has been directed, particularly since
1950, to the stylistic character of these great ornamented walls.
My own researches[15] have especially centered on the sequence of
metropolitan and regional styles or fashions in the retables of
Spain and Mexico in the eighteenth century, an era which produced an unusual number of basic formulae. Not since the Byzan-
tine period had there been such proliferation of art for the physical
enhancement of a religious setting. Especially after 1700, material
prodigality of gold, in a time of unparalleled mineral wealth, became a touchstone of personal pride—a curious combination of
seignorial splendor and bourgeois pretension. The term "gilded
grottos" of Mexico—as poetically minded writers have called
them—produces an image of ornamental fantasy, of sacred re-
treats with a dazzling richness of refulgent gold, in an age of surface.

Here again, although individual features had a climactic organization, there was general disinterest in the Baroque in terms of complex space and structural forms. The involvements of seventeenth-
century Rome, the telescoping octagons of Brazilian churches, the
melting curvilinear rhythms of eighteenth-century Bavaria and
Germany, were almost entirely lacking in Mexico (if one excepts a
few isolated churches in or near Mexico City).[16] The box-like interiors (even the *camarines* were often away from the church
proper so that this space-enhancing device of southern Spain
was made into a separate cubicle separated from the main fabric)
repeated an age-old preoccupation with Early Christian building

[15] Joseph A. Baird Jr., "The 18th Century Retable in the South of Spain,
Portugal and Mexico" (Diss. Harvard University, 1951; microfilm copies at
Bancroft Library, Berkeley, California and Department of the History of Art,
Yale University); "The 18th Century Retables of the Bajío: The Querétaro
Style," *Art Bulletin*, xxxv, 1953, pp. 195-216; "The Retables of Cádiz and
Jerez in the 17th and 18th Centuries," *Anales del Instituto de Investigaciones
Estéticas*, xxvi, 1957, pp. 39-49; "Style in 18th Century Mexico," *Journal of
Inter-American Studies*, i, 1959, pp. 261-76.

[16] Such as Santa Brígida, Mexico City (1740-44) by Luis Díez Navarro, and
the Capilla del Pocito (1777-91) by Francisco Antonio Guerrero y Torres.

types, rectangular in silhouette and lighted by a high clerestory. Use of the Gesú-inspired transept as chapels, and the deep apse, were common. The entire interior, then, was a convenient background for applied ornament, increasing in quantity with the richness of the patron or the eminence of the building; Taxco and Tepotzotlán are prime examples.

The frenzied multiplicity of retables in even the most modestly sized buildings (such as Santa Clara or Santa Rosa at Querétaro) created what at first glance might be called Rococo suffusion of the surface.[17] Indeed, in the later eighteenth century, something of Rococo exuberance invested these dazzling walls (Pl. LXVI, 7), as well as specific use of rocaille motifs. It is, however, important to note that consistency of interior design was never a major factor in Mexico, as it was in international Rococo terms (particularly in Austria, Germany, and Portugal). There were at least three major phases of later-eighteenth-century Mexican design fashions represented at Santa Rosa in Querétaro; and even Tepotzotlán had retables that were distinctly different from apse and transept to nave. The same thing was true of Taxco, where the nave retables were of a persuasion later than those of apse and transepts. San Cayetano de la Valenciana, near Guanajuato, had perhaps the most unified interior of the eighteenth century, but it never had any important nave retables. There were a few examples of apparent consistency, but more careful examination often reveals divergences of considerable importance within the complex framework of fashion sequences from 1700 to 1790.

The ornamented walls were conceived as a kind of historical picture gallery, with masterpieces of one school grouped in one area, and others strung along some convenient longer wall. Each was to be viewed in part and in sum as a finished design, which related to the others because the taste of the period united all in a common bond of competence[18] and splendor. This was par-

---

[17] Note also the importance in the 18th century of Jesuit builder-designers in the dissemination of the Rococo; see J. Evans, *op.cit.*, p. 95: "Only where Jesuitism had planted Baroque architecture in an alien soil—in Portugal, Germany and Poland (and Mexico)—did the Rocaille style have an unfettered vogue."

[18] E. Wilder Weismann, *Mexico in Sculpture*, Cambridge, Massachusetts, 1950, p. 83, characterizes this quality of competence: "Among retables, invention

ticularly true of seventeenth- and eighteenth-century revisions of sixteenth-century buildings (Acolman, Metztitlán, or Yanhuit-lán), where the apparent disparities of period were overcome by a common foundation in mixed sixteenth-century sources, no matter how modified. (The sixteenth-century ornamental sources of eighteenth-century Mexico are a subject unto themselves—particularly in reference to such a Mannerist-inspired eighteenth-century form as the *estípite*.)[19]

It is not my intent to catalogue again the nice distinctions of eighteenth-century styles or fashions. The change from twisted column (*Salomónica*), and its Renaissance and Baroque ornamental vocabulary, to *estípite*, with more Mannerist parts added to the lush foliation of the Baroque era, and the final dissolution of all tectonic interest in the magnificent Rococo-oriented ornamental niche-pilasters[20] or pilaster-niches of the 1770's and 1780's

---

and even naiveté are rare. The level of design and execution is high, but at the price of monotony. To make a fine retable was to make one that embodied the acceptable components assembled in the best manner, as if one were following the recipe for a perfect cake. If you could at the same time show originality, in a repeated emphasis on emerging triangles, let us say, true connoisseurs would no doubt applaud. If on the other hand, your altarpiece was put together with little creative feeling, if it was skimpy and dull, it would still be saved by the rules of proportion and the formulas of decoration." (Mrs. Weismann is referring especially to works of the period between 1735 and 1770, when the *estípite*—note 19 below—created a special uniformity of type. From 1770 to 1790, invention was of an unparalled brilliance, in the suites of enormous retables at San Agustín, Salamanca, in Santa Rosa and Santa Clara, Querétaro, etc.)

[19] A 16th century-inspired columnar or pilaster form, appearing in Spain in a developed form in the latter part of the 17th century (see A. Sancho Corbacho, *Dibujos arquitectonicos del siglo XVII*, Seville, 1947, figs. 89, 90). Its earliest use by José de Churriguera the Younger is still uncertainly dated; at any event it was subordinated to other articulative forms in most of his work. Gerónimo Balbás popularized it in Mexico (drawing upon still disputed sources, related to the early use of the *estípite* by the Hurtado circle at Granada); it was particularly employed in the mid-18th century works of Lorenzo Rodríguez, appearing first in Andalucía, but principally gaining his experience in Mexico. V. Villegas, *El gran signo formal del Barroco*, Mexico, 1956, attempts a comprehensive history of the *estípite*, with exaggerations of both sources and developments. There were sporadic examples of true *estípites* in interior and exterior projects over a long period of time; in Spain, after ca. 1685 and in Mexico, after ca. 1720-30. Its popularity waned by 1775 or 1780 in Mexico.

[20] Cf. J. A. Baird Jr., "The Ornamental Niche-Pilaster in the Hispanic World," *Journal of the Society of Architectural Historians*, xv, 1956, pp. 5-11.

is as easily seen on façades as on retables. It is relevant to note that an underlying continuity from one style to another helped to link retables within a given monument. The most glaring instance of non-compatibility was the replacing, after 1790 or 1795, of any of these varied fashions with Neoclassic works, which unfortunately were often simply less imaginative in their conception and execution, as well as being of a gelid purity alien to Mexico between 1530 and 1790.

Mexico was, is, and will always be, many things to many interpreters. Her artistic history has been so extraordinary and so varied, from pre-Conquest to contemporary, that one might have expected a kind of aesthetic trauma to have resulted long ago. Instead, in the viceregal period there were varied metropolitan and regional developments, drawing upon all the sources of Europe and yet resisting many of the Baroque implications growing out of those sources. A sense of organized pattern, an ability to relate infinite interpretations of established parts over a long period of time, and a mature craftsmanship of exceptional vigor— these combined to create certain works which will be memorable to anyone capable of accepting their challenging, imaginative qualities. No analysis can ever plumb the special psychology of variation (itself a craft heritage significant for any period of Mexican art) inherent here. To paraphrase a well-known *mot*, "Le Mexique a ses raisons que la raison ne connaît point."[21]

[21] I wish to express my appreciation to George Kubler and Justino Fernández for reading and commenting on this paper.

NEW DOCUMENTS ON
LORENZO RODRÍGUEZ AND HIS STYLE

MARGARET COLLIER

NEW documents on Lorenzo Rodríguez are so plenti-
ful at this moment that many of them are still on
unedited rolls of microfilm at Yale,[1] and the story of
this eighteenth-century architect's long and busy career[2] has
still to be disentangled from his payrolls, estimates, reports and
lawsuits which appear in almost every collection of documents

[1] Many of these documents came to me through the kindness of scholars in
Mexico, Spain and the United States. Full acknowledgment must await completion of a larger work on the Sagrario now under way, but I owe an especial
debt of gratitude to Mr. Heinrich Berlin, who at the very beginning of these
labors turned over to me his references to unstudied Rodríguez documents in
the archives of Mexico, and to Sr. Ignacio Rubio Mañé, who for many months
acted as almost daily guide and counselor to a novice in archival work. For
most of the material used in this paper, I am indebted to the Dean and Cabildo
of the Cathedral of Mexico who allowed me to study and photograph papers
in the cathedral archives. I wish especially to thank Monsignor Valdés and
Monsignor Dávila, and Padre Martinez of the Mitra archive, for their many
kindnesses to me during that time, and also Arq. José Espinosa, whose knowledge of the Mitra papers was of great help. The archive of the Vizcainas College was made available through the generous cooperation of Lic. Gonzalo
Obregón Jr.
A large collection of documents on microfilm recently came to Yale through
the efforts of Father Ernest J. Burrus, S.J., and Mr. Donald Cooper. These papers
are from the archive of the Secretaría de Salubridad in Mexico, and are referred
to here as Burrus-Cooper File, with an identifying number from Mr. Cooper's
index. Other archival references are: AGI—Archivo General de Indias, Seville;
AGN—Archivo General de la Nacion, Mexico; CMAM—Cathedral of Mexico,
Archivo de la Mitra; CMAC—Cathedral of Mexico, Archivo del Cabildo.

[2] Rodríguez was born about 1704 in Guadix, near Granada. His mother was
from Guadix; his father, Felipe Santiago Rodríguez, was a Corboban. (Information from Rodríguez' will, dated May 11, 1774, sent to me by Sr. Constantino
Reyes.) According to Rodríguez' statement of 1742, his father was "maestro
mayor de reales alcazares y fábricas del obispado de Guadix y Baza" (AGN,
Desagüe, vol. 11). The date of his arrival in Mexico is not known, and is involved with the complicated question of his activities in Cádiz which cannot
be explored in this paper. From 1731 until 1740 he is known to have worked at
the new mint in Mexico, first as carpenter, then as *maestro de moneda*, design-
ing machines for coining and supervising their operation (AGN, *Casa de
Moneda*, vols. 177, 195, 329, 372). The examination which admitted him to the
guild of architects is dated August 1, 1740 (Heinrich Berlin, "Three Master

in Mexico. The present study concerns architecture of the metropolitan area roughly between the years 1730-65, with emphasis on the emergence of a new style almost exactly at the mid-century, a style which first appeared in Rodríguez' design for the Sagrario Metropolitano.

The difficulties of working in this period are well known to those interested in the history of New Spain. The state of eighteenth-century studies is chaotic. Monographs and specialized works have never been made into an understandable structure. The enormous mass of documentary information is largely unstudied, and what has been studied has never been coordinated.[3] We know almost nothing of political events or cultural forces, nor of the men involved in either. In short, we must discuss works of art in a vacuum, as if they were acts of God, or *objets trouvés* left on a beach by the unpredictable motion of wind and waves.

Within this period, the Sagrario of the Cathedral of Mexico (Pl. LXVII, 1), the cathedral's parish church, is almost alone in being a well-documented work. There can be no doubt that Ro-

Architects in New Spain," *Hispanic American Historical Review*, XXVII, 1947, pp. 375-83; and Manuel Romero de Terreros, "La carta de examen de Lorenzo Rodríguez," *Anales del Instituto de Investigaciones Estéticas*, XV, 1947, pp. 105-8). Throughout the early forties he was involved in a series of lawsuits concerning property left to him by his wife's uncle, the architect Miguel de Rivera, who died in 1739 (AGN, *Hospital de Jesús*, vols. 25, 368). In 1744 he was paid for work on "las puertas de la crujía" in the cathedral, "en virtud de papel del Sr. Dean" (CMAM, *Libro de Fábrica 1730-1770*, fol. 202v). From 1743 to 1747 he made repairs and renovations on property belonging to the Convento de Jesús Maria (Burrus-Cooper File, 83-86). He submitted a design for an altarpiece to the Concepcionistas, but in January 1747 the design of Jerónimo Balbás was chosen "por la gran fama." (AGN, *Bienes Nacionales*, Leg. 85. Asúnçion Lavrin called my attention to this document, the only one we have which shows Rodríguez as a designer of altarpieces and in competition with the great Balbás.) In January 1749, the cabildo of the cathedral sent Rodríguez' plan for the Sagrario to the viceroy for approval, saying that it has been approved some years earlier by the late archbishop Vizarrón. Work began on the foundations five weeks later (Diego Angulo Iñiguez, *Estudios de los planos . . . existentes en el archivo de Indias*, Seville, 1933-39, III, pp. 157-63). For Rodríguez' later career see Berlin, *op.cit.* and "Artifices de la Catedral de Mexico," *Anales del Instituto . . .* XI, 1944, pp. 19-39.

[3] A basic work in the history of the period is now under way: Ignacio Rubio Mañé's *Introduccion al estudio de los virreyes de Nueva España*. Five volumes are planned; two have already appeared (Mexico, 1955 and 1959).

dríguez was its architect. The papers in the Archivo de Indias, published by Diego Angulo Iñiguez,[4] prove that Rodríguez drew the plan, and the account books preserved in the cathedral[5] show that he directed the work until the building was finished. The Sagrario is important for several reasons, not all of them architectural. In time, it coincided with the beginning of a period of great prosperity in New Spain. During the decades which followed, a fever of building swept the country, and through one regional development after another we can trace the influence of the Sagrario's richly ornamented façade: the stone altarpiece of the portada which exalts the gilt altarpiece within. This, of course, was no new idea in the Spanish world. Rich altarpiece façades existed in Spain and in Peru,[6] and there was one outstanding example in southern Mexico: the Soledad in Oaxaca (1689). In the capital the idea had long been accepted. The portals of the cathedral were referred to in 1688 as "retablos de las portadas," and these doorways (Pl. LXIX, 11), so much more sober than contemporary work in Peru, were the principal model for metropolitan church façades until the mid-eighteenth century.[7] They were based on the old altarpiece arrangement of static figures between pairs of columns. Rodríguez simply raised this theme to its nth power by using the new *estípite* altarpiece design[8] with all its

---

[4] Angulo, *op.cit.*

[5] CMAM, three volumes dated 1750-68. *Cuenta y razon de las cantidades de pesos que he resivido . . . para la fabrica de la iglesia del Sagrario* (80 fols.). *Cuenta y razon de las cantidades de pesos que . . . he entregado para la fábrica* (64 fols.). *Recaudos de comprobacion de la cuenta de la fábrica material del Sagrario . . .* (803 fols.).

[6] Outstanding examples in Spain: San Gregorio and San Pablo in Valladolid (late 15th century), San Esteban in Salamanca (16th century), San Miguel de los Reyes in Valencia, and the Cartuja of Jerez de la Frontera (17th century) façade of the cathedral of Santiago de Compostela (begun 1738), and façade of the cathedral of Murcia (drawing dated 1741). In Peru: Cathedral of Cuzco and la Compañia, Cuzco (both mid-17th century), and San Francisco, Lima (ca. 1670).

[7] Angulo, *op.cit.*, p. 165, and "Eighteenth Century Church Fronts in Mexico City," *Journal of the Society of Architectural Historians*, v, 1947, p. 27-32.

[8] For the history and development of the *estípite* altarpiece see Joseph Baird, *The 18th Century Retable in the South of Spain, Portugal and Mexico*. Diss., Harvard, 1951. See also Antonio Sancho Corbacho, *Arquitectura barroca sevillana del siglo XVIII*, Madrid, 1952, and Victor Manuel Villegas, *El gran signo formal del barroco*, Mexico, 1956. It should be noted that in spite of the great

depth and excitement (Pl. LXVII, 2), achieving in stone what had previously been attempted only in wood. Within a decade this new style had begun to change the aspect of the capital, and from there it spread to the rest of the country, constantly modified, renewed and enriched by local traditions and materials, reaching at last the missions of Arizona and Texas. It did not burn itself out until the end of the century. The style was exactly suited to the needs and tastes of Mexican artists and patrons. One might almost say that it was the idea they had been waiting for, so immediate was its acceptance and so far-reaching its development.

We do not know how Rodríguez obtained the commission for a work of this importance. His later fame has led to the assumption that he was the outstanding architect of the day, but this was hardly the case before 1747, the year in which Archbishop Vizarrón died, having already approved Rodríguez' plan.[9] He had not become an architect until 1740, and the existing documents indicate that he encountered difficulty in the early years of his new career. In 1742 he became involved in a violent professional quarrel with the senior architect of the guild, Custodio Durán, *maestro mas antigua,* as he called himself.[10] Durán accused Rodríguez of malpractice and misdemeanor, but especially of being an upstart who thought he knew everything. At the end of thirty pages of invective, the old architect let slip a phrase which explains much: *vino de otra clima*—he came from another part of the world. This long and bitter quarrel clearly indicates that the coming crisis in architectural style would involve not only age against youth, but criollo against Spaniard—the classic struggle of viceregal Mexico.

The crisis was especially bitter for the American-born masters of the guild because of what was happening in that other part of the world from which Rodríguez came, Andalucía. Important patrons of architecture came from there as well—Archbishop Vizarrón, for one, and Dr. Moreno y Castro, dean of the cathe-

---

popularity of *estípite* altarpieces in Spain, the free-standing *estípite* is very rare on Spanish façades and does not occur on the altarpiece façades mentioned above. See n. 15 below.

[9] Angulo, *Estudios de los planos . . .* , p. 158.

[10] AGN, *Desagüe,* vol. 11.

dral.[11] The criollo masters had their Serlio and Vignola, and the works of Padre Tosca and others, but they were at a great disadvantage when newly arrived patrons spoke of Figueroa and Diaz in Seville, of Hurtado's work in Córdoba and Granada, or Acero's new cathedral in Cádiz.[12] These Andalusian architects, no matter how distinctive in personal style, had in common a new quality of ornament, a three dimensional surface movement which would be very hard to understand from a drawing—unless you had seen something like it. The Mexican architects actually had one Andalusian work to study, as we shall see; but it took them a long time to turn it to architectural use and even then Rodríguez had to show them how to do it.

The Andalusian style is made up of two basic types of ornament which may be called the cut style and the modeled style, seen here on doorways in Córdoba[13] and Seville (Pl. LXVII, 3, 4). The styles can overlap in time, in place, in material, and sometimes in the work of the same man, so that any brief statement about them must be a great oversimplification. It seems to be generally true, however, that the modeled style arrived in Spain earlier through the work of Italian stuccoists and the engravings of ornamented ceilings, etc. It was especially popular in Seville where a long tradition of stucco ornament existed.

The cut style had its chief centers in Córdoba and Granada. It was derived from northern ornament books such as Dietterlin (Pl. LXVII, 5) and Vredeman de Vries, and perhaps from the marble decorations of the Low Countries. In this style the design

[11] Juan Antonio de Vizarrón was a native of Puerto Santa María on the bay of Cádiz. Before coming to Mexico in 1730 he was *arcedeano* of the cathedral of Seville. Alonso Francisco Moreno y Castro was from Motril in the kingdom of Granada. Vizarrón approved the Sagrario plan, but Moreno y Castro began the work *sede vacante*, that is between archbishops, and supervised its construction until his death in 1759. The account books show the extent of his devotion to the project. No architect could have asked for a better patron.

[12] For these architects see George Kubler, *Arquitectura de los siglos XVII y XVIII* (Ars Hispaniae, XIV), Madrid, 1957; Corbacho, *op.cit.*; René Taylor, "Francisco Hurtado and his School," *Art Bulletin*, XXXII, 1950, pp. 25-61; *idem*, "La sacristia de la Cartuja de Granada y sus autores," *Archivo Español de Arte*, XXXV, 138, 1962, pp. 135-72.

[13] For the Córdoba marble style, see René Taylor, "*Estudios del barroco andaluz*," *Cuadernos de Cultura*, IV, 1958 (Córdoba); idem, "La sacristia . . . ."

can sometimes be confined to only two planes, but more often it moves on several different levels. At its most elaborate it becomes prismatic, faceted, as if borrowing from the jewel cutter's art (Pl. lxviii, 6). It can be at home in brick, in marble and even in stucco.[14] A massive and stony variant of the style is found in the architecture of Galicia.

The modeled style can usually be recognized as something added, decoration applied to a clearly seen or sensed wall surface (Pl. lxx, 16). The cut style, on the other hand, is an exercise in depth. The wall is shown to have many surfaces, one beneath the other; the support is a cluster of prisms or geometric solids (Pl. lxx, 17).

These two major themes of eighteenth-century ornament arrived in Mexico very early, and in a sense they arrived together. In 1718 Jerónimo Balbás[15] came from Seville to build the Altar of the Kings in the apse of the cathedral of Mexico (Pl. lxviii, 7). Balbás was already famous in Andalucía, and long before the altarpiece was finished, his style had made a great impression. His architectonic background is made up of sharply edged geometric solids, but this is nearly concealed by an over-layer of swags and garlands, fruit, flowers and leaves, and a heavy population of angels and cherubs (Pl. lxviii, 8). These surface adornments caught the attention of Mexican artists, as did the new support, the *estípite*. In the thirties, *estípite* altarpieces became the fashion, and leafy ornament began to appear more frequently on façades. Yet the Balbás style remained essentially a means of interior enrichment. The architects of the capital continued to prefer a sober exterior.

The Vizcainas' college[16] (begun 1734) clearly introduced the second new theme: the cut style in a massive form which does not even acknowledge Balbás' existence (Pl. lxix, 10). The man who designed these walls was thinking only of Mexican stone, red *tezontle* and pale *chiluca*. His name is not documented, but

[14] For examples of these different materials as they occur in the Seville area, see Corbacho, *op.cit.*

[15] Corbacho, *op.cit.*, pp. 273-75, and Angulo, *Historia del arte hispanoamericano*, Barcelona, 1945-56, ii, pp. 558ff.

[16] Gonzalo Obregón Jr., *El real colegio de San Ignacio de México*, Mexico, 1949.

the architect who directed the work until his death was Miguel de Rivera, whose niece Rodríguez married and whose architectural books he inherited. The façades of the Sagrario owe a debt both to Rivera and to Balbás. The masterly contrast of *tezontle* and *chiluca*, the depth of carving and the bold scale of the ornament (though not its forms) derive from the Vizcainas façade, while the altarpiece portals refer to the Altar of the Kings.

The interior of the Sagrario[17] has always received less attention than its façades, yet it is probably unique in America—a spatial concept of the Cinquecento, the ideal Renaissance central plan with five domes, simple, austere and filled with light, based on a plan of Serlio (Pl. LXXI, 18-20). The contrast with the flamboyant exterior is startling, to say the least, and the effect is somehow reminiscent of those medieval reliquaries in which a holy object and its original container were enclosed in the extravagantly rich outer covering of a later century (Pl. LXX, 21).

The word *sagrario* is often used in the Spanish church to designate the container on or behind the altar in which.the Holy Sacra-

---

[17] The interior of the Sagrario is almost unknown to the present generation. The building has recently been reopened after extensive repairs which were necessary to save it from collapse. It has suffered fires, earthquakes and the constant settling caused by the unstable soil of Mexico. Funds for repairs are limited, and in order to use the building once more as a parish church, it has been necessary to build two temporary walls from either side of the main entrance to the altar. These, added to the remaining 19th century decorations, completely destroy Rodríguez' intention: the church as a great pavilion of many vistas whose architecture would inevitably dominate the added decoration of gilt altarpieces.

When Rodríguez' plan is aligned with Serlio's "Tempio quadrato in croce" in the Fifth Book, the proportions are seen to be virtually identical (Pl. LXXI, 18). Proportions in elevation are just as close (Pl. LXXI, 19), but the interior of the Sagrario departs from Serlio's design (Pl. LXXI, 20) and follows Mexican antecedents. The cathedral's doric order and fluted arches are used, and there are similarities with the "elongated square" plans of La Profesa and the Basilica of Guadalupe, especially in regard to the opening up of the corner chapels which are enclosed in Serlio's plan. In the perfect square of the Sagrario, this open arrangement, whether by accident or design, echoes older and more distant sources which cannot be discussed in this paper. It is interesting to note that the vaulting system used in all the buildings mentioned above (*bóvedas de cañon de lunetas*, barrel vaults with transverse ribs and lunettes) appears in Serlio immediately after the Tempio Quadrato, and also in the widely known Herrera engravings of the Escorial (Luis Cervera Vera, *Las estampas y el Sumario de el Escorial por Juan de Herrera*, Madrid, 1954).

ment is kept. In Spain these were frequently architectural in form: a round or square "temple" made of colored marbles. The sacramental character of Rodríguez' Sagrario is clearly stated. A monstrance surrounded by angels is carved on the highest point of the principal façade, and again over the great door leading from the cathedral into the Sagrario (Pls. LXVII, 2; LXX, 15a). Here the sacrament is enclosed in the clear geometry of space, a memory of Roman space, and then surrounded by an outer wall whose color and fantasy suggest an accumulation of all the riches of the Indies— yet only the stone and the *conjunto* are Mexican; the vocabulary of ornamental forms is purely European.

The forms are hard and clear, cut with a jeweler's precision to catch the light on a thousand sharp edges. Balbás' fruity garlands and perched angels are stripped away; foliage on the *estípites* is read not as leaves but as a solid mass on a raised panel (Pl. LXVIII, 9). The wall surface disappears among advancing and receding planes and a constant flicker of light. Not the least of Rodríguez' achievements was the organization of a crew of stonecutters who could master this difficult new technique with such virtuosity.

The design of the façade may perhaps be explained by a preference for Andalusian ornament on the part of the archibishop or the dean. As far as we now know, Rodríguez was the only Spanish-born architect in the city at that time. He was the son of a Cordoban master; he had been a boy in Guadix when Acero was *maestro mayor* of the cathedral there, and he probably followed Acero to Cádiz. He knew the style. There may, however, have been a more pressing reason for the sudden introduction of a new architectural style into Mexico. Work did not begin on the Sagrario until two years after the archbishop's death, and the documents concerning the events of February–June 1749 strongly suggest that the building not only introduced a new style but represented a break, public and ceremonial, with the old way of doing things. The plan was approved by the cabildo of the cathedral, the viceroy, the viceroy's financial adviser, the royal engineer, and a committee from the guild of architects, and work began on the foundations—all within five weeks.[18] These decisions were made and implemented in Mexico, without the king's permission

---

[18] Angulo, *Estudios de los planos* . . . , III, pp. 157ff.

or knowledge, a procedure which was not only extraordinary but illegal, as the king later pointed out in one of the most ill-tempered royal documents ever to issue from Buen Retiro.[19]

The explanation of the events of 1749 lies in the complicated financial history of the cathedral of Mexico. The cathedral was unfinished, and for more than half a century the work had been at a standstill while a succession of archbishops had attempted to obtain money from the royal treasury.[20] The need for a new Sagrario was particularly pressing.[21] Parish functions were carried on by four priests in two small chapels within the cathedral. The city was growing rapidly; crowds of parishioners blocked the aisles of the cathedral, and in the epidemic of 1737 the building was almost filled with bodies awaiting burial. The evidence of 1749 suggests that the dean had abandoned hope of obtaining money from the king, who as royal patron financed the building of all cathedral and parish churches,[22] and had instead embarked on a program designed to appeal to civic pride as well as to piety. We do not know what negotiations went on behind the scenes, but the project was remarkably well organized. The papers in the Archivo de Indias[23] show that more was accomplished in five weeks in obtaining approval to start work than in the preceding fifty years, and an account of the "ceremony of the first stone"[24] in May 1749, records an impressive alliance of sponsors who took part: the dean and cathedral clergy, the viceroy and his staff, the city government, and the *archicofradía* of the Santísimo Sacramento.[25] The *archicofradía* was composed of the wealthiest and and most influential laymen in the city. Many of them were bankers and merchants who were also members of the *consulado*,

[19] Royal *cédula* of March 15, 1758. AGN, *Obras Públicas*, vol. 34, fols. 44-49.
[20] An exhaustive review of the cathedral's finances is to be found in AGN, *Obras Públicas*, vol. 34.
[21] CMAC, *Libro 15*, no. 27, fol. 235v; AGI, *Audiencia de Mexico 805*. Letter from the king to the archbishop dated June 17, 1736; AGI, *Audiencia de Mexico 818*. Letter from Archbishop Vizarrón to the king, dated June 4, 1740.
[22] J. L. Mecham, *Church and State in Latin America*, Chapel Hill, 1934, pp. 1-44.
[23] Angulo, *Estudios de los planos . . .* , iii, pp. 157ff.
[24] Vizcainas archive, V-V-3, box 8. The ceremony is described by the secretary of the *archicofradía* of the Santísimo Sacramento.
[25] For the history of the *archicofradía* see José Maria Marroqui, *La ciudad de México*, Mexico, 1903, iii, pp. 432-47.

the "university" of businessmen who financed many civic projects and who contributed heavily to the building of the Sagrario.[26] In new Spain, such a group of sponsors would be more likely to rally to a grandiose project than to a purely utilitarian makeshift. If money had to be raised, if royal displeasure had to be risked, let it be done for a church worthy to stand beside the cathedral, facing the great plaza. Let it be so splendid that the people of Mexico, rich and poor, would contribute to its building. When the king was finally told about the Sagrario, he was assured that it would be "the wonder of America."[27]

The diary of Castro Santa-Anna[28] shows that public response was enthusiastic from the first. Rodríguez is mentioned several times, and referred to as the Sagrario's "diestro maestro."

The account books of the Sagrario[29] present an almost total record of the building program for eighteen years—July 1750 to May 1768. They include records of income and expenditure, and 1600 pages of payrolls, bills and receipts. In the income book we find the names of donors, the alms brought in day after day by Padre Sarmiento who went around the city on a mule, and the sums realized from lotteries whenever other sources of money failed. The record shows that not one peso came to the Sagrario from the royal treasury.[30]

The payroll book includes weekly purchases of materials and payments for cut stone. The masons were paid by the piece, and each piece was described and located, so that we can literally follow the progress of the work stone by stone as the walls rise. The influence of the Sagrario has always been discussed in relation to the terminal date, 1768, carved in the façade, but the payroll book shows that this is the date of dedication, and that the exterior of the building was completed long before.

[26] *Universidad de los mercaderes de Nueva España, Ordenanzas . . . del consulado . . .* , Mexico, 1772. See also Charles E. Chapman, "Consulados," *Hispanic American Essays*, Chapel Hill, 1942.

[27] Angulo, *Estudios de los planos . . .* , III, p. 162.

[28] José Manuel de Castro Santa-Anna, *Diario de sucesos notables* (*Documentos para la historia de México*, IV-VI), Mexico, 1854. See entries for October 1752, March 1753, September 1755.

[29] See n. 5.

[30] This is also stated by Fonseca and Urrutia in *Historia general de real hacienda*, Mexico, 1853, I, p. 535.

The main foundations were finished during 1751, and work began immediately on the bases of piers and pilasters. During the next two years, while the interior structure continued to rise, the exterior *tezontle* walls were in work. Some of the windows were completed in 1753 and probably one of the corner doors. The *estípite* façade panels (Pl. LXIX, 13) began to take shape very early. Foundations and bases of both façades were in work late in 1751; during the next year the pedestals were completed and two courses of the *estípites* themselves were carved and set in place—perhaps blocked in and finished in place. It is hard to be sure about the exact sculptural method, but three times during 1753 large pieces of wood were bought for a model of the portal. The façades continued to rise level by level, straight across the panel from buttress to buttress, at the rate of approximately three courses a year on each side. Each course was paid for as a unit, and the number and size of the stones is recorded in each case.

1756 was the year of greatest financial trouble, and work halted for a time on the portals, though not on the building itself. Then in 1757 the organization of the program was changed and Rodríguez undertook the completion of the work himself on a contract basis. Unfortunately for us, the payrolls were no longer kept by the treasurer, and we have only the receipts for large sums paid regularly to Rodríguez. The last of the receipts, in April 1760, includes the architect's statement that the archbishop and commissioners had inspected the building and were satisfied with the completion of the vaults and portals, and that he was satisfied with the money he had received—as well he might be, for it was a great deal.

The payrolls began again in 1761, and Rodríguez received his monthly salary of fifty pesos until early in 1762. Odds and ends of stone work were paid for, and one door was constructed, probably the great door into the cathedral. The last materials to be bought in quantity were paving stones and window glass. From 1764 through 1767 Isidro Vicente de Balbás, son of Jerónimo, supervised the carving, gilding, and painting of the main altarpiece and pulpits which he had designed. Finally, in February 1768, the church was cleaned and swept, and benches were moved in for the ceremony of dedication.

Rodríguez meanwhile had long since assumed his duties as *maestro mayor* of the cathedral and royal palace, a time-consuming job which meant involvement in all the royal works.[31] At present we have no document which shows him to have been the architect of another large church or another *estípite* façade. Yet the most troublesome problem concerning Rodríguez' ornamental style is its relation to the other façades which over the years have been attributed to him.[32] Our isolation from the realities of the eighteenth century is nowhere better shown than in this curious business which in the jargon of our day might be termed "The Case of the Missing Architects." This is not too fanciful a title because a sort of crime has been committed: ten or fifteen men have been obliterated—as individuals, that is—as artists with a personal style. On the one hand we have an extraordinary group of buildings; on the other hand we may, with a little effort, obtain a list of names—the roster of the guild of architects. Somewhere in this list are the names of two or three men of great achievement, but we do not know which names they are. Only their works remain, and these in a final irony have been credited to another man. The fame of Rodríguez as architect of the Sagrario managed to survive the disasters of the nineteenth century, and it became customary to attach all elaborate *estípite* façades in the Valley of Mexico to that one remembered name.

The solution of this stylistic puzzle must await more documentary evidence, but something can be said to indicate the unlikeliness of Rodríguez' participation in two of these façades at least. It may be helpful to consider for a moment what the decade 1755-65 must have been like for the guild of architects in the City of

[31] In 1765 Rodríguez requested an increase in salary because "a más de las obras corrientes y comunes, se han encomendado a mi cuidado todas las extraordinarias que se han ofrecido del Real Servicio." The burden of this work made it increasingly difficult for him to accept private commissions. AGN, *Obras Públicas*, vol. 35.

[32] The buildings most often mentioned are the church of the Santísima Trinidad (1755-83, façade undated), the Balvanera Chapel in the church of San Francisco (chapel dedicated 1766, façade undated) and the façade of the Jesuit seminary at Tepotzotlán (early 1760's). The façade of the oratorio of San Felipe Neri is concealed by a modern wall and can be studied only in photographs. Santa Vera Cruz is a more modest work, probably finished after Rodríguez' death. The *estípite* type is very close to that of the Sagrario.

Mexico—the end of one world and the beginning of another. Is this too dramatic a statement? I really do not think so. The scale of the Sagrario, the prominence of its position on the Plaza Mayor, the importance of its sponsors, the drive and determination of its chief patron and its architect, the final impact of the last two years of construction when the great façades were rushed to completion and when Juan de Viera[33] saw artists (*muchos artífices*) coming to copy the sculptural details of the façades—all these things, architecturally speaking, broke the century in two. Until then, startling innovations in the viceregal style had been left to Puebla and the South, while the maestros of the capital proceeded in their rather sober-sided classicizing manner. Public response to the Sagrario changed that forever, and the City of Mexico suddenly became the center from which a new development began to spread.

The crisis probably took the guild of architects by surprise, because events leading up to it had tapered off some years before. During the thirties there had been many important building programs and some new developments in the style of the capital. But the men responsible for these works had disappeared from the scene.[34] They had felt the first stirrings of a new style, a sort of uneasy preliminary movement in the soil of Mexico. When the earthquake came, what happened to their sons, pupils and followers, those shadowy figures on our list of names?

One way of dealing with the anonymous façades is to look at them as an answer to this question. It seems to me that in two of them especially, the Santísima and Tepotzotlán (Pl. LXIX, 12), we can see what happened to a man, or men, trained in one tradition and suddenly catapulted into another, whether by economic necessity or desire to master a new style. Both these façades are

---

[33] Juan de Viera, *Breve compendiosa narracion de la ciudad de Mexico*, ed. Gonzalo Obregón Jr., Mexico, 1952, p. 36.

[34] Pedro de Arrieta, the leading figure, died in 1738, followed by Rivera in 1739. The elder Alvarez and Herrera were dead before 1744, and Durán disappears from the records in the mid-40's. The royal engineer who created a stir with his oval plan for Santa Brígida, Diez Navarro, had been transferred to Guatemala. Balbás, *adelantor* of the new style, could not carry out any of his architectural ambitions. See Berlin, "Three master architects . . . ," and "Artifices de la catedral. . . ."

organized on the old principle favored for generations: an arrangement of rectangular areas within which one sets up a doorway with a large opening or relief panel above, and columns flanking niches on either side. In both façades, the columns have been replaced by *estípites*, and a layer of ornament in the modeled style (Pl. lxx, 15b, 16) has been added to the old design scheme. Both ignore the principle which underlies Rodríguez' use of ornament, a principle so old and so common in Spain as to be instinctive: on a façade, lavish ornament must be controlled in area and displayed against a plain background. The use of rusticated buttresses and towers weakens the effect of both the anonymous façades. Yet one must pay tribute to what these artists accomplished. Armed with a few pattern books and a love of surface richness they set themselves up as practitioners of the new style, and, in the case of Tepotzotlán at least, brought it off magnificently. When one is there on a sunny afternoon, Tepotzotlán has no faults, and one feels nothing but gratitude for the color and exuberance of this enormous tapestry. By manipulation of a great crowd of personages and scenes, the artist has given a new meaning to the old façade pattern, and his solution will be encountered in hundreds of provincial variants.

The Balvanera façade, the third important anonymous work (Pl. lxx, 14), is a very different matter: the design of an artist entirely committed to the new style, further committed even than Rodríguez, but leaning very heavily on certain details of the Sagrario façade. I would not remove the possibility that Rodríguez had a hand in this work, but it is so much less architectonic than the Sagrario design that it seems more likely to have been the work of a pupil or close collaborator. Like the Sagrario, the Balvanera façade uses an ornamental vocabulary derived from the cut style (Pl. lxx, 17) and is designed on an intricate and elaborate pattern of overlapping circles and triangles. It is strange that many critics find this style of visual ornament undisciplined and vulgar, yet regard the same technique in music as one of the highest forms of art. Perhaps the difficulties are less forbidding when listened to, a few notes at a time. In our bereft century we prefer to look at something simple; we cannot even approach the kind of controlled mental gymnastics required to construct counterpoint. This was a turn of mind not uncommon among artists of the seventeenth and eighteenth centuries, and in the Sagrario and Balvanera façades we have compositions in Baroque counterpoint *a lo grande*, proceeding through theme and episode, theme and episode, from base to pinnacle in one unbroken statement, massive yet precise, self-assured and self-disciplined. The theme of ascending motion is introduced and withdrawn, re-introduced in slightly different form, played in reverse and upside down, changed in scale and tempo, and finally restated clearly and released. The result is a purely intellectual representation of a strong emotion: the transcendental made tangible.

The desire to perform this miracle in stone transformed the architecture of New Spain in the last half of the eighteenth century.

The study of this architecture and this period in Mexico has lacked one thing above all—a viewpoint. The monuments which survived physical destruction have also outlasted hysterical disapproval, indifference, and condescension. Since none of these attitudes can be of any use to us, we must find another, and Justino Fernández has recently pointed it out. In his esthetic history of the period, *El Retablo de los Reyes*,[35] he has made a unique contribution to viceregal studies by establishing the importance of the concept of *grandeza* throughout the sixteenth, seventeenth, and eighteenth centuries. The point is proved not by argument but by massive evidence of what the people of Mexico thought and said about the grandeur of their city, and the impact of this idea on foreign visitors who recognized it for what it was until well into the nineteenth century. According to its poets, Mexico was a "city of palaces" for nearly three hundred years before Humboldt used the phrase. The theme of grandeur remains constant from Cervantes de Salazar's *Latin Dialogues* of 1554 ("Que adornada de altos y soberbios edificios . . . que regularidad! que belleza!") through Arias de Villalobos in 1603 ("En ti, nueva ciudad de Carlos Quinto/ halló nueva Venecia, Atenas nueva . . ."), and Balbuena's *Grandeza Mexicana* of 1604, a detailed and delightful description of the city in its golden age; through dozens

[35] Justino Fernández, *El Retablo de los Reyes*, Mexico, 1959.

of baroque apostrophes of later decades and finally the astonished letters of nineteenth-century travelers.[36] For our purposes some lines from Arias de Villalobos' *Mercurio* are particularly apt:

> Vamos a los retablos de su frente
> de Apeles y Parrasios propios nuestros;
> aqui el relieve y el pincel valiente
> vuelvan a lo inmortal por sus maestros. . . .

I think that the stylistic crisis of the century and the triumph of the Sagrario can only be understood within the framework of this tradition. The success of the style was the success of immediate recognition of the artist's intent: a restatement of the old idea of *grandeza mexicana* in a new and splendid form.

[36] *Ibid.*, pp. 18-119.

LA PINTURA EN VENEZUELA EN LOS SIGLOS XVII Y XVIII: NOTICIA PRELIMINA SOBRE UNA INVESTIGACION

ALFREDO BOULTON

DESEO presentar algunas consideraciones y resultados, aún provisionales, acerca de una investigación sobre la pintura en Venezuela durante los siglos XVI y XVIII. El tema, bueno es decirlo, no había sido abordado anteriormente, por lo que creo puede ser de interés para los especialistas y estudiosos de esa materia conocer algunos de sus aspectos sobresalientes. La historia de la pintura durante nuestro período colonial era un campo virgen que requería del lento y minucioso hurgar, entre documentos y lienzos, para indagar sus verdaderos orígenes, buscar sus huellas, y saber de su formación y crecimiento durante aquel período todavía tan escasamente conocido por los investigadores de arte. Al poner al descubierto las más tenues raíces de muestra tradición pictórica, estaremos en condiciones de comprender mejor los fundamentos de nuestra presente inquietud artística.

Las más antiguas manifestaciones de pintura occidental de que se tenga noticia en Venezuela ascienden a los alrededores de 1520, y han sido localizadas en la Isla de Cubagua. Esta fabulosa pequeña porción de tierra, que los historiadores designan con el nombre de Isla de las Perlas, fue la primera fuente de riqueza que la Corona de España obtuvo como premio del descubrimiento de América. En las ruinas de la ciudad de Nueva Cádiz se han encontrado fragmentos de dibujos hechos con grafito que han debido servir para adornar las paredes de la capilla del monasterio de los frailes franciscanos. Sobre la burda argamasa, un dibujante anónimo trazó con desenvoltura y sobriedad algunas figuras de las cuales sólo ha llegado hasta nuestros días esa muy pequeña muestra, testimonio del primer rasgo plástico de origen español hecho en tierra firme.

El caso de Cubagua en sí es un episodio pasajero, pero muy similar a lo que luego sucedió en la propia Provincia de Venezuela, pues aquello que se había iniciado bajo tan provechosos auspicios y alcanzado gran fama y riqueza fue de escasa duración. Si el bienestar de la isla tan sólo subsistió unos escasos veinte años, la prosperidad de la provincia sufrió un colapso después de 1810, a causa de la dura lucha por lograr su independencia política. En ambos casos el sosegado ritmo de las actividades creadoras se vio súbitamente afectado, hasta llegar a la paralización, por la crisis que alteró de manera substancial el giro de las principales normas de vida humana. Trescientos años habían transcurrido en el segundo de los casos, durante los cuales se había formado una conciencia cultural que tuvo su verdadera iniciación a partir solamente en las primeras décadas de 1600 cuando se consolidó la empresa conquistadora al convertirse la lucha guerrera en estabilidad y asentamiento provincial. El ritmo de vida segura y beneficiosa sólo pudo lograrse bien entrada esa centuria y fue a partir de entonces cuando en verdad la pintura floreció de manera ininterrumpida, si bien en modesta escala, en ninguna forma comparable con la de otros países americanos, donde ya existía en el nativo una alta tradición de carácter artístico. La pintura en nuestro medio fue producto exclusivo de la civilización occidental y por razones de la pobreza del suelo, de la incultura de nuestros aborígenes y por la prolongada resistencia que presentaron a los conquistadores, lo que trajo como resultado su tardía aparición en las fechas ya señaladas junto con las primeras muestras de arquitectura religiosa, a semejanza de lo ocurrido en el resto de América donde las artes plásticas formaron parte integral de los ritos cristianos.

En la investigación que se está efectuando surgen varios "Maestros de Arte de Pintor" que sirvieron a la Iglesia, construyendo retablos, pintando imágenes, y dorando altares. Los nombres de esos modestos artesanos, consignados en las Actas Capitulares, son los primeros que se registran en Venezuela: Tomás de Cocar, Pedro de la Peña y Juan Agustín Riera, activos los tres en Coro hacia 1602 y años inmediatos, cuando esta ciudad era la capital de la provincia y su sede episcopal. Por sus pinturas, hechas sobre lienzo de algodón, ellos recibían a veces en pago, harina, alojamiento, o una botija de vino.

Pasado ese primer período se tiene información de otras obras ejecutadas en Caracas, cabeza ya de la provincia, por artesanos, que, como era frecuente entonces en nuestro medio, ejercían a la vez diversas profesiones, entre las de albañil, pintor, tallista y dorador. Hasta uno de ellos, Fray Fernando de la Concepción, tuvo a su cargo los trabajos del acueducto de la ciudad. Juan de Medina, quien reedificó la catedral que el terremoto de 1641 había destruído, talló también sus altares. Juan Maldonado pintó una Sta Ana y un Apóstol Santiago para el Altar Mayor, sobre "bramante crudo."

El mencionado Fray Fernando, además de pintar y aliñar imágenes, dorar retablos, y estar activo durante más de veinte años—hacia 1660-80—en menesteres de religión y arte, era con frecuencia solicitado para el avalúo de pinturas en documentos testamentarios. Existen, asimismo, ciertos indicios de que fue el autor del retrato del Obispo Fray Antonio González de Acuña que se conserva actualmente en el Palacio Arzobispal de Caracas. Esa imagen es, posiblemente, la única de que se tengan suficientes motivos para atribuirla a alguno de aquellos primeros pintores.

Es desafortunado que los pocos lienzos de esa época que perduran no lleven firma alguna, pues eso nos impide apreciar mejor la obra de aquellos interesantes artistas, tan imbuídos del espíritu humanista de su tiempo y de quienes arrancan en verdad, en forma ininterrumpida, las actividades pictóricas en Venezuela. Se conoce un pequeño número de lienzos que por su estilo, carácter y técnica pueden ser atribuídos a artistas que estuvieron activos durante el período que reseñamos y que vienen a ser más que nada prueba material de esa actividad, testimonio más histórico que artístico. Su reducido número es prueba, también, de la inclemencia de nuestro clima tropical, de la condición limitada del ambiente cultural y de otros factores negativos que entrabaron aquellos días de génesis pictórico.

A la altura que va nuestra investigación hay razones para creer que no tuvimos en Caracas reglamentos de carácter gremial que rigiesen las actividades de los pintores; lo cual vendría a demostrar que tales actividades fueron de reducida importancia, puesto que las autoridades locales no se ocuparon en reglamentarlas, como en otras regiones de Hispanoamérica. Pero al lado de esos factores adversos existen otros que prueban un innegable interés por las manifestaciones plásticas de parte de esa pequeña población que para la última década del XVII solamente llegaba a los 6.000 habitantes. En los archivos testamentarios caraqueños han salido a luz datos que demuestran cómo en el transcurso de la décima-séptima centuria fueron legadas más de tres mil doscientas pinturas, y de esa cifra el 90% corresponde a la segunda mitad del siglo. Ahora bien, si comparamos el número de habitantes con la cantidad de cuadros mencionados en esos registros, podremos darnos cuenta de que 3.200 imágenes acumuladas en cincuenta años entre tan escasos pobladores demuestran a las claras una marcada inclinación hacia ese tipo de manifestación artística. Máxime, si se toma en cuenta que en ese total no están incluídas las imágenes que pertenecían entonces a quienes no habían aún testado, ni tampoco las que eran de las iglesias, de órdenes religiosas, de capillas y ermitas. Tenemos listas completas que nos muestran cuán frecuente era encontrar en las principales moradas un crecido número de pinturas que en algunos casos alcanzaban cifras tan elevadas como los noventa y nueve lienzos propiedad del Obispo González de Acuña, los ochenta y siete de don Francisco Aguirre de Liendo, los setenta y cuatro de Juan de la Torre o los setenta y siete de Domingo Hermoso de Mendoza. No todos eran de motivos religiosos, sino que trataban también de temas diversos como, por ejemplo, "las doce sibilas," países "flamencos," "los siete infantes de Lara," la "Reina nuestra Señora doña Mariana de Austria, de gala," países españoles, gitanas y hasta cuadros de cacería, que los avaluadores denominaban escuetamente "cuadros de perros." De Campeche venían pinturas y de Italia enviaban "láminas romanas." Con todo lo cual se puede en parte recrear la vida de las imágenes durante ese siglo XVII.

El indudable interés por la pintura que revelan las cifras anteriores se tradujo en la práctica ciudadana y efectiva en el incremento de pintores locales, entre los que se destacan a lo largo del siglo XVIII, ya por su buena calidad, Francisco José de Lerma, Juan Pedro López, Fernando Alvarez Carneiro, Francisco Narciso de Arévalo y Javier Flores. En algunos de ellos y especialmente en el primero, se advierte un estilo con visos de reminiscencia flamenca, acaso aprendidos en Sevilla o en las numerosas obras que nos llegaban de ultramar. Lerma estuvo activo hasta 1730 y fue un buen ejemplo de sensibilidad disciplinada en esos días alborales de nuestro tardío barroquismo (Pl. LXXII, 1).

En cambio, Juan Pedro López, personaje de importancia en la ciudad, fue el pintor más representativo de la que se ha denominado escuela de Caracas. Su estilo parece recrearse en los voluminosos ropajes y las ricas líneas de las composiciones barrocas ya en linde con el rocayesco, tan del gusto de nuestros principales tallistas. Javier Flores, hacia 1774, siguió el estilo y la huella marcada por López sin alcanzar sin embargo su amplitud artística ni su fuerte carácter, tan típico de nuestra pintura de esa época.

La investigación se ha llevado a cabo también en el propio campo de las imágenes. El número de ellas que subsiste es relativamente pequeño, pero ha sido posible examinar más de mil pinturas entre lienzos, tablas, grabados y cobres, de las cuales se han tomado más de seiscientas fotografías que sirven como material complementario para el estudio crítico que está en preparación. Creo que el resultado final puede revelar que la pintura fue, en el período estudiado, la actividad artística de mayor desarrollo en Venezuela, superior a la literatura o a la arquitectura. Bien servidos nos sentiríamos con tan sólo descorrer el espeso velo de ignorancia que nos enturbia la vista, para poder ver con precisión el pequeño y cautivador paisaje de la pintura colonial en Venezuela durante los siglos XVII y XVIII.

APPENDIX

225

226

APPENDIX

V O L U M E   I V

PROBLEMS OF THE 19TH AND 20TH CENTURIES

FRANK LLOYD WRIGHT AND ARCHITECTURE AROUND 1900

Introduction
HENRY-RUSSELL HITCHCOCK

Frank Lloyd Wright and Twentieth-Century Style
VINCENT SCULLY, JR.

The Prairie School, the Midwest Contemporaries of Frank Lloyd Wright
H. ALLEN BROOKS

California Contemporaries of Frank Lloyd Wright, 1885-1915
STEPHEN W. JACOBS

Wright's Eastern-Seaboard Contemporaries: Creative Eclecticism in the United States around 1900
CARROLL L. V. MEEKS

The British Contemporaries of Frank Lloyd Wright
JOHN SUMMERSON

THE REACTION AGAINST IMPRESSIONISM IN THE 1880's: ITS NATURE AND CAUSES

Introduction
MEYER SCHAPIRO

The Reaction against Impressionism from the Artistic Point of View
FRITZ NOVOTNY

The Changing Values of Light-Space-Form between 1876 and 1890
A. M. HAMMACHER

Symbolic Form: Symbolic Content
ROBERT GOLDWATER

La fin de l'Impressionnisme: Esthétique et causalité
PIERRE FRANCASTEL

THE AESTHETIC AND HISTORICAL ASPECTS OF THE PRESENTATION OF DAMAGED PICTURES

Introduction
CRAIG HUGH SMYTH, *Chairman*

Taste and Science in the Presentation of Damaged Pictures
PHILIP HENDY

Il trattamento delle lacune e la Gestalt psycologie
CESARE BRANDI

Restoration and Conservation
RICHARD OFFNER

DISCUSSION SESSION

MILLARD MEISS
PAUL B. COREMANS
SHELDON KECK
JOSÉ GUDIOL
CHARLES SEYMOUR, JR.
HENRI MARCEAU
TRENCHARD COX

JOHN COOLIDGE
GEORGE L. STOUT
JOHN MAXON
EDWARD S. KING

Conclusion
CRAIG HUGH SMYTH, *Chairman*

PLENARY SESSION: MOTIVES

KENNETH CLARK

INTERNATIONAL COMMITTEE
OF THE HISTORY OF ART

PLATES

1. Borromini, Fireplace, Sala di Ricreazione, Oratory, S. Filippo Neri

2. Base of column, S. Agnese fuori le Mura

3. Fountain, Flavian Palace on the Palatine

4. Circular temple, Baalbek

5. Tomb of the Caetenii. Excavation under St. Peter's

6. Sarcophagus, Melfi

7. Theater, Sabratha

8. Temple near Tivoli

9. Ancient building near via Labicana

10. Ancient building near via Labicana

11. Ancient building near Tivoli

8-11. G. B. Montanus, Engravings

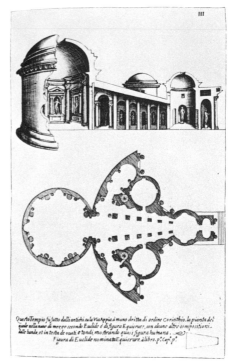

12. Design for a tabernacle   13. Ancient building on via Appia

12-13. G. B. Montanus, Engravings

14. The Conocchia, near Capua Vetere

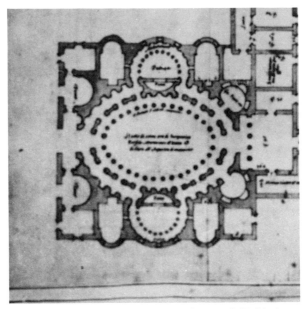

15. Pirro Ligorio, Reconstruction of part of Hadrian's
Villa. Windsor Castle, Royal Library

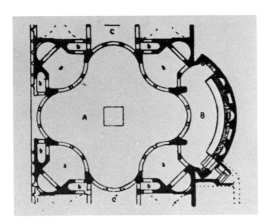

16. Plan, Piazza d'Oro, Hadrian's Villa, Tivoli

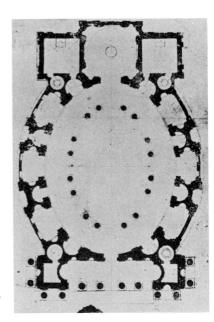

17. O. Mascherino, Plan for
Sto. Spirito dei Napoletani

18. Tomb, Ostia (Porto)

19. Borromini, S. Giovanni in Oleo

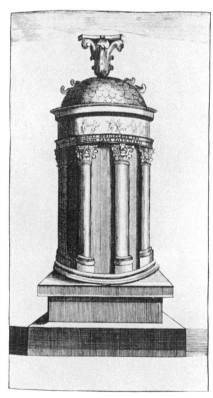

20. Choragic Monument of Lysicrates, Athens (engraving from Spon and Wheler)

1. Van Dyck, *Armida and the Sleeping Rinaldo* (drawing).
Formerly Fairfax Murray Collection

2. Baglione, *Armida and Rinaldo*
Rome, Casino Rospigliosi

3. After Van Dyck, *Armida and the Sleeping Rinaldo*. Los Angeles County Museum of Art

4. Endymion Sarcophagus. Rome, Casino Rospigliosi

6. Van Dyck, *Crucified Christ between St. Dominic and St. Catherine of Siena*

5. Cupid Quenching Inverted Torch (engraving) (from Bartoli and Bellori, *Admiranda romanarum* . . . , Rome, 1693, pl. 67)

7. Nereid sarcophagus, detail. Rome, Vatican

8. Rubens, *Arrival of Marie de Médicis at Marseilles*, detail

9. Harpocrates (from La Chausse, *Le grand cabinet romain* . . . , Amsterdam, 1706, fig. 26)

10. Brescia *Victory*

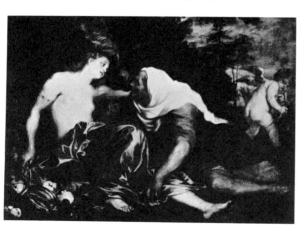

11. Van Dyck, *Vertumnus and Pomona*. Genoa, Collection of the Marchese Gustavo Doria

12. Van Dyck, after Titian. Chatsworth Sketchbook

13. Van Dyck, *Armida and the Sleeping Rinaldo*.
Baltimore Museum of Art, Epstein Collection

14. Van Dyck, after Titian, *Mars and Venus*.
Chatsworth Sketchbook

15. Van Dyck, after Titian, *Education
of Cupid*. Chatsworth Sketchbook

16. Van Dyck, *Rinaldo and Armida*. Paris, Louvre

17. Fresco from House of Mars and Venus, Pompeii

18. Carracci, *Rinaldo and Armida*. Naples, Pinacoteca

19. Fresco from House of Bronzes, Pompeii

20. Van Dyck, after Titian, *Toilet of Venus*.
Chatsworth Sketchbook

21. Veronese, after Titian (?), *Toilet of Venus*.
Collection of Viscount Lee of Fareham

22. Veronese (?), *Toilet of Venus*. Formerly
A. von Frey Collection, Paris

1. Jan Lievens, *Finding of Erichthonius*.
Emden, Ostfriesisches Landesmuseum

2. Antonio Tempesta, *Finding of Erichthonius*
(etching). New York, Metropolitan Museum of
Art (Whittelsey Fund, 1951)

3. Rembrandt, *Finding of Erichthonius* (drawing).
Private collection, U.S.A.

4. Rembrandt, *Finding of Erichthonius* (drawing).
Groningen, Museum (Copyright Piet Boonstra)

5. Engraving after Hendrick Goltzius, *Finding of Erichthonius*. New York, Metropolitan Museum of Art (Whittelsey Fund, 1949)

6. Rubens, *Finding of Erichthonius*. Vaduz, Collection Prince of Liechtenstein

7. Anthonie van Blocklandt, *Finding of Erichthonius*. The Art Institute of Chicago (The Leonora Hall Gurley Memorial Collection)

8. Paulus Bor, *Finding
of Erichthonius*. Where-
abouts unknown

9. Salvator Rosa, *Finding
of Erichthonius*. Oxford,
Christ Church

10. Rubens, *Finding of Erichthonius*. London,
Collection Count Antoine Seilern

11. Woodcut from J. Sambucus,
Emblemata, Leiden, 1599

12. Rubens, *Finding of Erichthonius*. Oberlin
College, Allen Memorial Art Museum

13. After Rubens, *Finding of Erichthonius*. Columbus (Georgia), Collection Edgar C. Mayo

1. So-called Antinoüs. Rome, Vatican
(engraving, after Bellori, 1672)

2. *Tragic Mask* (Roman mosaic).
Rome, Capitoline Museum

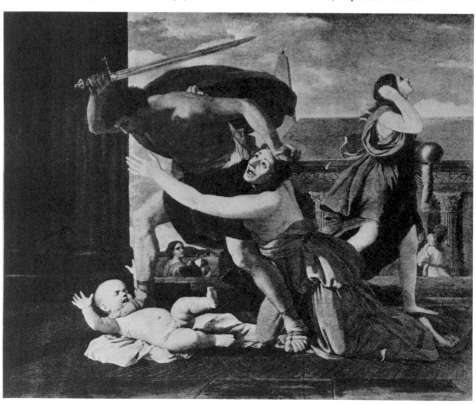

3. Poussin, *Massacre of the Innocents*. Chantilly, Musée Condé

4. *Creusa and Creon*, Roman Sarcophagus (detail). Paris, Louvre (engraving, after Bellori, 1693)

5. Poussin, *Massacre of the Innocents* (drawing). Lille, Palais des Beaux-Arts
(after Friedlaender)

6. Poussin, *Moses and the Daughters of Jethro* (drawing). London, private collection (after Friedlaender)

7a. Poussin, *Moses and the Daughters of Jethro* (drawing).
Paris, Louvre (after Friedlaender)

7b. *Juno and Niobids* (after Reinach)

8. Poussin, *Finding of Moses*, 1638. Paris, Louvre

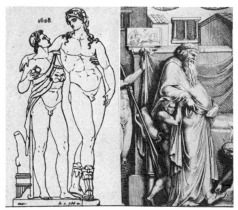

a. Ancient group   b. Detail of relief
(after Reinach)   (after Bellori, 1693)

9. *Bacchus and Satyr*

10. Poussin, *Theseus Finding the Sword of his Father*.
Chantilly, Musée Condé

11. Poussin, *Judgment of Solomon*. Paris, Louvre

12. Poussin, *Judgment of Solomon* (drawing). Paris, Ecole
des Beaux-Arts (after Friedlaender)

a. Orestes' Nurse (after Bellori, 1693) b. Althaea (after Robert, 1904)
13. Details of Roman Sarcophagi

14. Bernini, *Pluto and Proserpina*.
Rome, Villa Borghese

15. *Hercules* (Roman statue).
Rome, Capitoline Museum

16a. *Borghese Warrior*. Paris, Louvre; b. Bernini, *David*.
Rome, Villa Borghese

17a. Head of the *Apollo Belvedere*. Rome, Vatican
b. Bernini, Head of the *Apollo*. Rome, Villa Borghese

18. Bernini, *Longinus* (*bozzetto*).
Cambridge, Harvard University,
Fogg Art Museum

19. Bernini, *Angel with Superscription*.
Rome, S. Andrea delle Fratte

20a. Bernini, Head of the *Longinus*. Rome, St. Peter's
b. Head of the *Borghese Centaur*. Paris, Louvre

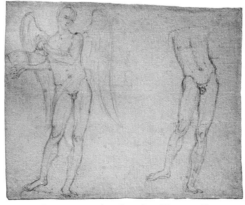

21. Preparatory drawing for Fig. 19. Rome,
Corsini Gallery (after Brauer-Wittkower)

22. Bernini, *Daniel*. Sta. Maria
del Popolo, Rome

23a. Head of the *Daniel*. b. Head of the *Laocoön*

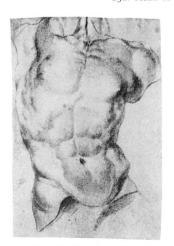  

24. Bernini, Drawing after the
Laocoön. Leipzig, Stadtbibliothek (after Brauer-Wittkower)

25-26. Bernini, *Daniel* (drawings). Leipzig,
Stadtbibliothek (after Brauer-Wittkower)

1. De Bisschop, *Bacchus and Faun*, formerly
Scholten Collection. London, Victoria and
Albert Museum (Crown Copyright Reserved)

2. De Bisschop, *Bacchus and Faun*,
formerly Scholten Collection
(from *Icones*, 1669)

3. De Bisschop, *Venus*, formerly Wlenburgh
Collection. London, Victoria and Albert
Museum (Crown Copyright Reserved)

4. De Bisschop, *Venus*, formerly Wlenburgh
Collection (from *Icones*, 1669)

5. De Bisschop, *Bacchus and Faun*, formerly Wlenburgh Collection (from *Icones*, 1669)

6. De Bisschop, *Actaeon*, formerly Scholten Collection (from *Icones*, 1669)

7. I. van Werven, *Gerard van Papenbroek's Collection as first shown at Leiden.*
Leiden, Gemeente-Archief

8. I. van Werven, *Gerard van Papenbroek's Collection*. Leiden, Gemeente-Archief

9. G. de Lairesse, *Roman Consul*, formerly Reynst Collection (from *Icones . . . Reynst*)
10. Fragment of Classical Statue, formerly Reynst Collection. Leiden, Museum van Oudheden
11. De Passe, *Human Proportions* (from *Luce del Dipingere*, 1643-44)

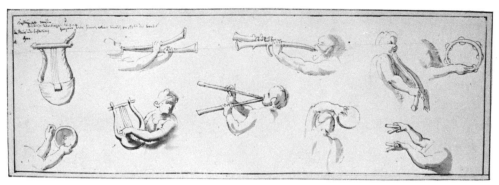

12. De Bisschop, *Studies after the Antique* (motifs from Perrier). London,
Victoria and Albert Museum (Crown Copyright Reserved)

13. De Bisschop, *Study after the Antique*
(motif from Perrier). London, Victoria
and Albert Museum (Crown
Copyright Reserved)

14. De Bisschop, *Reconstruction of a Roman Temple*.
London, Victoria and Albert Museum
(Crown Copyright Reserved)

15. De Bisschop, *Reconstruction of Domitian's Villa and Naumachia*. London,
Victoria and Albert Museum (Crown Copyright Reserved)

1. Rembrandt, *Minerva* (drawing). Amsterdam, Six Collection

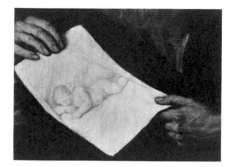

2. Detail of Fig. 1

1. Guercino, *"Disegno" and "Pittura."*
Dresden, Gemäldegalerie

3. Lorenzo Lotto, *"Lucretia."*
London, National Gallery

4. Detail of Fig. 3

5. Giovanni Francesco Caroto, *Child with Drawing*. Verona, Castelvecchio

6. Albrecht Dürer, *The Death of Orpheus*, 1494. Hamburg, Kunsthalle

7. Georg Hoefnagel, Frame for an early Flemish drawing then believed to be by Jan van Eyck. Copenhagen, Collection Count Moltke

8. Jan Wiericx, *Alexander and Apelles* (parchment). Antwerp,
Museum Mayer van den Bergh (Copyright ACL)

9. W. van Haecht, *The Collection of Cornelis van der Geest* (detail).
New York, Collection Mr. and Mrs. S. van Berg (Copyright)

1. Claude Lorrain, *View of Tivoli*. London, British Museum

2. View of Tivoli (modern photograph)

3. Claude Lorrain, *Trees and Rocks by a Waterfall*. London, British Museum

4. Claude Lorrain, *Two Pastoral Figures*.
London, British Museum

5. Claude Lorrain, *Two Figures* (after Raphael).
London, British Museum

6. Claude Lorrain, *Pastoral Landscape*. Kansas City, Missouri,
William Rockhill Nelson Gallery of Art

7. Claude Lorrain, Drawing from the *Liber Veritatis*
(No. 184). London, British Museum

9. Claude Lorrain, *Landscape with Brigands.*
London, British Museum

8. Claude Lorrain, *Study of a Tree.*
London, British Museum

10. Claude Lorrain, Drawing from the *Liber Veritatis*
(No. 3). London, British Museum

11. Claude Lorrain, *The Dismissal of Hagar*. Munich, Alte Pinakothek

12. Claude Lorrain, *The Dismissal of Hagar*
(verso). Cambridge, Fitzwilliam
Museum (Copyright)

13. Claude Lorrain, *The Dismissal of Hagar*
(recto). Cambridge, Fitzwilliam
Museum (Copyright)

14. Claude Lorrain, *The Arrival of Aeneas*.
Windsor Castle, Royal Library

1. Claude Lorrain, Preparatory Drawing for the etching *The Tempest*, 1630. London, British Museum

2. Claude Lorrain, *Morning Landscape* (drawing). Vienna, Albertina

3. Claude Lorrain, *Flight into Egypt* (four sketches). Haarlem, Teyler Museum

4. Claude Lorrain, Preparatory Sketch for *The Temple of Apollo at Delphi*. New York, Morgan Library

5. Claude Lorrain, Preparatory Drawing for *The Temple of Apollo at Delphi*. Paris, Louvre

6. Claude Lorrain, *The Calling of Peter and Andrew* (drawing). Vienna, Albertina

7. Claude Lorrain, *Mary Magdalene in Penitence*.
London, British Museum

8. Claude Lorrain, *Hill with Oak Trees*
(drawing). Haarlem, Teyler Museum

9. Claude Lorrain, *Shepherd and Shepherdess*
(etching). Vienna, Albertina

10. Claude Lorrain, *SS. Giovanni e Paolo* (drawing).
Windsor Castle, Royal Library

11. Claude Lorrain, *Herdsmen on the Campo Vaccino* (drawing). Windsor Castle, Royal Library

12. Claude Lorrain, *View in the Campagna* (drawing). Vienna, Albertina

13. Claude Lorrain, *Strada da Tivoli a Subiaco* (drawing), 1642. London, British Museum

14. Claude Lorrain, *Vista del Sasso* (drawing), 1649. Rotterdam, Boymans Museum

15. Claude Lorrain, *Figures on the Banks of a Stream near La Crescenza* (drawing), 1662. London, British Museum

17. Claude Lorrain, *Herdsman with Goats* (drawing), 1662. Haarlem, Teyler Museum

16. Claude Lorrain, *Riverside of the Tiber With Herdsmen Watering Cattle* (drawing). Vienna, Albertina

18. Claude Lorrain, *Woodland Scene with Two Wanderers* (drawing). Rotterdam, Boymans Museum

1. Jacques de Bellange, *Portia* (engraving).
Paris, Bibliothèque Nationale

2. Jacques de Bellange, *Woman Kneeling* (pen
drawing). Nancy, Musée Historique Lorrain

3. Jacques de Bellange,
Une Jardinière (pen and wash).
Stockholm, Nationalmuseum

4. Jacques de Bellange, *Une Jardinière*
(engraving). Paris,
Bibliothèque Nationale

5. Jacques de Bellange, *Hurdy-Gurdy Player* (engraving). Paris, Bibliothèque Nationale

6. Jacques de Bellange, *Hurdy-Gurdy Player* (pen drawing). London, Private collection

7. E. Sadeler after B. Spranger, *The Holy Women* (engraving). Paris, Bibliothèque Nationale

8. M. Merian the Younger after an engraving by Bellange, *The Holy Women* (engraving). Paris, Bibliothèque Nationale

9. R. Sadeler after F. Zuccaro, *St. Lawrence* (engraving). Paris, Bibliothèque Nationale

10. Jacques de Bellange, *Apostle* (engraving). Paris, Bibliothèque Nationale

11. Jacques de Bellange, *Saints* (pen and wash). Frankfurt, Städel Institut

12. School of Lagneau, *Centenarian*. Paris,
Bibliothèque Nationale

13. Lagneau, *La Monstrueuse* (caricature).
Paris, Bibliothèque Nationale

14. Lagneau, *Man with Skullcap*. Paris,
Bibliothèque Nationale

15. Lagneau, *Old Woman with a Cane*. Paris,
Bibliothèque Nationale

16. Lagneau, *Drinker, I*. Paris,
Bibliothèque Nationale

17. Lagneau, *Drinker, II*. Paris,
Bibliothèque Nationale

18. Lagneau, *Attentive Man*. Paris,
Bibliothèque Nationale

19. Lagneau, *Attentive Man*. Paris,
Bibliothèque Nationale

20. Lagneau, *Woman with Wide Face*. Paris, Bibliothèque Nationale

21. Lagneau, *Woman with Narrow Face*. Paris, Bibliothèque Nationale

22. Lagneau, *Person of Consequence*. Paris, Bibliothèque Nationale

23. Lagneau, *The Captain*. Paris, Bibliothèque Nationale

24. Lagneau, *Man with High Hat*. Rennes,
Musée des Beaux-Arts

25. School of Lagneau, *Rogue*. Paris,
Bibliothèque Nationale

26. School of George de La Tour, Woman with
Headdress, detail of *The Market*.
Private collection

27. School of Lagneau, *Woman with Headdress*.
Paris, Private collection

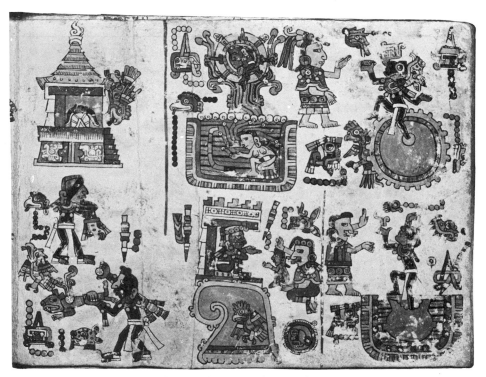

1. Codex Nuttall, p. 9. London, British Museum

2. Mixtec *policroma laca* tripod from Nochistlán,
Oaxaca. Mexico, Museo National de Antropología

3. Codex Borgia, p. 21. Rome, Vatican Library

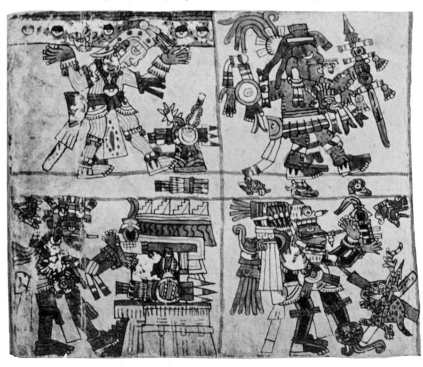

4. Codex Vaticanus B, p. 19. Rome, Vatican Library

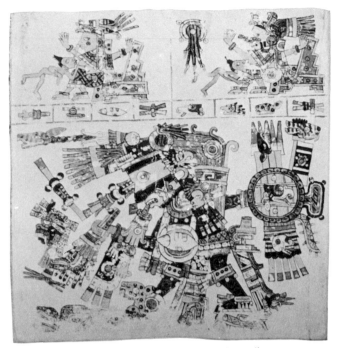

5. Codex Borgia, p. 17. Rome, Vatican Library

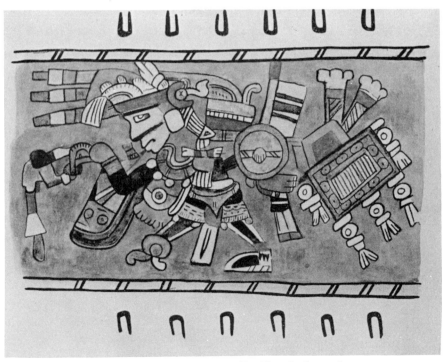

6. "Tezcatlipoca," Altar of Tizatlán, Tlaxcala Restoration.
Instituto Nacional de Antropología e Historia

7. Mitla, Oaxaca, Palace 1, Painting Fragments 1-10 (after Seler)

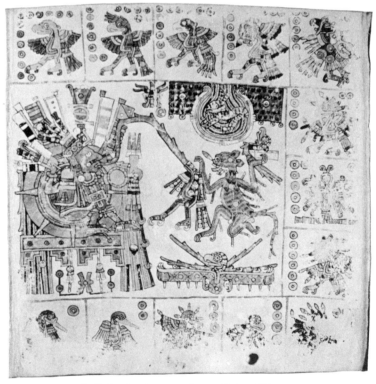

8. Codex Borgia, p. 71. Rome, Vatican Library

1. Retable of the High Altar, Cathedral, Portalegre, Portugal. Ca. 1590-1600

2. Retable of the Altar of St. Anthony, New Cathedral, Coimbra, Portugal. Ca. 1650-60

3. Retable of the High Altar, Cathedral, Salvador, Brazil. Ca. 1672

4. Retable of the High Altar, Carthusian Monastery, Évora, Portugal. 1729

5. Interior, S. António, Lagos, Portugal. Ca. 1700-20

6. Capela Dourada, Recife, Brazil. Ca. 1704

7. Detail of the Nave Wall, S. Bento, Rio de
Janeiro, Brazil. 1717-33

8. Detail of the Choir Stalls, S. Bento da
Vitoria, Oporto, Portugal. 1704

9. Interior, S. Francisco, Salvador,
Brazil. 1720-40

10. Retable of the High Altar, Cathedral,
Oporto, Portugal. 1726

11. Detail of a Lateral Retable, S. Miguel
de Alfama, Lisbon, Portugal

12. Detail of the Chancel, S. Francisco da Penitência,
Rio de Janeiro, Brazil. 1726-39

13. Retable of the High Altar, N. S. da Conceição da Praia, Salvador, Brazil. 1765
14. Retable of the High Altar, Benedictine Monastery, Tibães, Portugal. Carved 1667, gilded 1706
15. Retable of the High Altar, Church of the Third Order of St. Francis, Ouro Preto, Brazil. 1791

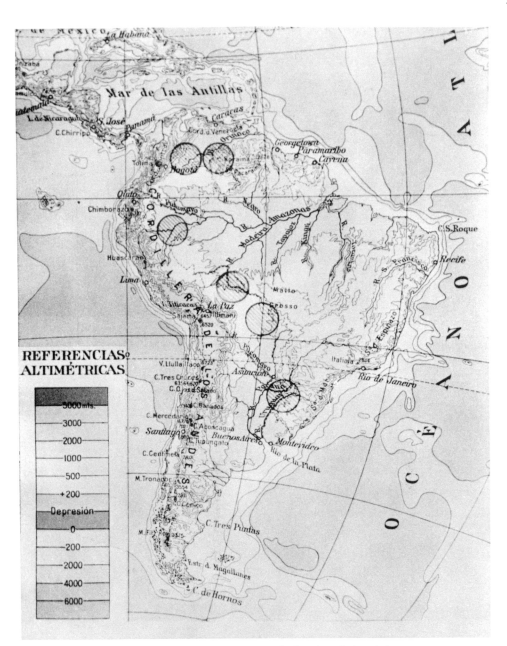

1. Map of South America showing the location of the missions

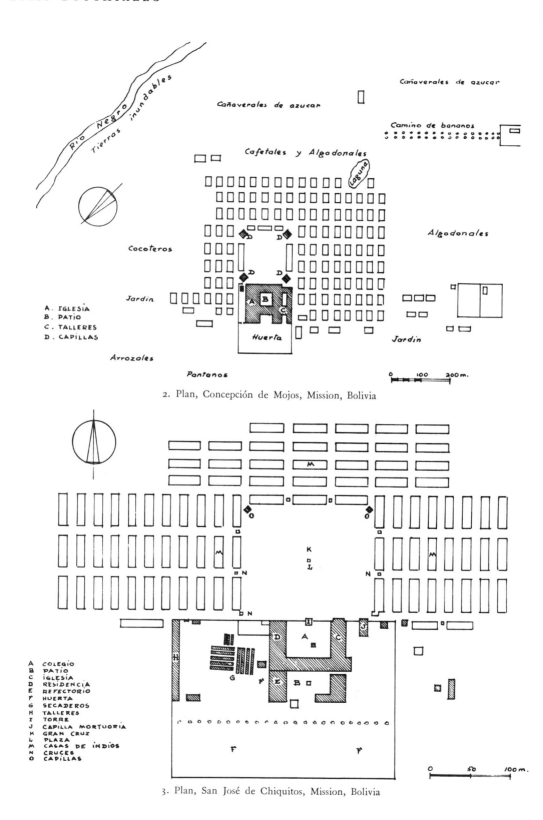

2. Plan, Concepción de Mojos, Mission, Bolivia

3. Plan, San José de Chiquitos, Mission, Bolivia

4. Entrance to the sacristy, San
Ignacio Miní, Argentina

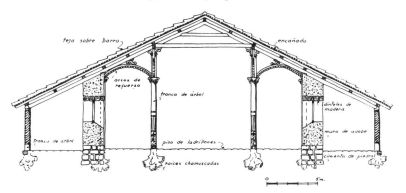

5. Transverse section of a typical church of the Jesuit
Missions of Paraguay, Mojos, Chiquitos, and Maynas

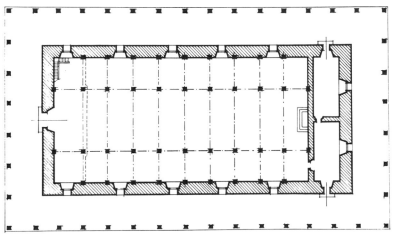

6. Plan of a church of the Jesuit Missions of
Paraguay, Mojos, Chiquitos, and Maynas

7. San Francisco, Santa Fé, Argentina

8. Ceiling, San Francisco, Santa Fé, Argentina

9. La Estanzuela de los Echagüe, Guadalupe, Santa Fé, Argentina

10. Sacristy, Church of Yagüaron, Paraguay

11. Presbytery, Church of Capiatá, Paraguay

12. Church of S. Andrés (demolished), Santa Cruz de la Sierra, Bolivia

13. Interior, Church of S. Andrés (demolished), Santa Cruz de la Sierra, Bolivia

14. Maté cup, Maguire Collection,
Buenos Aires

15. Detail from a column of the façade,
Church of Santa Cruz, Juli, Peru

16. Detail, lunette of the central vault, Church of Santiago, Pomata, Peru

1. Mexico City from the West. Oil painting on ten-panel screen. Ca. 1700

2. Cathedral, Morelia, Mexico. Lithograph. Mid-19th century

3. Basilica, Guadalupe, Mexico, with the dedication ceremonies
after its completion in 1709

4. Villa de Guadalupe, Mexico. Lithograph by C. Castro, in *México y sus alredededores*, 1855-56

5. Aerial Photograph of Guadalupe, Mexico, showing the Basilica, Hill of Tepeyac (upper center), Capilla del Pocito (right), with new paved atrium. Ca. 1950

6. Plaza Mayor, Mexico City. Lithograph by C. Castro, in *México y sus alrededores*, 1855-56

7. Retables of S. Agustín, Salamanca, Mexico.
Late XVIII cent.

1. Lorenzo Rodríguez, South façade, Sagrario Metropolitano, Mexico City. 1749-60

3

4

2. Lorenzo Rodríguez, Detail of south façade, Sagrario Metropolitano, Mexico City. 1749-60
3. Francisco Hurtado (?), Ornament in patio, La Compañia, Córdoba
4. Leonardo de Figueroa, Door, S. Pablo (now la Magdalena), Seville. 1691-1709
5. Wendel Dietterlin, Architectural detail from *Architectura*, 1598. pl. 85

5

6. Jaime Bort, Detail of façade, Cathedral, Murcia. 1741-54

7. Jerónimo Balbás, Altar of the Kings, 1718-37, Cathedral, Mexico City

8. Jerónimo Balbás, Detail, Altar of the Kings, 1718-37, Cathedral, Mexico City

9. Lorenzo Rodríguez, Detail of east façade, Sagrario Metropolitano, Mexico City, 1749-60

10. Miguel de Rivera (?), Detail of façade, Vizcainas College, Mexico City. 1734-53

11. Luis Gómez de Trasmonte (?), Main door, 1672, Cathedral, Mexico City (after M. Toussaint, *La Catedral de México y el Sagrario Metropolitano*, Mexico, 1948, p. 83)

12a. Anonymous, Façade, Santísima Trinidad, Mexico City. 1755-83
12b. Anonymous, Façade, Jesuit seminary, Tepotzotlán. 1760-62

13. Lorenzo Rodríguez, Central panel, south façade, Sagrario Metropolitano, Mexico City. 1749-60 (Photo Inah, Mexico)

14. Anonymous, Façade, Balvanera Chapel,
Church of S. Francisco, Mexico
City. Ca. 1766 (?)

15a. Lorenzo Rodríguez, Detail of door leading into the Sagrario, ca. 1763, Chapel of
S. Isidro, Cathedral of Mexico
15b. Anonymous, Detail of façade, Santísima
Trinidad, Mexico City. 1755-83

16. Anonymous, Detail of façade, Jesuit
seminary, Tepotzotlán. 1760-62

17. Anonymous, Detail of façade, Balvanera Chapel, Church
of S. Francisco, Mexico City. 1766 (?)

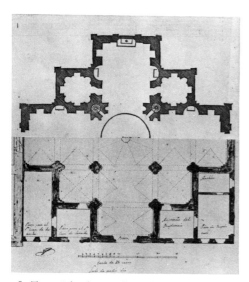

19. Left: Lorenzo Rodríguez, Rear elevation, Sagrario Metropolitano, Mexico City. 1749-60 (M. Toussaint, *La Catedral de México y el Sagrario Metropolitano*, Mexico, 1948)
Right: Sebastian Serlio, Elevation of a church, from *Quinto libro de architettura*, Venice, 1551

18. Top: Sebastian Serlio, Plan for a church, from *Quinto libro de architettura*, Venice, 1551
Bottom: Lorenzo Rodríguez, Plan of the Sagrario Metropolitano, Mexico City. 1749 (Diego Angulo Iñiguez, *Estudios de los Planos . . . Existentes en el Archivo de Indias*, Seville, 1933-39)

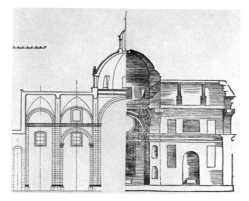

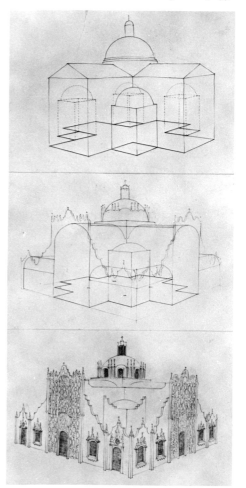

20. Left: Lorenzo Rodríguez, Section, Sagrario Metropolitano, Mexico City. 1749-60 (M. Toussaint, *La Catedral de México y el Sagrario Metropolitano*, Mexico, 1948)
Right: Sebastian Serlio, Interior of a church, from *Quinto libro de architettura*, Venice, 1551
21. Top: Sebastian Serlio, Tempio Quadrato in croce, from *Quinto libro de architettura*, Venice, 1551
Bottom: Lorenzo Rodríguez, Sagrario Metropolitano, Mexico City. 1749-60 (M. Toussaint, *La Catedral de México y el Sagrario Metropolitano*, Mexico, 1948)

1. Francisco José de Lerma, *Holy Family*. Caracas, Collection of Carlos Möller